STATES OF
EMERGENCY

Edited by

RUSS CASTRONOVO

and

SUSAN GILLMAN

STATES OF
EMERGENCY

THE OBJECT OF AMERICAN STUDIES

THE UNIVERSITY OF

NORTH CAROLINA PRESS

Chapel Hill

© 2009
THE UNIVERSITY OF NORTH CAROLINA PRESS
ALL RIGHTS RESERVED
Manufactured in the United States of America

Designed by Courtney Leigh Baker
Set in Garamond Premier Pro and Scala Sans
by Rebecca Evans

The paper in this book meets the guidelines for permanence and
durability of the Committee on Production Guidelines for Book
Longevity of the Council on Library Resources.

The University of North Carolina Press has been a member
of the Green Press Initiative since 2003.

Library of Congress Cataloging-in-Publication Data
States of emergency : the object of American studies /
edited by Russ Castronovo and Susan Gillman.
p. cm.
Includes bibliographical references and index.
ISBN 978-0-8078-3340-7 (cloth : alk. paper)
ISBN 978-0-8078-5985-8 (pbk. : alk. paper)
1. United States — Civilization. 2. United States — Study and teaching.
I. Castronovo, Russ, 1965– II. Gillman, Susan Kay.
E169.1.S76845 2009
973 — dc22
2009018544

cloth   13 12 11 10 09   5 4 3 2 1
paper   13 12 11 10 09   5 4 3 2 1

CONTENTS

ACKNOWLEDGMENTS

Ours is a collaborative effort that has been sustained at every turn by Sian Hunter, our editor at the University of North Carolina Press. Early on she lent her support and insight to this project in ways that have made a real difference. This volume emerged from intercampus conversations between the University of California at Santa Cruz and the University of Wisconsin at Madison, which were supported by the Center for Cultural Studies and the Jean Wall Bennett Fund. Vilashini Cooppan, Jane Gaines, Kirsten Silva Gruesz, Ursula Heise, Rob Nixon, and Susan Stanford Friedman were exemplary interlocutors at these events. Sebastian Frank helped provide the organization to get these initial efforts off the ground. We would also like to thank George Lipsitz for his inspiration at a crucial stage in the completion of this volume.

STATES OF
EMERGENCY

Introduction

The Study of the American Problems

RUSS CASTRONOVO & SUSAN GILLMAN

What is the object of American studies? This opening salvo really asks two questions. What does "American studies" study, and what does it want? Some would say that the question *is* the problem. "Must self-identification as an Americanist put one under the obligation to be an upholder or subverter of American institutions?"[1] Why should American studies take upon itself the call to endorse a program, especially one saddled with all sorts of nationalist connotations, more than any other field of literary and cultural studies? To say that the nation *is* the self-evident truth of the field simply states a tautology. W. E. B. Du Bois, author of "The Study of the Negro Problems" (1897), a foundational essay on the origins of his own methodological creativity and experimentation in studying an object, offers an answer. The scope of any problem, Du Bois recognizes, changes over time and across space — as surely as black life in the United States is conditioned by the long fetch of history that unfolded in the broader Atlantic world. "All Art is propaganda and ever must be," he wrote some twenty years later in "Criteria of Negro Art" (1926).[2] Translation: all American studies scholarship is ever propaganda. This is a place to start, not something either to celebrate or to decry.

In pressuring the object of American studies, we are questioning how the things that this interdisciplinary field studies — whether bits of material culture as small as a cigarette stub or as large as war — imply a political position or practice. Still following Du Bois, we could say that we do not care a damn for any methodology that is not used for political ends. For now, though, we advance the less controversial point that all politics have methodologies, and it is about time that American studies consciously evaluate the strategies, tactics, and assumptions with which it approaches culture. The fact that a long and rich research and curricular history exists in what is sometimes called "American cultures" programs makes this project at once more urgent and axiomatic. "The Study of the American Problems" may be just the ticket, a reformulation that looks back to Du Bois's problems and forward to its own future solutions.

A lifetime student of the singularly misnamed "Negro Problem," Du Bois provides a model for Americanists who would rather not be a member of the club. (Indeed, many of the contributors to this volume consider themselves interlopers to the field of American studies.) He remade the singular problem ("we ordinarily speak of the Negro problem as though it were one unchanged question") into a "plexus of social problems" and proceeded from there.[3] In Du Boisean spirit, instead of breast-beating about the name "America," we were inspired by the salutary boom across traditional interdisciplinary studies in the last three decades of the twentieth century. We started our project hoping to wed the object-centered field expansion of the 1970s and 1980s — all the hyphenated minority cultures and canons, histories and regions — with the theoretical work on nations, nationalism, and transnationalism of the 1980s and 1990s. The result turned out to be less a happy marriage than a healthy lack of consensus that extends to the naming of the field itself. U.S. cultural studies, American cultures, critical U.S. studies, Americas studies, Inter-American studies, and, of course, the default, American studies: the proliferation of possibilities suggests how this field has long defined itself through a lack of definition and routinely grounded its projects and methods in flux and transition.[4]

But despite moves toward some "outside" or postnational "beyond" that would define the discipline as impossibly external to itself, these new directions in American studies, we argue, are a part of a familiar pattern that, for all its disruptive energy, does not confront basic issues of scope and scale. Objects hold their place in archives and imaginations just as much as they endure in the form of course anthologies, surveys, and exam lists that we regularly require. In light of the challenges that interdisciplinary, transdisciplinary, and multidisciplinary scholarship presents to traditional ways of "doing" American studies, this volume examines how an object of study is set, identified, defined — or, most commonly, simply assumed. Even, or perhaps especially, when the canon has been opened up and expanded, as is undeniably the case with American studies today, the object itself multiplies yet remains, oddly, more or less static. Has inclusiveness, extending from our

RUSS CASTRONOVO & SUSAN GILLMAN

texts to the languages we acquire, become a substitution for methodology? As Du Bois would say, "A combination of social problems is far more than a matter of mere addition — the combination itself is a problem."[5] Likewise, for the study of the American problems, we are marking our difference from prevailing feel-good methods, which, too often, operate according to principles that are merely additive, a sort of scholarly liberal pluralism that fails to address how interdisciplinary practice might actually throw into question the disciplinary assumptions of history, textual analysis, and cultural studies from which they draw. Instead of envisioning such genuinely unsettling interdisciplinary agendas, American studies has often settled for a multidisciplinary regime as the mark of a comparativism that parades coverage in place of comparison and the totality of the nation-state in place of theory.[6]

If objects are often the focal point of desire, then our investigation is best taken as a variant of Freud's bafflement about what a woman wants. This question bears some adjustment, not the least because there were a lot of male professors around the seminar table at the institutional beginnings of American studies. What does an American studies scholar want? At first glance, the answer is nothing sexy: theory and praxis. But a closer look at alternative approaches to the field provided by this volume suggests that our desires to merge theory and praxis, our fantasy to make our objects of study coincide with our political goals or objects, might be rather risqué.

To recognize this possibility, we ask readers to engage in a thought experiment: imagine that you have an object and that you want to study it. The object could be anything, an artifact drawn from popular culture, a text culled from the archive, even something that is more of a moving target because of its location across or between cultures. In the pluralist ethos that characterizes the field, your object could be lowbrow or highbrow, material or virtual, national or transnational. The dime novels once unearthed by Henry Nash Smith that later become Michael Denning's mechanic accents, the fugitive expressions of sound recaptured by Stephen Best and Jonathan Sterne, the forms of affect explored as female complaint by Lauren Berlant or as hieroglyphs of black female flesh by Hortense Spillers, and the border narratives that have been so important to the work of José David Saldívar and other scholars of the Latin American-Latino diaspora exemplify one range of possibilities.[7] Another set emerges as a series of objects and people in motion, trafficked across alternative regions of study, including the Black Atlantic (itself pointing back to the earlier formulation Atlantic world), the circum-Caribbean and the global South.[8] Now that you have your object, which methodologies will contextualize and explain your selection? You might historicize the object or pay close attention to its language (and, of course, languages are not limited to print texts), but you also might set the object adrift, as it were, along the flows of capital, persons, and information that have characterized, albeit very differently, transoceanic worlds as well as digital and hyperreal spaces.

This positioning of the object quickly introduces another sense of object: what goal do you have in studying, recovering, or critiquing your object? Du Bois poses exactly this question as the initial charge of "Criteria of Negro Art." Addressing the Chicago NAACP, he asked "What do we want? What is the thing we are after?" Even if American studies cannot quite claim to be like the NAACP, "a group of radicals trying to bring new things into the world," this is not an innocent question. Like Du Bois, we "do not doubt but there are some in this audience who are a little disturbed at the subject" we have chosen. Just as he dismissed "the wailing of the purists" when it came to art, so too we doubt the existence of a mode of inquiry that could be described as pure scholarship or scientific truth.[9] Instead we see his advocacy for the ethical and political responsibility of art and literature as tied to the "things" that American studies wants to study.

While our objects have been expanding along with our names for the field, they are strangely static. It once looked to us as though the problem was that the category of time was missing amid the fixation with space in American studies, which as an interdiscipline often seems still profoundly wedded to the privileging of region that characterized the development of area studies in the postwar era. We wondered what happens to disciplinary critique when the transnational is described and deployed as primarily spatial, as a phenomenon of borders, rims, and spheres. As in Du Bois's understanding of problems, the transnational is also a temporal problem, its sudden appearance in recent years only the latest coordinate to be plotted on a map that includes points such as José Martí's "Nuestra América" (1892) and Randolph Bourne's "Trans-national America" (1916). But we need to do more than isolate temporality because such a singular focus would replicate the very one-dimensionality that we want to change. The spatiotemporal approaches adopted and adapted by the contributors to *States of Emergency*, in contrast, prioritize comparability as both the practice and the goal of American studies. And thinking through space-time helps to question the putative neutrality of comparison as a method. Objects, after all, are not only located in spaces such as archives and anthologies; objects are just as easily lost as found in time that, for commentators like Hegel reflecting on Africa, denies historicity to some people and that, for critics like Johannes Fabian, afflicts "the other" with difference.[10]

The issue is one of metrics, as units of study range from region to nation and from state to globe–hence, the ubiquitous formula of the local and the global. Units of study are also time bound, with their temporality expressed through conventional periods of study divided by major "events" into "pre" and "post" that partition history into a new, ever-updated sectionalism: the antebellum United States; the American Renaissance and its later companion period, the Harlem Renaissance; the post–World War Two era; and especially the global narrowly conceived as a purely contemporary phenomenon. But, in speaking of the "pre" and the "post," we could just as readily be speaking of space, which is broken down and opened up into the pre- and postnational, not to mention the transnational or even subnational.[11] The convertibility of these tags in marking units of space or geopolitical divisions suggests their overlap, in a kind of asymmetrical equivalence. For every spatial dimension, we should think in terms of an analogous temporal unit and vice versa. By putting pressure on the space-time of scale and comparison, the essays in this volume together represent an attempt to locate the study of American problems within a larger sociology of knowledge.

This thought experiment is what our contributors offer by collectively taking up an array of objects — the weather, oceans, cigarettes, archival material, AIDS, the enemy, extinct species, torture — and recalibrating the metrics of time and space with which we study these particular American problems. Nan Enstad locates cigarettes within a global economy, but spatial coordinates are not adequate to expressing how carcinogens and other toxins have an elongated temporality that inhabit the body for years. Rodrigo Lazo works from the other direction, at first concentrating on the temporal dimension of the archive as a historical accretion only to confront its stolid placement in the public institutions of the nation-state. Another kind of temporal tension underwrites Kenneth Warren's intervention on the Black Atlantic as both an object and a method of study, divided between historical periodization (the Atlantic world identified with the early modern and thus as the designation of a historical period) and transtemporal forms of identification (the cultural studies focus on the aesthetics and ethics of black identification or affiliation across space and time). Objects, for Anne McClintock, would seem to be irrefragably an issue of space. What could be more bound to a spatial location than tortured bodies imprisoned by the "War on Terror"— but McClintock's investigation leads simultaneously to the identification of a temporal malady, the persistent foreboding of a paranoid empire. By disrupting what we think we know about time and space, by questioning the disciplinary handholds to which we cling as Chris Castiglia does in writing about the "post" that is so dear to queer theory, by calling for new coordinates of analysis as Robert Levine does in writing about apocalypse, we come to have a revitalized sense not only of each of these objects but of our object, our goal, our commitments, our investments, as cultural critics.

As these examples make clear, the blending and crossing of space-time also involve competing metrics, a series of counterunits such as borders, diasporas, and contact zones. In the temporal realm, a variety of counterunits (the Janus face of history, historical return and repetition, uneven development, the "zigzag") have been proposed to offset the presentism that dogs teleological timelines and their linear metrics.[12] Frederick Cooper, for example, calls for a "history that compares" in contrast to an inert "Comparative History," one that is too flatfooted to consider transatlantic or global situations.[13] Units of time, such as the history of slavery, that trace synchronically whole systems or structures as though their building blocks remain static in a kind of monumental time create a need for counterunits, such as the history of slave revolt, that track more uneven, asymmetrical developments and phenomena. Questioning the category of nation is one thing, but there are limits, as well as possibilities, to the counterunits-of-study approach. Maybe, in addition, the efforts to retool U.S. studies have been overshadowed, skewed by all the frequent, if not ritual, uses of "post," "beyond," and "beneath." How to compare by putting space-time back together again?

Neoliberalism, both within and outside the academy, makes this task all the more difficult. Under neoliberalism, temporalities and spaces lose their multiplicity and are governed by a market sensibility of supposed individual freedom that in actuality is the abandonment of the social contract. Lacking the contexts of comparison, space and time are flattened out, and, as Enstad contends in her look at the invisible hand of the market, the frames available for analysis become severely limited. Not only does neoliberalism reduce competing worldviews to a singular American perspective, sometimes masked by the rubric of globalization, but it also enforces a hegemony that, as McClintock shows in her examination of torture, hides in plain sight. In each case, whether it is global circulation of toxins or the spectacle of torture, the body bears the brunt of neoliberal practice. And, if Srinivas Aravamudan is right in his assertion that we have entered a phase of "dominance without hegemony," then the task of decoupling the state and the discipline of American studies has become still more crucial. Working in conjunction with our other contributors, Enstad, McClintock, and Aravamudan suggest that while our methods, epistemological frames, and scales of analysis often are blind to and even complicit with force and violation, American studies practice also has a critical potential to fragment such accretions of power.

In the face of neoliberalism's hegemony, then, we need a robust and routine comparativism that does not just replicate the methods or the objects of comparative history, such as long-standing "two-country" pairings, but rather is attuned theoretically to questions of both time and space in its construction of analytical units. Nor can a systemic comparativism echo what has been traditionally called "comparative Literature" because the bases of comparison, which were ascendant in postwar culture, are no longer in place as they once were in the 1960s and 1970s. We think that American revolutionaries may have been on to something in devising a methodology whose watchword of "one if by land and two if by sea" tracked the movement of troops and other objects in a world that was global, colonial, and militaristic all at once. Updating this wisdom, we might say that we need transtemporal sites of comparison, such as those defined by oceans as well as by land, if we are to make visible both the global and the local routes that bring the objects of American studies — race, slavery, immigration, the state — into circulation. Such spatiotemporal paradigms would go a long way toward counteracting the tendency within conventional area studies, not only the older, pre–cultural studies variety but also the "new American studies," to privilege either space or time but never both at once.

The essays we have gathered together show how this theoretical dexterity operates in practice. In Benjaminian spirit, we envisage an innovative approach to the conventional, scholarly collection of essays. Rather than one, massive phone book, we propose instead a modest volume, with essays of different lengths, but none reaching the standard thirty-pages plus of the usual academic-journal article. It intersperses intervention-style, think pieces with manifestoes and keyword entries. With a philosophy of less-is-more, the object is less likely to overwhelm the methodology — or vice versa. Thus, we intend Warren's piece on the space and time of the Black Atlantic as a short suture — permanent, not the dissolvable kind — to the rest of the essays. Coming after McClintock's analysis of tortured bodies sequestered at sites in the Caribbean and Middle East and preceding Baucom's account of enemies manufactured by the philosophy and economy of the Atlantic world, Warren's Black Atlantic provides both a rupture and a bridge to the volume in the spirit of the very short gangplank that Toni Morrison envisions for the *Beloved* reader, the abrupt and unexpected "*in medias res* opening" that unfinished and open-ended political projects such as ours (and hers) warrant.[14] With Warren's Black Atlantic marking key lines of tension within black studies, our volume opens out, we hope, onto an interdisciplinary environment that our contributors all recognize as both utterly familiar and completely foreign. Wai Chee Dimock looks to the warming ocean air that becomes the engine for catastrophic hurricanes as a way of reconsidering nations, sovereignty, and other land-based notions. Also attentive to oceans and the crisscrossing currents of history, Baucom identifies the Atlantic as the spatiotemporal region from where contemporary understandings of "the unjust enemy" originate. From the perspective of Warren's Black Atlantic, Ian Baucom advances a view of history as both repetition and redemption, reflecting the paradoxical impulse to use history to overcome history that is centrally indebted to Walter Benjamin's philosophy of history. So, too, by translating the study of American problems into times and places that fail to abide by the regularities of U.S. history, the U.S. literary archive, or even the traditional interdisciplinary pairing of history and literature, these essays, like Aravamudan's examination of American studies' roguish past, seek a perspective on what Walter Benjamin called a "state of emergency."[15]

For Benjamin, living in a state of emergency requires a good deal of temporal flexibility. A supple view of the past is necessary in order to combat the exceptionalism that isolates a present crisis as somehow extraordinary, creating a situation that demands all sorts of extraordinary measures, not just civil and legal but also philosophical. Benjamin's assertion that the state of emergency "in which we live is not the exception but the rule" has uncanny relevance for both a nation and a field of study that has founded itself on exceptionalist narratives. This view is thus always implicitly comparativist, taking slices of the past and other objects and refusing their isolation, separateness, and partitioning from one another. But never should events or objects be strung together in a smooth, continuous sequence, like the "beads of a rosary" that allow for predestined stories of progress and overcoming.[16] Following this heretical spirit, the essays here do not string together one coherent method or theory. Nor is looking fixedly at the past a desired strategy. One's view must also be messianic, which is to say that any method for understanding culture then and now must also be concerned with what is coming. Thus, the ideal position is famously Janus-faced, like the angel of history, facing back toward the past but propelled toward the future.

As opposed to manufacturing an artificial state of emergency that plucks the present moment out of context, "our task [is] to bring about a real state of emergency," writes Benjamin in the present tense, directing his critical energies along an irregular timeline from the debt owed the past toward the future. In this sense, Benjamin's critique has an object, which is not the same thing as having a sure destination or even a plan. Like the object of Benjamin's critique, our volume has no lofty misconception that it points the way to a better interdisciplinary day or that it stands at brink of the new, waiting to usher in "the beginning of knowledge."[17] Our goal is more modest: to take the objects we study as problems, which, neither beyond comparison to other objects nor snugly fitting into a chain of events, make a problem out of the tools we would bring to the study of an event, phenomenon, performance, or artifact.

In short, what would it mean to understand the field of American studies as in a state of emergency? For Du Bois, the really crucial question is one of scale and time: to measure the many successive problems grouped around the object and the study of "America," and to trace their historical development and probable trend of further development.[18] For Benjamin, to say that the emergency is not exceptional suggests that it is routine, standard operating procedure, except that "standard operating procedure," like "state of emergency" itself, has morphed perversely in meaning. Both terms are now used virtually synonymously, to justify the increased extension of government power over questions of citizenship and individual rights after 9/11. Our contributors are hardly alone in looking at objects through the lenses of wreckage and destruction seen in New York City, Iraq, New Orleans, and elsewhere.[19] But when we asked Anne McClintock to consider the object of American studies, she encouraged us toward a type of critique that pays attention to the shadowy objects of present history, specifically the prisoners of Abu Ghraib, both occluded and hyperembodied by the state. Journalist Philip Gourevitch's 2008 *Standard Operating Procedure* notes the eerie absence of attention to torture in the whole spectacle of Abu Ghraib, asking: where's the anger?[20] He confirms the problem — a time of crisis has been transformed into a state of emergency that is not real but artificial, defined instead as standard operating procedure — that McClintock studies from a Du Boisean range of relative perspectives, including but not limited to her analysis of the photo archive. While Gourevitch opts for interviews and deliberately omits the photos from his book, McClintock concludes instead that the images *are* the necessary object of study that have the potential to move us through compassion and outrage to political action, the only way to stop the atrocities. Taken up in our double sense of object as both the topic and the point of critique, the Abu Ghraib photographs bring about a real state of emergency in defiance of official and artificial proclamations of the same.

While Benjamin inspired our title, it was actually Benedict Anderson who suggested the convergence of ideas about time, space, and the nation. Anderson's *Imagined Communities* — the subsequent editions that followed the original in 1983 — underlines both how critical it is to stress the New World origins of nationalism and why it has proved so difficult to do so.[21] Benjamin's concept of messianic time informed Anderson's focus in the 1983 *Imagined Communities* on the Americas as the locus of different structures of simultaneity underlying medieval and modern forms of imagining. But because "the crucial chapter on the originating Americas was largely ignored," Anderson explains in the 1991 preface, an additional chapter, "Memory and Forgetting," further develops the special nature of nationalism in relation to the newness of the New World. Rather than genealogical continuity *from* the old *to* the new, in the Americas "new" and "old" were understood "synchronically, coexisting within homogeneous empty time" as a sense of parallelism, simultaneity, or, in a nutshell, comparability.[22] The "doubleness of the Americas" accounts, Anderson concludes, for "why nationalism emerged first in the New World, not the Old"[23] — and, we would say, for why the key originating role for the Americas in the genesis of nationalism is so subject to memory and forgetting.

From this slightly askew spatiotemporal perspective, the old specter of American exceptionalism starts to have a new and charmed life. American difference turns out to be rooted in its special comparability. Anderson foregrounds both American difference, the particular novelty of its newness, and American comparability, how "Creole pioneers" of the New World imagined themselves as comparable to, existing synchronically alongside their Old World counterparts (see the retitled chapter 4, *Imagined Communities*). This "exhilarating doubleness" could reposition both the object and disciplinary method of American studies.[24] First, it avoids the trap of the two Americas, sometimes associated with Latin American intellectual history, which pits one against the "other America" [*la otra América*].[25] Instead, this American doubleness makes comparability both internal and external to the Americas, the object studied in relation to Europe, Asia, and Africa, to the Atlantic and Pacific worlds, as well as to itself. Temporally and spatially, American doubleness multiplies into a simultaneity of times, places, and languages coexisting unevenly across the multiple national states of the Americas. Second, from this perspective the early United States is "just another creole-led revolutionary state" and the Civil War a minor conflagration at the periphery of worldwide explosions of anarchist violence in the last quarter of the nineteenth century. Finally, the doubleness of the Americas sidesteps the "spectre of comparison" that haunts other colonial-imperial histories, in which the worlds outside Europe are condemned to see themselves through the small end of the telescope, a kind of second-order doubling, shadowed by the ghosts of European modernity. Offering perfect arguments against both national incomparability and Eurocentrism, this model accounts for why the specter of comparison is so palpable and elusive, so formative and forgettable in the Americas context.[26]

Our essays take up Anderson's challenge and show how the object of American studies benefits from a structure of comparability, meaning a theory of space and time that recognizes how changing apprehensions of both coordinates produce new thinking about the nation in local and global contexts. In practice, "nationalism's undivorcible marriage to internationalism" also means that we do not have to throw out the baby with the bathwater in order to "transnationalize" American studies.[27] Nations and other "old" units remain in play even as comparative spaces (such as oceans or borders) and times (such as nostalgia or amnesia) can change the standard operating procedures of American studies. Considering toxicity allows Enstad to pay new attention to the problem of scale: is the object a chemical, a body, a particular human or animal population, a geographic location of consumption, or a global network? Thus bridging the analytic dichotomy between local reactions and global forces, "toxin" is by definition a relational term that can track the effects of global capitalism in particular times and places. If the study of AIDS raises its own question of scale, in Castiglia's formula, "too big for queer theory and too small for American studies," then not just AIDS but the history of sexual liberation struggles may fall through the cracks of institutional memory. In objecting to trauma as a countertemporal term that does not respond to the cry of the past, Castiglia questions the standard yardsticks used to measure a crisis.

As the scale of analysis fluctuates, old objects enter the archive in new ways. Lazo advances this argument by turning his attention to texts that require translation — that is, they move across borders of language, nations, and generations — to ask how our methods change the objects that we study. But it also might be the case, as Levine shows in his essay in this volume, that our present methodologies lack proper calibration for studying the usual cataclysms — you know, little things like species extinction, global warming, the day of judgment, or the end of the universe — that in one form or another have contributed to postapocalyptic visions since at least the era of Edgar Allan Poe and Nathaniel Hawthorne.

Nor do all the essays mechanically or slavishly fill in the dotted lines between the coordinates of "Space New and Old" and "Time New and Old."[28] The view from the volume's bridge shows historical changes envisaged as simultaneous yet capable of producing configurations of difference, to the extent that comparisons highlight the local meaning of each event and, sometimes, the exceptionality of each case. Sovereignty and historiography undergo specific material and conceptual explosions in the oceanic histories of Warren's Black Atlantic, Baucom's "crucially Atlantic" figure of the unjust enemy, and Dimock's "flooded" world. Baucom locates three corners of an Atlantic triangle in Europe, America, and Africa of the late sixteenth, seventeenth, and twenty-first centuries as the simultaneous space-time of the figure of the unjust enemy. In this strange hybrid crossing of modern imperial history with humanist jurisprudence and ancient Roman law, Baucom finds the precedent for America's enemies, the so-called unlawful combatant, just one of the ghosts haunting a body of international law that exempts the "conflict zones" of the Americas and Africa from the normative regulations of the laws of war. Dimock writes her own "nonsovereign history" from the watery standpoint of global climatological catastrophe — hurricanes, floods, soil erosion, loss of wetlands — that have the potential to produce an analogously enlarged sense of democracy, rooted, asymmetrically, in microevidence and bottom-up chronologies. If Warren's Black Atlantic seeks to bridge "then" and "now" by writing the slave past as a history of and for the present, likewise Baucom and Dimock join McClintock in their attempts to make sense through different states of exception to our contemporary experiences of law, violence, human and inhuman, and sovereignty. Each finds the wolves inside the sheepfold that, as Aravamudan would have it, confuse sovereign right and the unjust enemy. They are all practitioners of rogue studies, making the study of the United States unfamiliar to itself and finding some form of political hope in so doing.

This preview of the volume's essays brings us to our final sense of "object."

RUSS CASTRONOVO & SUSAN GILLMAN

Up to this point, we have been using "object" in a double sense to denote both the things we study and the aims implicit in methodologies of scale that we employ to tackle the coordinates of space-time. But "object" can also be used as a verb to signal disagreement or voice opposition. It is in this sense that *States of Emergency* objects to American studies, its history of exceptionalism, its often dogged fixation on spatial questions over temporal ones, its affected innocence about the political implications of methodological choices, or, vice versa, its unquestioning adherence to an assumed political righteousness, regardless of methodology. The posture of critique has become an endgame, a substitute for self-criticism. Then there is the tendency to repetition that no one seems to notice or resist: call after call for the new, the post, the beyond, none of which states of disciplinary consciousness we ever actually get to or get to live in. Take the nation, for example. Despite the fact that Anderson's *Imagined Communities* (itself only the most traveled of many theories of nationalism) has now gone through three editions, we do not have to look very far to find Americanists still scratching their heads in wonder at all the field shaking that will take place once we shift away from nation-based frameworks. Yet many scholars in allied disciplines are working with and after the news that (as Anderson puts it) nations have their own biography, just like the race concept. (Du Bois was already writing his own "essay toward an autobiography of a race concept" in the "dusk of dawn" of 1940.)[29] The fact that African American studies has long gone from being a subsidiary of the national corporation and moved through key changes from black studies to diaspora studies to black literary and cultural studies has had, as Warren suggests, surprisingly little impact on the mother lode.

Our response: don't object, just correct. Just say yes! In this spirit, several of our contributors suggest models for methods and objects of study from specific disciplinary constellations. Srinivas Aravamudan and Ian Baucom work in eighteenth-century British literature from a perspective informed by ocean and postcolonial studies, while Warren, working in African American studies, travels a similar route but asks a different question: what happened to that field in the wake of diaspora and comparative ethnic studies? Together they point to the burgeoning of Atlantic world as an analytic that crosses national literatures, races, histories, and languages as well as spans several centuries. So, too, Anne McClintock's work has traveled from its nominal origin in postcolonial studies to such unexpected places as the field of world history, which is itself undergoing radical disciplinary reinvention. Nan Enstad approaches toxicity from her own view as a cultural historian, showing how work on consumer culture interfaces with a new interdisciplinary influx emerging around environmental studies, via fields traditionally underrepresented in American studies, such as geography (again), history of science and medicine, epidemiology, and biology. Wai Chee Dimock uses an interdisciplinary discussion of climate change, human health, and environment to address the "scale politics" of American studies. Such studies further the time-honored tradition of shifting the object and disciplinary mix of American studies work in order to respond to current states of emergency.

Thus, neither the critique of any of our contributors nor ours here is negative. It is not really the effect of some being outsiders to American studies "proper," because we have tried to show how object matter depends on different scales rather than being determined by area of study. All of us would rather have improper relations to our different fields. We believe that it would be somewhat perverse and altogether shortsighted to oppose this interdiscipline without seeing an inverse potential in using American studies to object to the standard operating procedures — the toxicity of everyday life, amnesia, excesses of state power, and torture — of our own particular, but surely not exceptional, location in space-time. That location is nothing less than the here and the now.

NOTES

1. Lawrence Buell, "Introduction: American Literary Globalism?" in "American Literary Globalism," ed. Wai Chee Dimock and Lawrence Buell, special issue, *ESQ* 50, nos. 1–3 (2004): 1.

2. W. E. B. Du Bois, "Criteria of Negro Art," in *The Norton Anthology of African American Literature*, ed. Henry Louis Gates Jr. and Nellie Y. McKay (New York: Norton, 1997), 757.

3. The first quotation is from "The Study of the Negro Problems," in *W. E. B. Du Bois, On Sociology and the Black Community*, ed. Dan S. Driver and Edwin D. Driver (Chicago: University of Chicago Press, 1978), 72; the second quotation is from *The Philadelphia Negro* (1899), excerpted in *The Oxford W. E. B. Du Bois Reader*, ed. Eric J. Sundquist (New York: Oxford University Press, 1996), 346. While Du Bois offers a prospective for an American studies methodology, our attempt here is not to produce a retrospective as a bookend. Contributions to mapping the field in these ways include *Keywords for American Cultural Studies*, ed. Bruce Burgett and Glenn Hendler (New York: New York University Press, 2007); *American Literary Studies: A Methodological Reader*, ed. Michael Elliott and Claudia Stokes (New York: New York University Press, 2003); *The Futures of American Studies*, ed. Donald E. Pease and Robyn Wiegman (Durham: Duke University Press, 2002); *Post-Nationalist American Studies*, ed. John Carlos Rowe (Berkeley: University of California Press, 2000).

RUSS CASTRONOVO & SUSAN GILLMAN

4. The most important contribution to this debate is Janice Radway, "What's in a Name? Presidential Address to the American Studies Association, 20 November 1998," *American Quarterly* 51, no. 1 (1999): 1–32.

5. Du Bois, *Oxford W. E. B. Du Bois Reader*, 346.

6. On the spatiotemporal relation and the viability of comparative study, see Harry Harootunian, "Some Thoughts on Comparability and the Space-Time Problem," in "Problems of Comparability/Possibilities for Comparative Studies," ed. Harry Harootunian and Hyun Ok Park, special issue, *boundary 2* 32 (Summer 2005): 23–52.

7. Henry Nash Smith, *Virgin Land: The American West as Symbol and Myth* (1950; repr. Cambridge, Mass.: Harvard University Press, 1978); Michael Denning, *Mechanic Accents: Dime Novels and Working-Class Culture in America*, 2nd ed. (New York: Verso, 1998); Hortense Spillers, *Black, White, and in Color: Essays on American Literature and Culture* (Chicago: University of Chicago Press, 2003); Lauren Berlant, *The Female Complaint: The Unfinished Business of Sentimentality in American Culture* (Durham: Duke University Press, 2008); Stephen Best, *The Fugitive's Properties: Law and the Poetics of Possession* (Chicago: University of Chicago Press, 2003); Jonathan Sterne, *The Audible Past: Cultural Origins of Sound Reproduction* (Durham: Duke University Press 2003); José David Saldívar, *Border Matters: Remapping American Cultural Studies* (Berkeley: University of California Press, 1997); Walter Mignolo, *Local Histories/Global Designs: Coloniality, Subaltern Knowledges, and Border Thinking* (Princeton, N.J.: Princeton University Press, 2000); Gustavo Pérez Firmat, *The Cuban Condition: Translation and Identity in Modern Cuban Literature* (1989; repr., Cambridge: Cambridge University Press, 2006); Gustavo Pérez Firmat, *Life on the Hyphen: The Cuban-American Way* (Austin: University of Texas Press, 1994), translated as *Vidas en vilo: La cultura cubanoamericana* (Madrid: Colibrí Editorial, 2000); Anna Brickhouse, *Transamerican Literary Relations and the Nineteenth-Century Public Sphere* (Cambridge: Cambridge University Press, 2004).

8. See, for example, Paul Gilroy, *The Black Atlantic: Modernity and Double Consciousness* (Cambridge, Mass.: Harvard University Press, 1993); Jon Smith and Deborah Cohn, eds., *Look Away! The U.S. South in New World Studies* (Durham: Duke University Press, 2004); Brent Hayes Edwards, *The Practice of Diaspora: Literature, Translation, and the Rise of Black Internationalism* (Cambridge, Mass.: Harvard University Press, 1993).

9. Du Bois, "Criteria of Negro Art," 752, 757.

10. Johannes Fabian, *Time and the Other: How Anthropology Makes Its Object* (New York: Columbia University Press, 1983). Africa, for Hegel, "is no part of the historical World; it has no movement of development to exhibit" (*Philosophy of History*, trans. J. Sibree [New York: American Home Library, 1902], 157).

11. See Wai Chee Dimock, "Scales of Aggregation: Prenational, Subnational, Transnational," *ALH* 18, no. 2 (Summer 2006): 219–28.

12. The Janus face is associated with Walter Benjamin's angel of history as well as with Tom Nairn's work on nationalism. On the zigzag, see Benedict Anderson, *Under Three Flags: Anarchism and the Anti-Colonial Imagination* (New York: Verso, 2005).

13. Frederick Cooper, "Race, Ideology, and the Perils of Comparative History," *American Historical Review* 101 (October 1996): 1135.

14. Toni Morrison, "Unspeakable Things Unspoken: The Afro-American Presence in American Literature," *Michigan Quarterly Review* 28 (Winter 1989): 32.

15. Walter Benjamin, "Theses on the Philosophy of History," in *Illuminations: Essays and Reflections* (New York: Schocken Books, 1968), 257.

16. Ibid.

17. Ibid.

18. See Du Bois, "Study of the Negro Problems," 72–75.

19. See George Lipsitz, "Learning from New Orleans: The Social Warrant of Hostile Privatism and Competitive Consumer Citizenship," *Cultural Anthropology* 21, no. 3 (2006): 451–68. This essay is exemplary in moving between the different senses of object as both thing and political aim: focusing on New Orleans and Iraq, Lipsitz seeks to invest scholarly practice with the spirit of public political discussion, as he does in *American Studies in a Moment of Danger* (Minneapolis: University of Minnesota Press, 2001), a book whose title is indebted to Benjamin.

20. Philip Gourevitch and Errol Morris, *Standard Operating Procedure* (New York: Penguin, 2008).

21. Benedict Anderson, *Imagined Communities: Reflections on the Origin and Spread of Nationalism*, 2nd and 3rd eds. (London: Verso, 1991, 2006).

22. Ibid., 187.

23. Ibid., 191.

24. Ibid., 195.

25. On "the other America," see J. Michael Dash, *The Other America: Caribbean Literature in a New World Context* (Charlottesville: University Press of Virginia, 1998), and an unpublished conference paper by Peter Hulme, "Expanding the Caribbean" (keynote address at "Writing the Other America: Comparative Approaches to Caribbean and Latin American Literature," Humanities Research Centre, University of Warwick, February 2006).

26. On the United States as "just another creole-led revolutionary state," see Anderson, *Imagined Communities*, 210, and on the Civil War as one of "the three longest and bloodiest wars . . . on the periphery of the world-system," see Anderson, *Under Three Flags*, 3. See also Anderson, *The Spectre of Comparisons: Nationalism, Southeast Asia, and the World* (London: Verso, 1998).

27. Anderson, *Spectre of Comparisons*, 207.

28. See ibid., 187, 192.

29. See W. E. B. Du Bois, *Dusk of Dawn: An Essay toward an Autobiography of a Race Concept* (1940; repr., New York: Schocken, 1968).

Rogue States and Emergent Disciplines

SRINIVAS ARAVAMUDAN

The relationship between the state and the discipline is always at issue for the interdisciplinary venture of American studies, from past inception to current obsession. Is the venture an ontology of the nation, an instrument in the tool kit of the state, or a paradigm for the liberation of citizen-subjects from the state's clutches? A responsible scholarly procedure would map the internal dynamics of the discipline and measure the long arm of the state through various temporal moments of knowledge production, eventually producing a diachronic account of the development of American studies. Thereby situating itself, the discipline could map its own emergence, evolution, and teleology. However, what if we chose to be irresponsible and instead reoriented the discipline to its wild side, through a puckish, perhaps even roguish desire, to have the discipline swallow its own tail? Rather than trying to shake free of its genealogy, what if American studies pursued the wildest aspects of its genealogy as current and future object? In what follows, I propose a new name and focus for this kind of research program, answering the call of the discipline at the same time as the call of the wild. The wildness I hint at comes in part from my being an interloper, maybe even an inter*loup*er, especially as I will be taking up the question of whether there is indeed a wolf at the door of American studies. What is at stake through such an exercise is an alternative temporality for American studies, one that arises from a foundational incommensurability at the very heart of the project, where the old and the new, the compromised and the promissory, the domesticated and the wild, compete equally for attention. Bringing the wild card into American studies by referencing the wildness of early U.S. history would certainly be a risky proposition. The calculable balance sheets of inspired investment and debilitating loss define the conventional world of risk.

However, what might be disciplinarily at stake through such speculation? Perhaps we will discern, even if only fleetingly, another realm of disjuncture, discontinuity, and strange pleasure, one that comes into being when practitioners can no longer find themselves "back at the ranch" of disciplinary and national familiarity.

IT IS NO SURPRISE that the field imaginary of American studies is still caught between critical breast-beating and redemptive utopianism, both of which replicate symptomatically, at another remove, that which was earlier disavowed. American studies may merit a name change, as Janice Radway has proposed, to "U.S. studies," "Inter-American studies," "transnational cultural studies," or "critical U.S. studies." Beginning with the ideologically homogeneous accounts of the myth-and-symbol school, American studies predates the Cold War when it was fully institutionalized in major university settings.[1]

At an early stage, an intellectual-historical synthesis of multiple traditions was accompanied by an object-centered analysis of the U.S. nation-state. Myths of Anglo-American man's presence in the genocidally evacuated "virginity" of the New World were bolstered by essentializing notions regarding the "American" mind, and particular attention to puritanism, transcendentalism, pragmatism, constitutionalism, liberalism, and individualism. Vernon Parrington is frequently credited with originating the intellectual-historical component of the field as a veritable movement, even as Perry Miller initiated the academic discourse of myth and symbol that drew upon earlier New England Puritan roots.[2] The Cold War context gave this nationalist intellectual tendency within the United States an interdisciplinary institutional home and a state-sponsored social movement in parallel. As the scholarship recounts, the enterprise of American studies almost immediately fell into the clutches of the state. The missionary project of garnering materials celebrating the virtues, traditions, and heritage of the United States was instrumental for the conduct of an aggressive propaganda war on the Soviet Union and its global satellites from the 1950s to the 1970s.

After the first twenty years of apologia and expansion, the field witnessed a reversal of the celebratory paradigm. The professionalization of the field, followed by the entry of a number of politicized and progressive scholars, led to a revision of the field's debt to the U.S. imperial vision during the Cold War. The formation of interdisciplinary scholarship in the humanities and social sciences since the 1960s, as well as the decline of Cold War area studies configurations, contributed vastly to this development. Ethnic studies, women's studies, sexuality studies, film and cultural studies, as well as postcolonial and Third World criticism, New Historicism, and critiques of nationalism and empire fragmented whatever homogeneity the field of American stud-ies had exhibited through the antihistoricist myth-and-symbol paradigm. By the time of her 1998 American Studies Association (ASA) presidential address, Radway questions the field's beleaguered state-centeredness, instead suggesting that "ethnic, queer, feminist, or working-class identities cannot be conceived as separate essences sheltered within a capacious, ontologically prior American identity. Rather, they must be seen as cross-cutting, insurgent, oftentimes oppositional identifications."[3] Multiple radical political imaginaries had begun to interrupt the consolidating and largely antipolitical field imaginary. Radway's proposal for a name change led to some furious reactions even while the tendency toward greater pluralization that she was representing appeared to be both diagnostic and prescriptive with respect to new disciplinary norms.

The entry of progressive thought into the field imaginary led to a reversal that mimicked the earlier dominant discourse. The New World Puritan genre of the American jeremiad morphed into left-liberal jeremiads against U.S. tyranny. In retrospect, such gestures of scholarly self-location after excoriating self-criticism suggest a performative contradiction. This hair-shirt logic characterizes much contemporary left-wing American studies, and a residual, if chastened, national self returns after conducting obligatory penance in order to shore up a progressive outcome. To what extent does contemporary American studies rely on a negative theology of the U.S. nation-state — or empire — as the overarching colossus in need of constant berating as a kind of captive golem to be taken out in chains, whipped, and then put back in the national closet? After the dismantling, there is reconstruction according to progressive aspirations fueled by featuring suppressed archives within the earlier historiography. Critiques of right-wing and hegemonic nationalism offer inclusive liberal or radical alternatives, even if the initial critiques already have the insurgent function of the "intricate interdependency" that Radway delineates. A left-leaning American studies seems fated to play out a counterhegemonic script, by proclaiming an open-ended radical democracy opposing the appropriating state-form of an earlier generation.[4] However, this game of insurgent oppositionality (turning into political revindication) confronts two notions of the nation against each other — the expanded and socially progressive version that aims to enfranchise the disenfranchised and give a political life to those who had previously suffered a social death against the consolidating, antipolitical, and constitutional form of American-ness, one that wishes to create managerial consensus around an animating national vision that can allow all these multiple newly identified actors to "get along" with each other superficially — if not substantively — in Rodney King's famous words.[5] The U.S. Left's predilection for multicultural differ-ence reveals itself as deeply nationalist despite occasional attempts to go beyond the national paradigm.

While there has been a history of pieties expressed in various ASA presi-dential addresses regarding U.S. scholars paying insufficient attention to the scholarship of non-U.S.-based American studies scholarly ventures, the rela-tivism of the observer's respective standpoint is given symbolic play even as actual publication practices reveal that disciplinary professionalization and its circuits of citation trump such goodwill gestures. As Paul Giles suggests, there is a residual cultural transcendentalism within Americanist discourse.[6] Or, as Lawrence Buell argues, American studies is destined to thrive and writhe, because its general institutional health has always to be tempered by an identificatory political guilt.[7] Buell holds out for the slipperiness within the discourse of American studies that resists embodiment and enacts a criti-cal distance and disaffiliation from reductive state-identified ventures of me-diation that is exemplary.

Despite some sage disidentifications such as Buell's, or those by Amy Kaplan or Donald Pease, much of American studies, especially in its literary-critical mode, is caught up in a short-leash redemptive logic of an accelerated if not instant gratification, and a recognizable but teasingly elusive future of social justice and participatory democracy. To be sure, the mobilizing power of the United States' founding ideals involving liberty, justice, equality, and individuality-within-community is still evident around the world. The initial moves that critically defamiliarize the discourse in order to populate it with other subjects and sensibilities are already part of an instrumentalizing meth-odology that wishes to recognize, respect, and celebrate differences in the place of a previous logic of homogeneity, conformity, and identity. In much of the literature, there is not enough attention being paid to the symptomatic nature of such desires for difference — even if there is something commend-able about having these desires. Indeed, one might ask, along with the title of Alberto Moreiras's perceptive book on Latin American cultural studies, whether all this focus on and fetishization of multiple identities, leads, ul-timately, to something like a veritable "exhaustion of difference."[8] As critics of corporate multiculturalism have begun to argue, a politics of difference plays back into a managerial discourse of social consensus.[9] Despite calls for a robust dissensus in the literature, the administrative structure of the university favors collaboration with a consensual postpolitics. Putting a benign face on the market-driven differentiation of society under late capitalism, managerialism does not push hard enough on the incommensurabilities of various visions because that would otherwise break apart the social contract and reveal the real fissures that are otherwise papered over. The U.S. academy's intellectual ventures are, at least in part, funded through the vagaries of global finance capital localized through bonds, endowments, and soft money, along with skyrocketing student fees, variously driven by deficits and unsustainable consumption patterns alike.

In the midst of this generalized post-Fordist ethos, the call to resituate American studies within a critical internationalism, when suggested by Jane Desmond and Virginia Dominguez, ought to lead to a non-U.S.-centric comparativism that might shed additional if indirect light.[10] However, this has not happened. A recent turn to transnationalism (Shelley Fisher Fishkin's 2004 ASA address, or Robert Gross's "The Transnational Turn") in lieu of critical internationalism seems dangerously symptomatic in an era when the U.S. state has been reneging on its international obligations and arguing for its super-sovereignty in international contexts.[11] Why is transnationalism an emergent — perhaps now even dominant — disciplinary method in the social sciences at a moment when global fears about the U.S. state's unilateralism and hyperpower (amid a pick-and-choose liberal internationalism) have been widespread? As Leerom Medovoi argues, our current post-Fordist conjuncture in political economy enables this transnational turn in the criticism: we are now caught in a new global narrative that "does not presume a world protagonist subject to interpellation." As a result, Medovoi counsels that we ought to pay far more attention to the future-tense narratives of globalization *in* and *as* American studies rather than to continue the repetitive exposures of the past-tense justification of American studies as a product of the Cold War standoff with the Soviet Union. Globalization studies, in other words, is American studies writ large but pretending to be about everything and everyone else.[12]

There are considerable analytical differences to be identified, with respect to the changes from the old U.S. exceptionalism to the focus on new global transnationalisms. Denationalization cannot really be practiced epistemologically through good intentions, given the power asymmetries politically and globally that still write the United States into every narrative as the sole hyperpower on the world stage. Karen Halttunen's 2005 ASA address (that hopes to explore and reverse the power geometries that juxtapose capitalist transformation of place into amorphous placelessness) finds redemption through the localization of identity. However, it is worth asking if such localization of place is what many nation-state-centered narratives nonetheless tend to favor as another form of masking the national narrative and presenting it under another guise.[13] If one version of globalization expands the United States into the world, making American studies inescapable but also uncontainable, the version of the transnational turn proposed by some scholars as localism defamiliarizes — but does not dissolve — the nation through the abstract flows of multiple local interactions.

Recognizing multiple dynamics at work in terms of the projected temporalities of American studies in their comprehensive anthology, *The Futures of American Studies*, Pease and Wiegman identify four broad categories of "future talk" regarding the field.[14] "Posthegemonic" positions are, to some degree, positions that recognize a perpetual critical distance that separates the field's critical intentions from its ostensible object, even as "counterhegemonic" ones argue somewhat more hopefully that recognizing and including progressive movements and suppressed pasts can actually lay claim to a redemptive and expansive nation-state narrative. The other two categorizations of articles in their anthology are "comparativist" and "differentialist." Comparativist American studies is a move outward from a single object such as the United States — however complicated — toward hemispheric and transnational forms of comparative area studies and interdisciplinarity, in order to see better the multiple intersections among social, academic, and political movements, whereas a differentialist American studies stages the failure of the ready referentiality enabled by such comparative area studies work. To some degree, if posthegemonic and counterhegemonic logics are caught up in something like a political ontology of failure and success within the political and representational discourse of the nation-state, comparative and differentialist logics are caught up in the metadisciplinary epistemology of a globalized area studies discourse customized for Americanist and non-Americanist settings. Such a global comparison might need a veritable Archimedean lever that enables the scholar to assess incommensurabilities differently from complicities. Area studies epistemologies seek to connect and referentialize theoretical discourses with political practices. By enacting an integration of the sphere of intellectual production and the sphere of political systems, such disciplines fix meanings comparatively even as differentialist logics seek to unfix them through critique. These important classifications reveal the extent to which American studies is caught up within vectors of time and space: the posthegemonic and counterhegemonic tendencies are about retroactive generational battles regarding the internal dynamics of the nation-state, even as comparative and differentialist tendencies are about the revealed limits of spatialization when taken as the primary mode of epistemological understanding.

I WANT TO turn from this disciplinarily internal discussion of the simultaneous "thriving and writhing" of American studies (Buell) to the external factor of the rogue state as animating concept and condition of knowledge. Since Richard Slotkin's documentation of the dirty tricks of both the state and the nonstate actors that enabled U.S. expansion, American studies appears to alternate between an alienated and angry posthegemonic narrative and a redemptive and revisionary counterhegemonic narrative.[15] Hegemony requires consent, but lately consent is increasingly absent. Neoliberalism assaults time and space by erasing particular histories of domination and resistance, instead substituting a model of spatialized governance. The political history of democracy in various places features how "the part that is no part" can begin to speak and claim a political voice as the synecdoche of the whole, a "dis-agreement" in Jacques Rancière's terms.[16] Once we focus on the actions of the United States as a rogue state, we become aware of comparativist and differentialist analyses. It is a truism that the global security state increasingly functions outside frameworks of hegemony. Neoliberalism aims to ensure the smooth functioning of globalized markets even as neoconservatism identifies enemies of Western suzerainty. Ironically, even as neoliberalism suppresses or ignores historical difference for the chimera of seamless global economic unification, neoconservatism engineers the assault on cultural and civilizational enemies, thereby recognizing the continuation of history even if through a distorted way.

The history of the rise of the United States as an arch-rogue state forces an alternative temporality onto U.S. studies. In anticipation of the persistent and irreducible power of the state beyond any Gramscian project of the war of positions, Ranajit Guha proposed a fuller analysis of the relationship between coercion and consent and, alternately, the forms of collaboration and resistance to state power that violate the overriding category of consent that doctrines of hegemony and counterhegemony rely upon. It is therefore compelling to describe the global script of the United States today as one of dominance without hegemony.[17] As a declining hegemon, the United States can either participate in the newer structures of global multipolarity in the twenty-first century or react through a desire for dominance without hegemony, lashing out militarily against real and imaginary foes. Thinking of the United States and American studies in this way is to route it "irresponsibly" through South Asian and subaltern studies, a procedure that may yield new insights about the manner in which state formation generates surplus effects that are persistent and yet invisible from within self-understandings of the structure created by the polity.

The rogue state appellation has arisen in the context of the decline of the Cold War. Even as the United States has at various times deemed specific adversaries including preinvasion Iraq, Iran, North Korea, Cuba, Libya, and others as rogue states, the United States' own global actions writ large resemble the illegality that is projected onto others. The United States' refusal to accede to various internationalist protocols from Kyoto to the International Criminal Court and the Law of the Sea, and the rise of complicitous scholarship that queries the very existence and normative force of international law can be cited as evidence of the decline of a hegemonic framework on the international stage, just as much as the United States' recent floutings of the United Nations charter and the Geneva Conventions.[18] These developments represent a major challenge to the conduct of international law and the regime of international liberal institutions that the United States nonetheless largely supports, even if such law is deemed by the United States as necessary for others rather than for itself. Jacques Derrida, Giorgio Agamben, and Judith Butler have analyzed the philosophical implications of these exceptional forms of behavior.[19]

However, this is not necessarily just a post-9/11 tendency as some have recently argued; rather, 9/11 only exacerbated a long history of the United States' deliberate flouting of international law. International legal scholar Philippe Sands, in his book, *Lawless World*, suggests, with copious evidence, that the United States has systematically undermined the very global order that it created and supported after 1945.[20] It is a mistake to assume that this is a temporary aberration of George W. Bush's regime, and its flamboyant neoconservative experiment of exporting "democracy" through war and invasion. Witness 24 March 1999, a date identified by Sands as one during which NATO began its illegal bombing campaign in Serbia and also, coincidentally, when the liberal *New York Times* published an editorial condemning Britain's arrest of former Chilean president Auguste Pinochet as "sovereignty's worst day in memory." The U.S. intervention in Kosovo and Serbia is often defended as politically legitimate even if technically illegal as its intention was to prevent genocide, even though the postwar evidence points to the war as having pre- cipitated the scale of the genocide. If Bill Clinton's Serbian escapade anticipates George W. Bush's Iraq misadventure, no U.S. soldier died in combat operations during the Serbian war, and Clinton escaped the domestic and international political scrutiny that was later given to George W. Bush and Dick Cheney's imperial conduct of the presidency. In retrospect, if Clinton's military strategy was postmodern in that he bombed but did not occupy, his decision to go to war without explicit UN approval was no less illegal than Bush's.

These complicities across Democratic and Republican regimes are important to emphasize in order to understand the imperialist assumptions of the U.S. political mainstream. While it is important to appreciate the nuances, as left internationalists have tried to justify humanitarian intervention in the worst cases where dictators abuse their captive populations and hide behind sovereignty doctrine, it is equally worth realizing that regional and local interventions have been known to work far better than those orchestrated on a global scale by the United States with the baggage of vested interests it represents. The UN failure to intervene in Rwanda, Palestine, and Congo, alongside successful interventions in Sierra Leone and East Timor, and problematic U.S. involvements in Haiti, Afghanistan, and Iraq in the past decade, demonstrate at best a mixed legacy of internationalist intervention.

It is no wonder that William Blum's book, *Rogue State: A Guide to the World's Only Superpower* documenting U.S. and CIA dirty tricks from 1945 onward vaulted onto the *New York Times* best-seller list along with news of its influence on Osama Bin Laden, who cited it in one of his anti–United States missives.[21] Noam Chomsky also documents illegal U.S. actions copiously in his *Rogue States: The Rule of Force in Foreign Affairs*.[22] According to Chomsky, the United States is the most roguish of all states especially when it designates others as rogue states in order to declare war against its enemies.[23] It appears as if liberal internationalism and its aim to replace older mechanisms of sovereignty with governmentality was largely the United States' creation. This internationalism is designated by the United States as law for others who are politically and militarily subordinated, whereas the U.S. state's own persistent desire is for an old-fashioned and untethered sovereignty, kept largely for itself and, occasionally, some choice international friends, such as Israel.

Jacques Derrida points out that the United States' recent diatribe against rogue states began in the speeches of Bill Clinton and Madeleine Albright after 1997. Robert S. Litwak, who worked for the Clinton administration and subsequently became a scholar at the Woodrow Wilson Center, also published a book entitled *Rogue States and US Foreign Policy: Containment after the Cold War.*[24] Litwak's argument is thoroughly circular: rogue states are defined as those who oppose the United States and who are named by the United States as rogues. The United States arrogates to itself the power to name, pursue, and punish the rogue, and it also retains the right to re-scind such a designation as it did with Libya. Once the former rogue state has expressed adequate contrition and paid compensation for its previous crimes, it is readmitted and domesticated into the family of nation-states under the United States' auspices as a client. According to Derrida, this logic of the naming of rogue states relies ironically on the dictum of Jean de La Fontaine's fable, "The Wolf and the Lamb," which begins with the proposition that might is right.[25]

Legal scholar John Yoo (who drafted the sophistical torture memo jus-tifying anything less than organ failure or death as allowable side effects of interrogation techniques under the Geneva Conventions) similarly argues for an imperial presidency in his book, *The Powers of War and Peace: The Constitution and Foreign Affairs after 9/11.*[26] Yoo's argument is for original understanding rather than original intent, but the drift of his reasoning pegs Congress back to its task of appropriating monies rather than "interfering" with the presidential executive, whose powers are deemed as entirely unfet-tered despite the rich constitutional debate about the doctrine of mixed sovereignty laid out by Articles 1 and 2 of the U.S. Constitution. A careful reading of Yoo's argument will reveal that his project is a repudiation of the modern administrative state that arises under FDR, along with its various forms of governmentality, welfare, and legal delegation. Wanting the com-fort and the transparency of a fully hierarchical and embodied sovereignty in the institution of the presidency, Yoo is obsessed with an ipsocentric political theology of sovereignty as representing pure indivisibility and the suspen-sion of time and history. In this regard, we might find that even committed neoliberals express nostalgia for this kind of sovereignty when faced with national crisis. This much-hankered-for model of sovereignty goes back to Jean Bodin and earlier justifications of absolutism in Europe, rather than the alternative tradition inspired by Montesquieu's resuscitation of republican ideas of mixed government that actually inspired the writers of the U.S. Constitution and Jeffersonian democracy in their creation of a system of checks and balances across different branches of government.

Of relevance here is Judith Butler's recent attempt to discuss full sovereignty as anachronistic in her recent book *Precarious Life: The Powers of Mourning and Violence*, and especially her chapter on the U.S. state's incarceration facilities at Guantánamo that turns to this issue of the indivisibility of sovereignty. Butler follows Foucault's line of argumentation, one that sees a succession of stages from sovereignty to discipline to governmentality, followed by a problematization of that chronology with the discovery of the coexistence of these modes of power. In this situation, Butler suggests that "sovereignty, under emergency conditions in which the rule of the law is suspended, would re-emerge in the context of governmentality with the vengeance of an anachronism that refuses to die . . . *the historical time that we thought was past turns out to structure the contemporary field with a persistence that gives the lie to history as chronology*."[27] Butler's account names the resurgence of U.S. sovereignty under a state of emergency as precisely anachronistic, justified in revisionist terms by the likes of Yoo and other neoconservative apologists. The anachronism of sovereignty comes home to roost amid the dulcet strains of neoliberal governmentality that was, until then, singing the praises of the global marketplace.[28]

THE RICH national imaginary of the United States, as Richard Slotkin already demonstrated, pertains to the permanent frontier, populated by criminals, rogues, and runaways. The settlement of the West has been recently unsettled in relation to the rest of the world, and the positioning of space as the final frontier in the television series *Star Trek* and its spinoffs has now been reterritorialized in terms of the Global War against Terror. It is as if the Wild West is now projected externally on "failed states" seen as enacting a Hobbesian "state of nature" where violence is both imminent and immanent.

We need to remember the roguish contexts of the United States' early settlement as a genealogy of the recent flirtation with global super-sovereignty. Such a hypothesis might crosswire the material of the myth-and-symbol school, reading it against the grain and connecting it to social history, while at the same time reflecting on the functionality of such mythmaking. This might turn into a dialogue with the presence of the past, something that is frequently excluded in contemporary discussion of foreign policy. The early

American rogue might then serve as mythistorical analogue of Hobbes's monstrous Leviathan, containing the body politic within himself, his actions, and tendencies, even as he anticipates the U.S. state's emotional comprehension of the world outside of itself. "Land pirates" such as John Murrell, Samuel Mason, Joseph Hare, Micajah and Wiley Harpe, and other famous criminals and renegades, including Bampfylde-Moore Carew, transported twice to the colonies whereupon he escaped to lead a life of crime,[29] and Joshua Tefft, a renegade in King Phillip's war who was executed in Rhode Island for siding with the Narragansetts, present us with rich prefigurations of roguishness that is exemplary of national character. Tom Bell was perhaps the most famous rogue of eighteenth-century British America, about whom there were at least a hundred newspaper articles from 1738 to 1755. Committing many thefts, impostures, and impersonations, Bell's reputation as quintessential wild American was partly celebrated and excoriated in a manner that suggests the germ of media fascination with great criminals including serial killers.[30] What later became enshrined in Melville's *The Confidence-Man* can be discerned in several early figures including William Riddlesden, who cheated Benjamin Franklin's father-in-law; John Underhill, a captain of the militia during the Pequot war, whose sexual escapades and involvement in the Antinomian Controversy aroused considerable interest; and Gilbert Imlay, the land speculator and confidence trickster who escaped to England, where he had an affair with Mary Wollstonecraft and plotted an invasion of Louisiana with the early French Revolutionaries. Matching the connection between roguery and criminality in the United States with the milieu of the early English novel, Henry Tufts wrote *The Autobiography of a Criminal* (1807).[31] These criminal figures are politically "vitalist," resonating with the country's heritage and rationalizing its future actions.

These colonial rogues, some of whom precede the declaration of the formal U.S. nation-state, are not necessarily unique in European terms: from the Renaissance, the picaresque genre purveyed Spanish rogues, and writers such as Richard Head produced *The English Rogue*, even as parallel fictions of *The French Rogue* and *The Dutch Rogue* also came about.[32] It is not surprising that Thomas Jefferson's chapter on "Religion" in *Notes on the State of Virginia* cautions its readers about the widespread persistence of roguish identity in early America. Perhaps this background of roguery demonstrates more adequately the United States' alternation, since its inception, from "secured innocent nation to a wounded, insecure emergency state," in the words of Donald Pease. The demetaphorization of the virgin land in terms of current political discourse is spectacular, and as Pease suggests, the current spectatorial public is being returned to a prenational moment of atavistic memory regarding the clearing of Indian territory that is then appropriated as homeland over against the notion of the terrorist wolf outside the fold. The quasi-permanent biological arrangement of the homeland in relation to the juridical-political apparatus of the state is the renewed discovery of a pastoralism as the state's function over and beyond that of sovereignty, a reconstitution of a citizenry as a biological population or flock to be tended to by the state-shepherd.[33]

Derrida chose the late seventeenth-century fable of "The Wolf and the Lamb" to showcase the United States' self-aggrandizing super-sovereignty since 9/11, echoing the Hobbesian world of the state of nature within which man is a wolf to fellow man (*Homo homini lupus*). The same metaphor can be extended via Michel Foucault to the topic of governmentality with a somewhat different twist. Governmentality speaks of a world of sheep protected by the pastoralism of the shepherd-monarch, along with the protection of sheepdogs. In this world, the roguery of wolves on the run — such as the terrorist network al Qaeda — can be kept at bay, even if the lone wolf can occasionally catch the defenseless stray lamb.[34] The leaders of men are as pastors to their flocks, but these pastors keep their animals in order to eat them voraciously at a moment of their choosing.[35] As Foucault puts it, in political philosophy, the city-citizen game is always supplemented by the shepherd-flock game, and the question of sovereignty always has to be supplemented by an analysis of the art of governmentality.[36]

Given the rich history of wolfish roguery in the United States' exceptionalist past and its contemporary present as the shepherd anchoring the new transnationalism, what kind of emergent interdisciplines can really do battle with the metaphysics and politics of the anachronistic return of sovereignty? At this moment, a neoliberal consensus regarding markets, free trade, and international institutions coexists alongside a neoconservative belief in the imperial presidency and the resurrected powers of the executive and imperial monarch-president, a wolf and a shepherd at once. It remains to be seen whether future presidents will renounce the powers arrogated to the office by Bush and Cheney.

Which emergent interdiscipline is adequate to studying the category of the rogue state, ruled over by a shepherd-monarch-wolf? This question might be a rubric that oversees any future intervention into the huge and bewildering terrain of American studies. A particular kind of interdiscipline is required to study the anachronistic resuscitation of early modern sovereign tendencies in a postmodern era. Or, are these tendencies not that anachronistic after all, revealing the compressed multichronic time that Ernst Bloch called *Ungleichzeitigkeit*? The symbolic formation of the U.S. state in the early twenty-first century consists of arcane metaphysics as well as the economics of derivatives, old-fashioned criminality and newfangled bio-politicality. The objects to be studied include xenophobic fear of the Islamic terrorist amid unmitigated greed for the nonrenewable oil revenues and resources of the Islamic world; nuclear supremacism over nonnuclear and nuclear-aspiring states while espousing messianic rhetoric regarding the primacy of Judeo-Christian civilization over all others; and imposing a "Washington Consensus" debtor's medicine on Third World countries even as large-scale banking bailouts are planned to rescue those on Wall Street who invented large-scale Ponzi schemes through exotic financial instruments called collateralized debt obligations. The emergent interdiscipline renames American studies with a frisson, thereby marking the guilty pleasure of secret enjoyment that frequently accompanies narratives of power. A critical combination of political philosophy, cultural history, and literary theory, we might call this new form of American studies, "rogue studies."

Rogue studies would have come full circle, beginning with the other side of the myth-and-symbol school, and showing us the obverse face of the nation-state with its self-justifications and hegemonic ambitions. Realists might be very unhappy with this form of rogue criticism, an exercise of shadow puppetry outside the boundary recognition of the scholarly frontier. The territory is that of the state of exception, a shadow world where legal norm is suspended, and the suspended form of detention without trial is the norm. There is nothing more mythical than the wolf, and yet, does not the power of that fabulous beast strangely connect the domesticated fold and the wild frontier, the shepherd-state and the nonstate actor–terrorist? Tariq Ali's *The Clash of Fundamentalisms* has a witty cover showing Osama Bin Laden in Bush garb and George W. Bush in Bin Laden garb.[37] This reveals the wolf in shepherd's — rather than sheep's — clothing. Ali's witty cover shows the custodian of the state in terrorist drag and the terrorist in presidential attire. Who's zooming who? Between the Bushes and the Bin Ladens, there is a strange confusion of roles, and the crossing of family complicities and economic interests. The shady connections of the Carlyle Group, Halliburton, and various oil-based oligarchies collide with the adoption of bio-terrorist strategies by state and nonstate actors alike that mutually confuse righteous sovereign and unjust enemy, shepherd and wolf, agent and actor. The myth-and-symbol school is easy to beat up on, except when the reality of fear-mongering begins to draw upon myths and symbols much more energetically than in the recent past, and when the shadow history of the nation, replete with rogues and mountebanks — a history marginal until now except for its celebration in certain segments of popular culture — strangely begins to resemble the actual hijacking of the state apparatus by oil reconstruction companies, mercenary armies, and fundamentalist preachers. These were the very internal wolves that in "normal" (read, secular humanist) circumstances might have been placed outside the sheepfold because they represented the unjust enemy rather than the homeland itself.

Rogue studies might appear very threatening, as if it might blow apart the entire scholarly venture of American studies, but if we look at it closely, it is nothing more than a redescription of the phenomena by way of a hyperrealist provocation. However, the progressive Americanist seeking counterhegemony might very legitimately ask: where is the hope?

Not yet, not now, answers the practitioner of Rogue studies, indexing the current situation of dominance without hegemony. Rogue studies would be about the roguishness of U.S. foreign policy, the rogue as generative national figure in the country's past and present, and the serendipitous convergences of political emergency, financial crime, and social deviancy. Rogue studies has a considerable future, taking into its purview the neoliberal globalization of Bill Clinton, the neoconservative backlash of George W. Bush, and the post-meltdown pragmatism of Barack Obama. A series of global crises might not just culminate in the disciplinary emergency of the inadequacy of American studies, but could instead paradoxically result in the windfall of the emergent discipline that we can affectionately and provocatively call: Rogue studies.

NOTES

1. See Donald Pease and Robyn Wiegman, eds., *The Futures of American Studies* (Durham: Duke University Press, 2002), and Janice Radway, "What's in a Name," in ibid., 45–75. Radway's article is a revised and expanded version of her 1998 American Studies Association presidential address.

2. See Vernon Parrington, *Main Currents in American Thought: An Interpretation of American Literature from the Beginnings to 1920* (New York: Harcourt, 1958); Perry Miller, *Errand into the Wilderness: An Address* (Providence, R.I.: John Carter Brown Library, 1952).

3. Radway, "What's in a Name," 58–59.

4. There are, of course, several exceptions to be noted against any such generalization, and many of these are discussed here. Two significant scholars who have resisted celebratory resistance narratives are George Lipsitz and Amy Kaplan.

5. See Orlando Patterson, *Slavery and Social Death: A Comparative Study* (Cambridge, Mass.: Harvard University Press, 1982); for influential critiques of Patterson's position, see Russ Castronovo, *Necro Citizenship: Death, Eroticism and the Public Sphere in the Nineteenth-Century United States* (Durham: Duke University Press, 2001), and Vincent Brown, *The Reaper's Garden: Death and Power in the World of Atlantic Slavery* (Cambridge, Mass.: Harvard University Press, 2007).

6. Paul Giles, "Reconstructing American Studies: Transnational Paradoxes, Comparative Perspectives," *Journal of American Studies* 28 (1994): 335, 344.

7. See Lawrence Buell, "Theorizing the National in a Spirit of Due Reluctance," in *Theories of American Culture, Theories of American Studies*, ed. Winfried Fluck and Thomas Claviez (Tübingen: G. Nar, 2003), 177–99, 180. See also Lawrence Buell, "The Timeliness of Place," *American Quarterly* 58, no. 1 (March 2006): 17–22.

8. Alberto Moreiras, *The Exhaustion of Difference: The Politics of Latin American Cultural Studies* (Durham: Duke University Press, 2001).

9. See David Theo Goldberg, *Multiculturalism: A Critical Reader* (Oxford: Blackwell, 1994); and Chris Newfield, *Ivy and Industry: Business and the Making of the American University, 1880–1980* (Durham: Duke University Press, 2004).

10. Jane C. Desmond and Virginia C. Dominguez, "Resituating American Studies in a Critical Internationalism," *American Quarterly* 48, no. 3 (1996): 475–90.

11. Shelley Fisher Fishkin, "Crossroads of Cultures: The Transnational Turn in American Studies," *American Quarterly* 57, no. 1 (March 2005): 17–57. This was the 2004 ASA Presidential Address. See Robert Gross, "The Transnational Turn: Rediscovering American Studies in a Wider World," *Journal of American Studies* 34, no. 3 (2000): 373–93.

12. See Leerom Medovoi, "Nation, Globe, Hegemony: Post-Fordist Preconditions of the Transnational Turn in American Studies," *Interventions* 7, no. 2 (2005): 162–79, quotation from 169.

13. Karen Halttunen, "Groundwork: American Studies in Place," *American Quarterly* 58, no. 1 (March 2006): 1–15.

14. Donald Pease and Robyn Wiegman, "Futures," in Pease and Wiegman, *The Futures of American Studies*, 1–42.

15. See Richard Slotkin, *Regeneration through Violence: The Mythology of the American Frontier, 1600–1800* (Middletown, Conn.: Wesleyan University Press, 1973).

16. Jacques Rancière, *Dis-Agreement: Philosophy and Politics*, trans. Julie Rose (Minneapolis: University of Minnesota Press, 1998).

17. Ranajit Guha, *Dominance without Hegemony: History and Power in Colonial India* (Cambridge, Mass.: Harvard University Press, 1997).

18. See Curtis A. Bradley and Jack L. Goldsmith, "Customary International Law as Federal Common Law: A Critique of the Modern Position," *Harvard Law Review* 110, no. 4 (February 1997): 815–76; Jack L. Goldsmith and Eric A. Posner, *The Limits of International Law* (New York: Oxford University Press, 2005); Ernest A. Young, "Sorting Out the Debate over Customary International Law," *Virginia International Law Journal* 42

(Winter 2002): esp. 365; and Ernest A. Young, "The Trouble with Global Constitutional-ism," *Texas International Law Journal* 38 (2003): esp. 527.

19. See Jacques Derrida, *Rogues: Two Essays on Reason*, trans. Pascale-Anne Brault and Michael Naas (Stanford: Stanford University Press, 2005); Giorgio Agamben, *Homo Sacer: Sovereign Power and Bare Life*, trans. Daniel Heller-Roazen (Stanford: Stanford University Press, 1998); and Judith Butler, *Precarious Life: The Powers of Mourning and Violence* (New York: Verso, 2004).

20. Philippe Sands, *Lawless World: America and the Making and Breaking of Global Rules from FDR's Atlantic Charter to George W. Bush's Illegal War* (New York: Viking, 2005); see also Jordan J. Paust, *Beyond the Law: The Bush Administration's Unlawful Responses in the "War" on Terror* (New York: Cambridge University Press, 2007).

21. William Blum, *Rogue State: A Guide to the World's Only Superpower* (Monroe, Maine: Common Courage Press, 2005).

22. Noam Chomsky, *Rogue States: The Rule of Force in Foreign Affairs* (Cambridge, Mass.: South End Press, 2000); and Noam Chomsky, *Acts of Aggression: Policing Rogue States* (New York: Seven Stories, 1999).

23. Amusingly, Hugo Chavez waved a Spanish translation of Chomsky's *Hegemony or Survival: America's Quest for Global Dominance* (New York: Henry Holt, 2003) during his UN address in September 2006, while excoriating Bush.

24. Robert S. Litwak, *Rogue States and US Foreign Policy: Containment after the Cold War* (Washington, D.C.: Woodrow Wilson Center, 2000). For a more general bibliography on the rich references to rogue nations and rogue states in the current context, see also, T. D. Allman, *Rogue State: America at War with the World* (New York: Nation Books, 2004); Peter Brooks, *A Devil's Triangle: Terrorism, Weapons of Mass Destruction, Rogue States* (Lanham: Rowan and Littlefield, 2005); Gary J. Dorrien, *Imperial Designs: Neoconservatism and the New Pax Americana* (New York: Routledge, 2004); S. P. Fullinwider, *Towards a Rogue Reality: Kant to Freud, and Beyond* (New York: P. Lang, 1998); Geoffrey Household, *Rogue Justice* (Boston: Little, Brown, 1982); Koichi Iwabuchi and Many Thomas, *Rogue Flows: Trans-Asian Cultural Traffic* (Hong Kong: Hong Kong University Press, 2004); Alexandra Kura, ed., *Rogue Countries: Background and Current Issues* (Huntington, N.Y.: Nova Science Publishers, 2001); James M. Lindsay, *Defending America: The Case for Limited National Missile Defense* (Washington, D.C.: Brookings Institute Press, 2001); Miroslav Nincic, *Renegade Regimes: Confronting Deviant Behavior in World Politics* (New York: Columbia University Press, 2005); Solve Ohlander and Gunnar Bergh, "Taliban — A Rogue Word in Present-Day English Grammar," *English Studies: A Journal of English Language and Literature* 85, no. 3 (June 2004): 206–29; Clyde V. Prestowitz, *Rogue Nation: American Unilateralism and the Failure of Good Intentions* (New York: Basic Books, 2003); Peter Scowen, *Rogue Nation: The America the Rest of the World Knows* (Toronto: M&S, 2003); Gerry J. Simpson, *Great Powers and Outlaw States: Unequal Sovereigns in the International Legal Order* (Cambridge: Cambridge University Press, 2004); and Raymond Tanter, *Rogue Regimes: Terrorism and Proliferation* (New York: St. Martin's Press, 1998).

25. "La raison du plus fort est toujours la meilleure / Nous l'allons montrer tout à l'heure" (Derrida, *Rogues*, xi). In La Fontaine's fable, the lamb appears to represent enlightened

reason even as the wolf represents brute force. Three times the lamb reasons with the wolf's specious reasoning: the lamb is drinking from the water downstream from the wolf, and therefore cannot soil his water as he initially alleges; the lamb could not have insulted him last year as the wolf suggests, as he was not yet born then; and the lamb does not have a brother even though the wolf charges him with assuming the guilt of his brother's having insulted him earlier. However, the wolf's fourth charge is equivalent to a capital sentence: the lamb is deemed guilty by association because the lamb's friends — shepherds and sheepdogs — are necessarily the wolf's sworn enemies. The lamb's reasonings that attempted to get him out of a sticky situation where he does not bear personal responsibility are insufficient, and tragically so, as the wolf drags him into the woods and devours him before he can even respond to the charge of guilt by virtue of group identity. On the surface, this fable demonstrates, with considerable irony, that might is right. The wolf's self-legitimating reason always manages to trump the lamb's defensive legalisms that create alibis, but these alibis cannot adequately preserve the lamb. The wolf makes law according to his strength and is creating new norms with every utterance in a manner that forces the lamb onto the defensive.

26. John Yoo, *The Powers of War and Peace: The Constitution and Foreign Affairs after 9/11* (Chicago: University of Chicago Press, 2005).

27. Butler, *Precarious Life*, 54.

28. President Bush reportedly asserted, in a manner that uncannily echoes the first words of Schmitt's *Political Theology*, "I am the decider, and I decide what's best. And what's best is for Don Rumsfeld to remain as the secretary of defense." *New York Times*, 19 April 2006, A1.

29. "The Life and Adventures of Bampfylde-Moore Carew, Commonly Called the King of Beggars" (London: J. Buckland, C. Bathurst, and T. Davies, 1793), available at Eighteenth Century Collections Online.

30. See Carl Bridenbaugh, "The Famous Infamous Vagrant Tom Bell," in *Early Americans* (New York: Henry Holt, 1981), 121–49; and Steven C. Bullock, "A Mumper among the Gentle: Tom Bell, Colonial Confidence Man," *William & Mary Quarterly* 55, no. 2 (April 1998): 231–58.

31. For other sources regarding early American rogues in addition to Bridenbaugh, see Frank Wadleigh Chandler, *The Literature of Roguery* (New York: Houghton Mifflin, 1907); Daniel E. Cohen, ed., *"The Female Marine" and Related Works: Narratives of Cross-Dressing and Public Vice in America's Early Republic* (Amherst: University of Massachusetts Press, 1997); Peter Linebaugh and Marcus Rediker, *The Many-Headed Hydra: Sailors, Slaves, Commoners and the Hidden History of the Revolutionary Atlantic* (Boston: Beacon Press, 2000); and A. J. Wright, *Criminal Activity in the Deep South, 1700–1930, an Annotated Bibliography* (New York: Greenwood Press, 1989).

32. See Jeffrey Knapp, "Rogue Nationalism," in *Centuries' Ends, Narrative Means*, ed. Robert Newman (Stanford: Stanford University Press, 1996), 138–50.

33. See Donald E. Pease, "The Global Homeland State: Bush's Biopolitical Settlement," *boundary 2* 30, no. 3 (2003): 1–18, quotation from 3. See also Amy Kaplan, "Homeland Insecurities: Reflections on Language and Space," *Radical History Review* 85 (Winter 2003): 82–93.

34. In the essay, "La bête et le souverain," Derrida suggests the ominous future of such governmentality through his meditation on the complicity and, indeed, the uncanny resemblance of the figures of the beast, the criminal, and the sovereign. Jacques Derrida, "La bête et le souverain," in *Démocratie à venir: Autour de Jacques Derrida*, ed. Marie-Louise Mallet (Paris: Galilée, 2004), 433–76.

35. For Derrida, the wolf's gait is an expression in French (*pas de loup*) that suggests the silent stalking of prey, and a true history of sovereignty might involve tracing this wolf's gait back to a lycology from book VIII of Plato's *Republic*, to the myth regarding the founding of Rome by Romulus and Remus suckled by a she-wolf, and a genealogy of the lupine *topoi* of sovereignty from Plautus, Rabelais, Montaigne, and Bacon up to Hobbes. Giorgio Agamben has partly attempted this as well. This is not just a European genealogy but an Indo-European one, including the devouring wolf of the *Rig-Veda* and the deep structural implication of devoration with vociferation, or "the carnivorous sacrifice [that] is essential to the structure of subjectivity." Jacques Derrida, "Force of Law," in *Acts of Religion*, ed. Gil Anidjar (New York: Routledge, 2002), 247.

36. The figure of the lone wolf, the Leviathan, or the sovereign legislator at the origin of the state is recited and reiterated by narratives of political philosophy in a manner that introduces a differential contamination of founding violence and preserving violence (or *rechtsetzende Gewalt* and *rechtserhaltende Gewalt* according to Walter Benjamin). In his reading of Benjamin's "Critique of Violence," Derrida suggests that founding and preserving violence cannot be kept apart, as their iterability collapses into their foundational origin. The police function of the state emerges as spectral in ways that demonstrate the police as increasingly without face or figure, formless and everywhere in a manner that plays out the police's involvement in a "mystical foundation of authority." For a fuller argument concerning these ideas, see Srinivas Aravamudan, "Sovereignty: Between Embodiment and Detranscendentalization," *Texas International Law Journal* 41, no. 3 (Summer 2006): 427–46; and Srinivas Aravamudan, "Subjects/Sovereigns/Rogues," in "Derrida's Eighteenth Century," special issue, *Eighteenth-Century Studies* 40, no. 3 (Spring 2007): 457–65. For close connections between the terrorist and the pirate, see Ileana M. Porras, "On Terrorism: Reflections on Violence and the Outlaw," in *After Identity: A Reader in Law and Culture*, ed. Dan Danielsen and Karen Engle (New York: Routledge, 1995), 294–313; Noam Chomsky, *Pirates and Emperors, Old and New: International Terrorism in the Real World* (Boston: South End Press, 2002).

37. Tariq Ali, *The Clash of Fundamentalisms: Crusades, Jihad, and Modernity* (London: Verso, 2002).

Migrant Archives

New Routes in and out of American Studies

RODRIGO LAZO

The history of the modern archive is inextricable from the establishment of nation-states. In various parts of the world, including France in 1790 and numerous countries in the nineteenth and twentieth centuries, the establishment of a "national archive" followed a revolutionary break from monarchy or colonialism. Archive and nation came together to grant each other authority and credibility: the archive contained documents and records that supposedly spoke to and about the state, while the nation granted a certain cachet to an archive, elevating it above its local and regional counterparts. The continuing influence of that institutional formation is evident in a statement produced by the International Council on Archives, a professional society for archivists and their institutions: "Archives constitute the memory of nations and of societies, shape their identity, and are a cornerstone of the information society."[1] The high stakes of such a claim begin to explain the sustained examination and critique of archives by theorists, most prominently Jacques Derrida, and by historians, librarians, and other scholars.[2] If archives do indeed "constitute" memory rather than just contain it or record it and if they are crucial in disseminating information, a variety of questions emerges. How do archives develop procedures for the inclusion and exclusion of materials, for the preservation and even inadvertent destruction of information? How do archives wield authority over what is considered important in public institutions and educational settings? Who has access to archives, and what types of identity claims are made by the people who control and disperse the information? Most pertinent to the goals of this essay, how can we conceive of archives in new ways so that research agendas are no longer contained by the parameters of the archival frame?

The physical manifestation of archival parameters in the modern period has been a building, which literally housed the materials and served metaphorically to delimit the information. The records office or rare-book library provided safekeeping for documents and became a place where archive rats could gather empirical evidence for their accounts of the past.[3] In the United States, the National Archives occupies both a modern research facility in College Park, Maryland, and a museum facing Constitution Avenue in Washington, D.C., not far from the Capitol. The latter location features copies of the Declaration of Independence, the U.S. Constitution, and the Bill of Rights.[4] This tourist attraction, resembling the Parthenon and featuring New Deal–era engravings on its facade, provides an image of the nation that is connected to a grand narrative of freedom stemming from 1776. The main chamber where the Declaration and other documents are displayed is known as the Rotunda for the Charters of Freedom. By contrast, the facility in College Park, opened in 1994, is a research center that holds many of the records of government agencies. Although some records are still in the Washington, D.C., location, the separation into buildings known as Archives I and Archives II in effect divides visitors into tourist and researcher.

But that division is breaking down as the archive building shares space with the archive Web page. With rare documents, including everything from nineteenth-century immigration records to seventeenth-century books, increasingly becoming available through online databases, archives are now accessible to someone in his or her house, a potential alternative (and more classical) site for archive construction. Visitors to the U.S. National Archives Web page can now "collect records to create your own archive of American history."[5] A personal archive has the potential to challenge the authority of the national building. And scholars who conceptualize archives in ways that displace the terms under which a singular archive is constructed can open new routes for research agendas.

For American studies, these new routes allow for a way to move in and out of the nation rather than privileging national study as the defining point of the field. It is my contention that these paths will lead us to what I call "migrant archives." Migrant archives reside in obscurity and are always at the edge of annihilation. They are the texts of the past that have not been written into the official spaces of archivization, even though they weave in and out of the buildings that house documents. Migrant archives are oxymoronic because one of the functions of archival organization is storage in a specific (safe) place. Migration, by contrast, connotes a journey. And "migrant archives" call for a journey, if not on the part of the researcher, then certainly on the part of a text that will have to travel from one place to another. The contemporary association of migration with border crossings and movement of people in and out of nation-states at great personal risk emphasizes that migration is not safe. Certainly, it is at odds with a storage vault, which historically has been one of the constituting elements of an archive.

The move toward migrant archives calls for the ongoing examination of how memory is constituted, how history is written, and how research is connected to identity. In other words, control of the archive has epistemological and political ramifications. For American studies to move beyond the fixed archive of an Anglo-American nation, scholars will have to undertake more multilingual work in migrant archives. Writing in languages other than English can lead scholars to alternative ways of remembering the past, new ways of naming multiple nations and communities, and even the invention of new ontologies. The writing itself — in Spanish, for example — can constitute a different archive that calls attention to the political choices of writers and also implies that they were unable or unwilling to write in English. More than a record of social processes or a representation of experiences, the writing itself, whether in book form or scraps of paper, is a site where migrant conditions take material form. As writing moves to the de facto official language of a discipline or area, translation becomes a particularly important but unpredictable and vexing type of work. Translation can integrate marginalized and forgotten people into the authorized archive, even as it threatens to alter the content of a migrant archive and erase, however gently, language difference. Given the importance of translation, I begin my discussion by focusing on *Mis Memorias*, a book whose recent republication involved movement out of a migrant archive across decades and languages. I pair this with a return to Derrida's *Mal d'archive*, a fruitful critique of the archive that has inspired lively responses. I conclude with a consideration of how migrant archives emerged from the Recovering the U.S. Hispanic Literary Heritage project.

IN 1935 Luis G. Gómez published *Mis Memorias*, a Spanish-language memoir that recounted Gómez's experiences crossing the border from Mexico to the United States and working as an accountant and contractor in southeast Texas. For many years, the few known remaining copies of *Mis Memorias* were kept by Gómez's descendants but were not circulated among the general public. In 1991 Gómez's grandson presented information about the book at a meeting of the Spanish American Genealogical Association in Corpus Christi, Texas. That presentation drew the attention of Thomas H. Kreneck, associate director for special collections and archives at Texas A&M University, Corpus Christi, who discovered that the book was not listed in library catalogs. Working with Gómez's family, Kreneck helped usher a translation of the memoir into publication. The result was *Crossing the Rio Grande*, a book out of a migrant archive that crossed decades, generations, and languages.[6]

Mis Memorias resided in a migrant archive because it not only was kept privately and faced the risk of being lost or destroyed but was written in a language other than English, another mark of migrancy in the U.S. context. The editors of the book attempt to counter the lack of attention to the Spanish language by undertaking two archival functions: the establishment of a lineage for the book (in this case one based on a family) and the storage of information in an official repository. In his introduction to the volume, Kreneck describes the process of translation and republication as a "labor of love and family devotion." He characterizes the book as "truly a product of two men," Gómez and his translator, Guadalupe Valdez, who was also Gómez's grandson. "By making these memoirs available to a wider audience, Valdez has done much not only for his grandfather's memory and for his family's heritage but for scholarship as well," Kreneck writes.[7] Like Kreneck, Valdez emphasizes the importance of family lineage while explaining why and how he took on the project: "Because of my special relationship with my grandfather and because I am the last living member of his family who knew him personally, it has naturally fallen to me to translate his memoirs."[8] In claiming a "natural" reason for undertaking such work, Valdez conflates academic labor and genealogical connections. That perspective celebrates the regenerative potential of family history even as it overlooks the responsibility of professional scholars to do such work. Why should professors not be engaged in that type of recuperative republication and translation? In placing familial ties at the center of the archival process, Kreneck and Valdez actually turn to a classical notion of the archive, one that links the archive to the archivist's house.

The family, connected to living quarters and offering a genealogical connection from the present to the past, is an important dimension of the archive. The etymology of the word "archive," as Jacques Derrida notes, goes back to an association in ancient Greece between records and a house run by a patriarch known as an archon. Derrida writes, "As is the case for the Latin *archivum* or *archium* (a word that is used in the singular, as was the French *archive*, formerly employed as a masculine singular: *un archive*) the meaning of 'archive,' its only meaning, comes to it from the Greek *arkheion*: initially a house, a domicile, an address, the residence of the superior magistrates, the *archons*, those who commanded."[9] *Arkhe* can be translated as a commandment. By this account, the father's position in the house (and his commandment) was linked to the maintenance of records. In the modern period, the rise of the nation-state transfers the archon's authority to public institutions, and not just national archives but also regional historical societies and local records offices. The public repository continues to imply a common legacy, with the nation or local community taking the place of the family. Thus, it is no surprise that the editors of *Crossing the Rio Grande* are overt in communicating the relationship developed by Gómez's descendants with various archival establishments.

As *Crossing the Rio Grande*'s introductory material makes clear, one of the goals of the publication is to situate the book in various types of archives. *Mis Memorias/Crossing* moves into a rare-book repository, a card catalog, and even a field of study. In conjunction with the new publication, the family bestows a copy of the Spanish-language edition on Texas A&M library, to the delight of Kreneck, the archivist. The English-language edition becomes part of another archive, the library catalog; libraries across the country take on the archival function of organizing and legitimating published material. The book enters a third archival space through the participation of a university press. Published by Texas A&M in an attractive hardcover edition, *Crossing the Rio Grande* has the potential to move into the archive created by disciplines and fields of study. The book can become part of the reading material of American studies, Texas history, labor studies, and Hispanic literary heritage, among others fields.

My usage of "archive" here is in keeping with a pronounced slippage in the meaning of the word in recent years. Once invoked in certain disciplines to distinguish repositories of rare documents from libraries, "archive" is now used in reference to a record of Web postings, historical memory, libraries, and even a set of readings with a theme. Scholars in American studies regularly now refer to an "alternative archive" that will help the field reconsider its assumptions and practices for selecting texts. Two related forces are at work here, writes Marlene Manoff: "One is the conflation of libraries, museums, and archives; and the other is the inflation of the term 'archive,' which has become a kind of loose signifier for a disparate set of concepts."[10] The term is being used more widely, I would argue, because the physical archive is associated with authority and is a locus of power in research. Calling a selected group of readings "my archive" claims legitimacy but can also invoke the types of critiques that have been leveled at archive, the building. Perhaps writers use the term ironically. But does a site that recovers and collects texts for public use justifiably stake a more serious claim on the use of "archive" than individual researchers who use the word loosely? When I say that *Crossing the Rio Grande* enters several archives, it is to note that the library and university press can grant visibility in academic or other public discourse to what might otherwise remain a family heirloom.

Crossing the Rio Grande enters various archives because the new English edition has the potential to reach a reading audience that includes monolingual scholars. Translation becomes an important process in the recovery of migrant archives. Like migrancy, translation implies movement — literally, "to carry across." In the case of American studies, the movement in and out of migrant archives calls for the transferring of little-known documents into the more visible spaces of the field's debates and also for the carrying of those documents across languages. In the United States, archives hold a wealth of textual riches in languages other than English. A decade ago, Marc Shell and Werner Sollors attempted to "make visible the most glaring blind spot in American letters" by publishing *The Multilingual Anthology of American Literature*, which included selections in French, Navajo, and German, among other languages.[11] This anthology invoked literary history as a kind of memory that could intervene in contemporary debates about the United States' relationship to English-only movements. Multilingualism calls for an opposition to the national fixation on a single language and opens avenues for transnational connections.

Materials in languages other than English written in the past face the possibility of disappearance and annihilation because historically the United States has not established official channels for study and archivization. With the din of a call for English as an "official language" persistently in the background, the papers of multilingual America remain in the obscurity of archival vaults, if we can assume they have been gathered and kept. In addition, the demands of working in multiple languages means that relatively few scholars can approach the multilingual past; a project for a multilingual America would involve extensive collaboration. It is difficult enough to inspire bilingual approaches. Because many, if not most, practitioners of

American studies work predominantly or exclusively in English, documents require translation, which is always intertwined with interpretation, in order to enter the field. In other words, translation helps formulate a recognizable body of work that the field can share. As the case of *Crossing the Rio Grande* illustrates, translation also becomes part of the process of building archives (field of study and library holding).

But how does a field of study resemble a repository of documents? What exactly is the relationship between American studies and the U.S. National Archives? That question is an important dimension of Derrida's *Mal d'archive*, which seeks to posit a homology between the field of psychoanalysis and the archive proper. With a founding father (Freud) who bestows authority on the operations of interpretation, psychoanalysis offers an institutional narrative that is comparable to that of the national or local archive. Derrida argues that in both cases the archive posits an origin (a primal scene, the founding of the nation) and frames a narrative on the basis of that claim. As such, Derrida seeks to undo the ontology of the archive.

MAL D'ARCHIVE runs through a gamut of associations, connecting the archival setting with everything from politics to e-mail. Derrida's trail links the following: the aforementioned ancient Greek house as repository of archival material, the keeper of the archive as a kind of father or authority, the institution as a protector of the archival function, an academic and scientific field of study as an archival impression, and the storage of material as a process of violent exclusion. In turning to psychoanalysis, Derrida attempts to combat the privileging of origins and familial connections. At the same time, his broad strokes turn the archive into a question of memory, both personal and collective. The Derridean dispersal of the archive differs significantly from Michel Foucault's use of "archive." In *The Archeology of Knowledge*, Foucault presents the "archive" as a discursive system that permits certain things to be said.[12] By contrast, Derrida would grant no such presence to the "archive," and his critique helps us unpack the relationship (and distinction) between archive as a place with research materials and reading desks and archive as metonym for the organization of information.

To develop his critique of official sources of knowledge, Derrida turns to Yosef Hayim Yerushalmi's *Freud's Moses: Judaism Terminable and Interminable* and thus intertwines history (Yerushalmi's discipline) with Judaism and psychoanalysis. Much of Derrida's discussion leads to a confrontation with Yerushalmi's question: is psychoanalysis a Jewish science? Descent and legacy, to which I have already alluded in relation to *Mis Memorias/Crossing the Rio Grande*, would seem constitutive elements in both Judaism and psychoanalysis. One relies on biology and the other on the name of Freud as an intellectual father, but Derrida also calls attention to how the ethnos and father come together in a field of study and how that has ramifications for the construction of an ethnic archive. Challenging this association, Derrida writes,

> But the structure of the theoretical, philosophical, scientific statement, and even when it concerns history, does not have, should not in principle have, an intrinsic and essential need for the archive, and for what binds the archive in all its forms to some proper name or to some body proper, to some (familial or national) filiation, to covenants, to secrets. It has no such need, in any case, in its relationship or in its claim to truth — in the classical sense of the term.[13]

The point here is that language, a statement linked to a proposition, does not need an archive to stake its claim on truth. In other words, a scientific or philosophical finding would not need Judaism or Freud for justification. For our purposes, we could say that the textual record, the scraps that might emerge from migrant archives, does not need "some body proper" (an author) or some place (a national archive) for the validation that we would associate with a claim to truth. More concretely, Luis G. Gómez should not need the archival setup established by his descendants. But is that actually the condition of scholarly work in the United States at this time? Does a book such as *Crossing the Rio Grande* actually need filiation in order for its claims to enter a public discussion? Does it need a home for that claim to be heard, and, if so, what type of archive?

Derrida would allow no such filiations. The stakes of his argument against the archive become clear when, deploying the language of psychoanalysis, he associates the archival function with the death drive. On the one hand, the drive to establish archives, archive fever, is related to a kind of conservation and preservation. But, according to Derrida, it also erases what came before. The effects of the death drive are not confined to the exclusionary effect of collecting some materials and not others in an archive. Rather, Derrida posits that the archival process releases a type of aggression; the archive is an impression that alters a previous impression. More than excluding something, the archive destroys the archive that preceded it. One need not go far here to come up with examples for Derrida's theoretical point. Surely, the

preservation of English as a kind of official language has led to the annihilation of American Indian languages that have been forgotten. With English
as a language of America, the country or hemisphere's more ancient copy is
subjected to erasure.

The association of archival construction with the death drive begins to
explain Derrida's provocative line that "archive fever verges on radical evil."[14]
From a Kantian perspective, the notion of "radical evil" refers not to an in-
comprehensible or momentous example of evil but rather a kind of conduct
that proceeds only from personal inclination or interest. Radical evil is not
about committing atrocities, no matter how heinous. It is about acting in a
way that discounts the possibility of a higher principle.[15] The Derridean critique, then, would appear to rest on a sense of the archivist as someone who
conforms to the structure of the archive for some benefit, which could be
personal but not necessarily imply malicious conduct. One might consider
here the pleasure of hoarding books or the patriotic feeling of running a national repository as self-serving personal rewards that also create the boundaries of authoritative thinking. In effect, archive collections can inhibit avenues of research that might move closer to alternate truth claims.

The introduction of an ethical dimension calls attention to the different
associations created when *Mal d'archive* (1995) was translated into the English *Archive Fever* (1996). The French *mal* not only connotes a kind of illness but also can be synonymous with "evil." As a connotative sign, it is more
varied and rich than "fever." If anything, the translation of the title of Derrida's
book into English opts for a satirical effect. "Archive fever" sounds like a kind
of fad, perhaps a headline in a newsweekly; it is reminiscent of the 1970s song
"Boogie Fever." The translated title emphasizes a critique of the archival turn
as a form of empirical research and thus differs from the engagement of *mal*
with European philosophy. With the focus on Yerushalmi, a historian, and
the use of "fever," it is not surprising that Derrida inspired responses from
researchers who are invested in archival work, namely, historians.

In her critique of Derrida, Carolyn Steedman calls attention to the material realities of labor (within and without the archive), at times connecting the physical experience of going to and working in the archive with the
bodily effects of production. Running with Derrida's fever metaphor, Steedman notes that sometimes the dust in archives can make people sick. More
important, dust is itself a metaphor for the residue of the laboring classes.
Reading the historian Michelet alongside Derrida, Steedman calls attention
to "the dust of the workers who made the papers and parchments; the dust

of the animals who provided the skins for their leather bindings."[16] Michelet, she notes, "inhaled the by-product of all the filthy trades that have, by circuitous routes, deposited their end-products in the archives."[17] As one who actually goes to archives, Steedman shifts the focus away from the Derridean concern with the archive as a locus of authority in language. In other words, the archive can also contain information about those who do not have authority and even those whose authority has been forgotten. Yet Steedman's critique does not negate Derrida's point that the archive does claim an authority, usually on a foundation stemming from a nation, a locality, an institution, or a person. This locus of authority becomes the familiar point that frames the archival holding, including the migrant archives that might be contained within.

Making a book familiar is one of the goals of *Crossing the Rio Grande*. In moving the family book into the public space of libraries and doing so in standard English, Gómez's descendants desire to move an ancestral authority into an official archive. The translation of the book's title is important and, in some ways, more radical than the change from "*mal*" to "fever." "*Mis Memorias*" emphasizes the subjective and very personal claim made by its author. A literal translation, "my memories," does not have the right intonation, but other possibilities, "a memoir" or "my experiences," would have retained the generic and personal emphasis. The title *Crossing the Rio Grande*, by contrast, chooses a common trope that describes the passage from Mexico to the United States and thus situates the book in a public discussion of immigration and the experiences of those who make the trek across that angry river. Here we see the importance of translation to the archival function because the title helps situate the book in the archive of immigration. But the change also prompts a question about how translation might be the type of act that Derrida calls "radical evil." I emphasize that evil here is not about heinous acts. But if Derrida's use of "radical evil" speaks to an automatic following of the norm, that which is accepted, then displacing the Spanish original with a translation into the official language does negate the presence of the Spanish language in U.S. publication history.

Perhaps that new impression, with its potential to obliterate, is an inevitable effect of translation, a point that has inspired lengthy discussion in translation studies. Lawrence Venuti, for example, has written, "Translators are very much aware that any sense of authorial presence in a translation is an illusion, an effect of transparent discourse, comparable to a 'stunt,' but they nonetheless assert that they participate in a 'psychological' relationship with the author in which they repress their own 'personality.'"[18] Gómez's translator takes that relationship to a grand Oedipal degree, simultaneously asserting a blood connection to the author, a claim to the author's presence (without an acknowledgment of illusion), and a foregrounding of his own presence as descendant-translator. The translator-grandson thus carries across the book from migrant archives to a singular archive that demands a standard language. That integration of language difference into a norm (English) is one reason why scholars of hemispheric American studies have increasingly called for attention to translation studies and sought new ways to conceive of the transformation created by translation, including "adaptation."[19]

Despite the effects of the impression created by the new English version of *Mis Memorias*, something is also gained by bringing this document out of migrant archives. Given the anti-immigrant sentiments that surface repeatedly in U.S. history, the translation and public dissemination of the Gómez memoir is a necessary evil. In other words, the evil is idiomatic more than ethical. The necessity here is about political participation in U.S. society. In a footnote early in his book Derrida gestures to an important claim that he does not follow. He writes, "There is no political power without control of the archive, if not memory."[20] Here Derrida reminds us that archives are also part of a political arena in which people vie for power and recognition. If we take this statement as a reference to the archive as a repository of historical documents (although the usage there is more diffuse), questions emerge about the relationship between research emphasis and the exercising of power in a contemporary liberal society. Derrida's point would then be that political power derives in part from such a national institution because the archivist interprets meanings and associations. In some ways, the archive defines the nation, and participation in the archive is one gauge of democratization.

Still, Derrida's sentence raises an additional problem, that of memory. "Nul pouvoir politique sans contrôle de l'archive, sinon de la mémoire."[21] The phrase "if not memory," not quite conditional and almost an afterthought, adds a complication. Is it national memory? Personal memory? Your memory? Given the subjective thrust of memory, the point would be that political power rests on the control of the memories of others. When *Mis Memorias* is translated into *Crossing the Rio Grande*, Gómez's account becomes part of a different archive, one that is in dialogue with the recent resurgence of anti-immigrant discourse. It is not surprising that *Crossing the Rio Grande*'s editors emphasize the importance of immigrant labor, and thus the book's subtitle, *An Immigrant's Life in the 1880s*. This type of book is a necessity in a society that routinely seeks to forget its immigrant past and its multilingual background.

And yet the archive of immigration, with its monument at Ellis Island and reading lists of immigrant novels, would seem to bind some of the energy of *Mis Memorias*. An "immigrant life" has traditionally implied integration or even assimilation into a national panorama. The translation integrates Gómez's book into an archive rather than emphasizing the multiple locations of the book's publication history and its content. *Mis Memorias*'s episodes recount movement within Texas and note that returning to Mexico is an important consideration for the author and his friends. The change into an immigrant life deemphasizes what may be its most interesting dimension of the book's social panorama: the importance of a Spanish-speaking work force that is not easily assimilated into Texas society in the late nineteenth century.

THE CHALLENGE not just for American studies but also for many scholarly efforts that recover texts from the past is how to bring forth historical and linguistic differences without allowing the present discourse to dominate. The archival claim, meaning the terms under which an archive is constructed, always threatens to become hegemonic, but some texts may contain a difference emphatic enough to prompt a reconsideration of the archive's limits. Let me be more specific by looking at the case of a very important archive developed in the past fifteen years: the Recovering the U.S. Hispanic Literary Heritage project.

The "recovery project" is an example of an archive that collects, houses, and circulates a variety of documents under the rubric of ethnic identity. The project is authoritative, in the sense that Derrida uses the term, because it gains legitimacy from describing its object of study as the textual record left behind by people of Hispanic descent. Although the project is capacious in its definition of "Hispanic" and is also sensitive to the variety of populations that might be part of that group historically, the claim to heritage retroactively organizes the project's texts under the rubric of a contemporary identity formation. One of the salutary effects of such an archive construction is that the recovery project has brought into circulation materials that were previously available only in the rarest of library stacks. It was the recovery project that published in the 1990s María Amparo Ruiz de Burton's novels *Who Would Have Thought It?* (1872) and *The Squatter and the Don*

(1885), as well as the anonymous *Jicoténcal* (1826). Housed at the University of Houston, the recovery project now holds originals, photocopies, and microfilms of a thousands of documents, thus functioning both as a repository of rare materials and as an institutional home.[22]

The goal in establishing the recovery project was not only to identify the Hispanic past but also to restore it, presumably as an important component of the nation, if not memory. This was, like so much of American literary revision in the 1980s and 1990s, an attempt to broaden the texts that made up a literary past. In the introduction to the first volume of the recovery series, Ramón A. Gutiérrez and Genaro M. Padilla write, "The long forgotten editorials these men and women wrote, their manifestoes for better wages and better working conditions, their private thoughts and emotions committed to diaries, their moral tales disguised as comedies and farces, their tersely measured lyrical poems, and their pauses and silence in the textual record are the collective object of our study." This expansion into beyond-literary genres and the public sphere of newspapers and pamphlets moved interdisciplinary scholarship into "privates thoughts and emotions," the terrain of memory and lived experiences. In some cases the "literary" would give way to Hispanic heritage, defined as the cultural background of "these men and women." In working against the "long forgotten," the memory lapses and the destruction, the recovery project could simultaneously make visible a documentary history of a people.

Despite what we might call the archival threat of this scholarly effort, the project was a great necessity in that it promoted a type of research that was not being carried out on a large scale. More than a century before the recovery project, Walt Whitman had articulated, on commemorating the 333rd anniversary of the settlement of Santa Fe, New Mexico, a need to consider the Hispanic past: "We Americans have yet to really learn our own antecedents, and sort them, to unify them."[23] Calling on the nation to move beyond its Anglocentrism, Whitman argued, "To that composite American identity of the future, Spanish character will supply some of the most needed parts."[24] Whitman's statement calls attention to the ongoing need for recovery projects of various sorts and also poses one of the problems of an authoritative archive. In the Whitmanian schema, the search for a Hispanic antecedent would recover parts of a "composite" U.S. identity; the goal would be unification into what we might call a multicultural nation. By contrast, the work done by scholars points to numerous identities that also intersect with national, regional, and local influences outside of the United States.

RODRIGO LAZO

The counterclaim to national hegemony was also contained in Gutié-rrez and Padilla's statement explaining the research project. "Our mission and goal is nothing less than to recover the Hispanic literary heritage of the United States, to document its regional and national diversity, to view from various perspectives and angles the matrix of power in which it was created, and to celebrate its hybridity, its intertextuality and its polyvocality."[25] That diversity would point toward difference that moved in other directions, away from the U.S. nation. The gesture toward intertextual connections and poly-vocal productions paved the way for considering how certain writers and print culture formations did not respect national boundaries. In actuality, some of this Hispanic textual heritage would point simultaneously to two or more sites (Mexico, Cuba, and other countries), bringing forward trans-national print culture formations and traveling writers. In addition, efforts to associate the texts from the past with post-1960s archival claims to liberation projects came under scrutiny as scholars unearthed complicated political alliances and positions in other centuries, most evident in the debates over María Amparo Ruiz de Burton, whose position in Chicano literary history clashes with her flirtations with the Confederacy.

Migrant archives began to emerge in the differences of the past. Experi-ences, writings, and contexts from other centuries did not always fit the para-digm, and not only because these writers may have invented other national or hemispheric American affiliations but also because they participated in intel-lectual traditions and political alliances that could not be classified within the dynamics of contemporary Hispanic cultural and political dimensions. Newspapers, an additional migrant element, often printed anonymous ar-ticles, making it difficult to connect a piece of writing to an author, compli-cating the very idea of Hispanic literary heritage, and calling attention to the ease with which Hispanic could become Hispanophone U.S. literary heri-tage. Rather than see the emphasis on language difference as a disciplinary boundary, many of the scholars associated with the recovery project took the opportunity to seek out multiple avenues of research. We are still moving, I would argue, into migrant archives that will ultimately displace the subjec-tivity that sustains the project.

What emerged was a tension between the necessary evil of the archive, the building that houses the materials, and the challenge of migrant archives. The recovery project gathered authority from something that is commodifi-able and commonly commodified: the Hispanic subject of the United States as conceived after the 1960s. Would it have been possible to bring the materials of the recovery project into national circulation without this archive? Could the documents have staked a claim to truth without the edifice of the project, which has been supported by prestigious foundations and the influence in U.S. society of a growing Latino population? Like the nation and the national archive, an ethnicity and an ethnic archive validate and sustain each other.[26]

Although the phrase "U.S. Hispanic Literary Heritage" claims an association with national literature, it was clear from the beginning that we would need to move outside the boundaries of the nation-state to do recovery work. The project held that door open from the beginning because both temporally and spatially the Hispanic heritage of the United States has connections to other countries. Those connections sometimes are evident in the content of a text but are also in the print culture conditions or even in the biographies of writers. The recovery project has always moved in an interdisciplinary and even indeterminable field, into and beyond American studies, Latin American studies, Spanish-language literature, American literature, and literature of the Americas. In other words, an ethnic subject is a heuristic for a textual reality that is much more complicated. The "Hispanic" in Hispanic literary heritage is like the museum-on-the-Mall version of National Archives: an edifice that stands in for the intricacies of the many archives held in other locations. The museum is not necessarily an impediment. Actually, it could be a door into migrant archives.

MIGRANT ARCHIVES are not widely available, nor is their existence known by a large number of people. They are sometimes in someone's garage or held by a descendant of the person who produced the document. These documents contain stories, experiences, and languages that are not part of easily recognized narratives of institutions. They break out of standard language and official stories. But that is not to say they are completely outside of the physical archive. They move in and out of repositories of rare documents and other libraries. The Beinecke library contains migrant archives. So does the Library of Congress. At the Library Company of Philadelphia, founded by Benjamin Franklin in 1731, a collection of German-language documents from the colonial and early republican period are part of a migrant collection. It is migrant because it complicates the common understanding of Philadelphia and of the corpus of myths and stories associated with Benjamin Franklin. It also moves a conception of the early United States outside of the local geography and into a dialogue with the Germanic antecedents of the local print culture.

The documents of migrant archives do not need to be discovered; discovery implies that they are not known and located. Some documents are already cataloged and part of official collections, even though migrant archives do not have their own catalogs. The point is that their presence might not be readily apparent within the existing discourses of academic or political inquiry. In that sense, they differ from new documents by or about well-known historical figures. In the 1980s, for example, a stash of Melville family documents was found in a barn and became part of the lore of research on Melville. Unlike the stuff of migrant archives, these documents had a home in an existing academic fields, Melville studies and, more generally, American literature.[27] While fields of study provide insight into the interests and commitments of those who practice within them, who defend them eagerly and/or viciously, migrant archives can contain the writings and visual cultures of those who are dismissed and overlooked by the keepers of the archive. In some cases, the writers are migrants, literally speaking. But they might also be members of elite groups who travel first class but whose texts also open a variety of views of the past. Sometimes the routes of migrant archives will lead to new understandings of who and what is excluded from the archive.

The physical archive (the national archive, the official archive) provides many opportunities. As a rare institution, an archive stipulates who can enter. Some archives require registration, others ask for letters of reference. To locate the dusty texts of migrant archives you might have to pass through the door and sign yourself in as a reader at the archive run by the city or the state. The old archive persists. Derrida's injunction against the archive per se calls for a necessary move away from something that might be unavoidable. (The legal problems that arose in relation to the "Derrida archive" are a reminder of the archive's presence.)[28] Furthermore, as the case of the Hispanic literary heritage project shows, some groups do not have the luxury of ignoring or dismissing the importance of archives, nor would it be politically astute to do so.

Migrant archives are calling for the work of those who would go into them and do the careful reading and contextualization that the finest research requires. As pressure builds on national or ethnic archives to account for transnational, exile, and diasporic influences, scholars will have to follow migrant routes rather than revert to the inclusion of a text into a preexisting model. That work is not the primary purview of relatives and descendants of the producers from other decades and centuries but of scholars who seek to fan the flames of the past so as to create light for the present. Because migrant archives do not have buildings devoted to them, it is up to committed Americanists to locate their contents, read them carefully, and provide contexts for their emergence.

NOTES

1. International Council on Archives, ⟨http://www.ica.org/⟩.

2. In this article I discuss Jacques Derrida, *Archive Fever: A Freudian Impression*, trans. Eric Prenowitz (Chicago: University of Chicago Press, 1996). For an overview of debates about the archive, see Marlene Manoff, "Theories of the Archive from across the Disciplines," *Portal: Libraries and the Academy* 4 (2004): 9–25.

3. Thomas Osborne has argued that the physical reality of an archive, in tension with the abstract conception of what it implies, grants credibility to certain archival configurations and even disciplines. See Osborne, "The Ordinariness of the Archive," *History of the Human Sciences* 12 (May 1999): 51–55. That physical credibility is one factor behind what some have called an archival turn in literary and cultural studies. While historicist methodologies and the decentering of the literary text have also contributed to this archival turn, the lack of a consensus as to what constitutes literary studies has led to a privileging of the recovery of texts and contexts that have not been considered in the recent past. Jane Gallop has criticized this historical turn by establishing a dichotomy between close reading and "archival work." Actually, the best historical work would deploy close-reading techniques on documents that might otherwise be taken as factual evidence for historical narratives. See Gallop, "The Historicization of Literary Studies and the Fate of Close Reading," *Profession 2007* (New York: MLA, 2007), 181–86.

4. The National Archives also has connections to regional archives and presidential libraries. The United States offers a curious case of archive construction. Unlike other nations, the United States did not establish the institution called National Archives until more than a century after the country's founding. Individual government agencies had been in charge of their own records before Congress created the National Archives and Records Administration in 1934. ⟨http://www.archives.gov/about/history/⟩. I would argue that the first U.S. "national archive" was the Library of Congress, founded in 1800 when the capital was transferred from Philadelphia to Washington, D.C. Originally intended to house books for use by the government, the Library of Congress became a national library that was to provide information on all subjects, meaning all subjects would be of interest to the nation. For an account of the founding of the Library of Congress, see John Y. Cole, *Jefferson's Legacy: A Brief History of the Library of Congress* (Washington, D.C.: Library of Congress, 1993).

5. ⟨http://www.digitalvaults.org/⟩.

6. Thomas H. Kreneck, preface to *Crossing the Rio Grande: An Immigrant's Life in the 1880s* (College Station: Texas A&M University Press, 2007), ix–xii.

7. Ibid., x.

8. Guadalupe Valdez Jr., "Memories of My Grandfather: Luis G. Gómez," in *Crossing the Rio Grande*, 14.

RODRIGO LAZO

9. Derrida, *Archive Fever*, 2.

10. Manoff, "Theories of the Archive," 10.

11. Marc Shell and Werner Sollors, *The Multilingual Anthology of American Literature* (New York: New York University Press, 2000). See also Werner Sollors, ed., *Multilingual America: Transnationalism, Ethnicity, and the Languages of American Literature* (New York: New York University Press, 1998).

12. "By this term [archive]," Foucault writes, "I do not mean the sum of all the texts that a culture has kept upon its person as documents attesting to its own past, or as evidence of a continuing identity; nor do I mean the institutions, which, in a given society, make it possible to record and preserve those discourses that one wishes to remember and keep in circulation." Michel Foucault, *The Archeology of Knowledge* (New York: Pantheon, 1972), 128–29. Instead, Foucault would focus on the historical discursive system (assumptions, connections, relationships) that permits a particular statement. Libraries and academic disciplines or fields are the product of the archive but are not the archive themselves. If a national archive implies continuity and tradition, Foucault's "archive" functions in a particular context. Rather than focusing on the content of an archive or the person who inaugurates or promotes it, Foucault seeks to understand how the archive delimits what and how something can be said.

13. Derrida, *Archive Fever*, 45.

14. Ibid., 20.

15. For a discussion of "radical evil" in various strains of philosophy, see Richard J. Bernstein, *Radical Evil: A Philosophical Investigation* (Cambridge: Polity, 2002). For a brief explanation of Kant's concepts in relation to other uses of "evil," see Christoph Cox, "On Evil: An Interview of Alenka Zupancic," *Cabinet* 5 (Winter 2001–2), ⟨http://cabinetmagazine.org/issues/5/alenkazupancic/.php⟩.

16. Carolyn Steedman, *Dust: The Archive and Cultural History* (New Brunswick, N.J.: Rutgers University Press, 2002), 27.

17. Ibid., 27.

18. Lawrence Venuti, *The Translator's Invisibility: A History of Translation* (New York: Routledge, 1995), 7.

19. Kirsten Silva Gruesz calls for overcoming a "lack of interest in questions of language difference and translation in most Americanist work at present." See "Translation: A Key(word) into the Language of America(nists)," *American Literary History* 16 (2004): 90. In developing an approach toward hemispheric studies, Susan Gillman argues that *adaptation* rather than translation may be a more fruitful way to think about texts that are incommensurable and affected not only by different literary histories but also by uneven economic and social conditions in the Americas. See Gillman, "Otra Vez Caliban/ Encore Caliban: Adaptation, Translation, Americas Studies," *American Literary History* 20(Spring–Summer 2008): 187–209.

20. Derrida, *Archive Fever*, 4–5.

21. Jacques Derrida, *Mal d'archive: Une impression freudienne* (Paris: Galilée, 1995), 15–16.

22. The project has also awarded many fellowships for research and sponsored a bi-annual conference that has become a central gathering place for many scholars interested

in the Hispanic past. The conferences, in turn, have led to a series of volumes of critical articles.

23. Walt Whitman, "The Spanish Element in Our Nationality," in *Poetry and Prose* (New York: Library of America, 1996), 1146.

24. Ibid., 1147.

25. Ramón A. Gutiérrez and Genaro M. Padilla, introduction to *Recovering the US Hispanic Literary Heritage* (Houston: Arte Público Press, 1993), 21.

26. A similar process is evident in the racial authorization of African American studies, although not without its own debates. As Xiomara Santamarina has noted, a methodological paradox emerges in that field when scholars develop an archive presumably about a racial group at the same time that certain practitioners deconstruct the racial particularity that propels such a search. "[T]he field encompasses reprinting and reinterpreting long out-of-print and forgotten texts, in combination with textual and contextual analyses that recover the instability and contingency of racial discourses across space and time." In response, Santamarina argues for the ongoing recuperation of archival materials that call attention and speak to the need for specific analyses — in this case, historicizing practices that place discourses on race in the particular conditions faced by the writers. But one has to wonder whether in African American studies race remains as the category that sustains the archival process. By contrast, migrant archives move away from racial formations. See Santamarina, "'Are We There Yet?'": Archives, History, and Specificity in African-American Literary Studies," *American Literary History* 20 (Spring–Summer 2008): 304.

27. Hershel Parker opens the first volume of his monumental biography of Melville by emphasizing the importance of that discovery. See *Herman Melville: A Biography*, vol. 1 (Baltimore: Johns Hopkins University Press, 1996), xi.

28. The competing claims on Derrida's papers and Derrida's response to institutional injunctions show just how important and even scandalous archives continue to be. For a newspaper account of these troubles, see Thomas Bartlett, "Archive Fever," *Chronicle of Higher Education*, 20 July 2007, A8.

Toxicity and the Consuming Subject

NAN ENSTAD

In October 2006, *National Geographic Magazine* featured an article and photographic spread entitled "Pollution Within." Reporter David Ewing Duncan had himself tested for 320 toxic chemicals and found that 165 of them lurked within his body, including PCBs, DDT, dioxin, mercury, and PBDEs (polybrominated diphenyl ethers) found in flame retardants. In fact, Duncan's level of one particularly toxic PBDE was ten times the estimated average in U.S. citizens, and two hundred times the estimated average in Sweden, where the chemical is banned. PBDEs are found in, among other things, "mattresses, carpets, the plastic casing of televisions, electronic circuit boards, automobiles," and the "plastic and fabric interiors" of airplanes. While it is common knowledge that we all have a body burden of numerous chemicals that come to us through air, water, and the commodities we utilize daily, only recently have a few laboratories developed sophisticated testing apparatuses that can ascertain the presence or absence of so many different compounds in trace amounts, generating detailed new knowledge about the self.

National Geographic Magazine's shifting attention signals a broad-based new anxiety about globalization and its perils, one that holds multiple political and scholarly possibilities for rethinking self and society. From the magazine's historic emphasis on the exotic natural environment and customs of imperialism's "other," *National Geographic* turns its gaze to the toxic debris that has migrated to and is deposited in a U.S. citizen's body from transnationally circulating commodities. U.S. readers of *National Geographic* no longer imagine the global "out there," but, disturbingly, the global "within us." This shift in scale redefines the geoscape, not only including the United States — a move *National Geographic* made some time ago — but replacing the exotic body of the "foreigner" with the interior, biochemical body of a U.S. citizen. *National Geographic* paired its in-depth interior gaze on Duncan's body with photos and prose about people who have experienced acute toxic exposures: women in Richmond, California, who attribute their breast cancer to the many factories and oil refineries there; tobacco farm workers in Nicaragua exposed daily to pesticides; and children in Vietnam with birth defects attributable to Agent Orange.[1] *National Geographic*'s gaze, at once encompassing the biochemical self and the transnational, reflects broad shifts in our political and ecological reality.[2] I suggest that considering toxicity might open up a new critical engagement with subjectivity, commodity consumption, and transnational capitalism.

Changing directions in my own work have led me to these concerns. My prior work examined clothing and dime novels as items of collective and personal consumption that both shaped workers' imaginations according to the logics of capital and provided them with narratives and tropes that they could utilize in the larger process of forming oppositional politicized subjectivities. My current project similarly looks at the collective consumption of a highly personalized commodity — cigarettes. Here, however, I find it impossible to focus exclusively on style, pleasure, and sexuality, though those are all clearly essential aspects of cigarettes' meanings. Cigarettes' toxicity — their remarkably efficient carcinogen-delivery system — caused a global health disaster in the twentieth century.[3] A cultural history of cigarette consumption would have to confront toxicity; such an endeavor offers an opportunity to link personal experience — the very construction of the body and the self — with corporate decision making at the highest level. Cigarettes demand a broader view of consumption, one that engages the global and the cellular, the moment of product use and its unintended consequences, and the ways the eventual knowledge of cigarettes' toxicity changes the story we tell.

This short essay, then, is a meditation on the ramifications of studying toxicity for newly refracting our categories of global and local, consumer culture, subjectivity, and the formation of knowledge. Because it is based in my own work and interests, this essay is idiosyncratic rather than comprehensive. Although it begins with my own work, it gestures outward to the broader endeavor of American studies scholarship to indicate some salient points of scholarly possibility. While my first book drew me to study film theory, British cultural studies, and gender theory, this question propels me to consult scholars who study environmental history, environmental justice, and illness narratives. Many of these scholars already participate in American studies conversations, so I do not intend to introduce strangers but rather to weave connections that may prove provocative in an American studies context. American studies scholars specialize in creating narratives of possibility: through story and critique, American studies participates in envisioning what democracy and justice look like. I draw attention, therefore, to the tethers between epistemologies and politics to suggest possible openings to change where American studies scholars might work. In choosing the essay format for my ideas, I have necessarily opted against the comprehensive literature review format; however, notes do point to excellent sources that might provide a starting point for further reading in the interdisciplinary study of toxicity. My own interest in toxicity, however, begins with the global corporation's triumph in the twentieth century and capitalism's remarkable success at infusing lives and bodies around the world with its products and by-products.

As manifest ways in which capitalism becomes part of our bodies, toxic chemicals seem to fulfill the utopian and fantastical promises of globalization more than any other aspect of multinational corporate capitalism, albeit in a dark and clandestine way. Global capitalism promises mobility, flexible accumulation, and wealth to stockholders while generating an ever-rising economic tide. Toxic chemicals realize many of these promises: they move silently with a giddy freedom from place to place, exceeding the mobility of physical plants and workers as well as commodities and advertisements. Collectively, they are present at every stage of the process of production, distribution, and consumption. If the goal and methods of contemporary global capitalism are flexible accumulation as opposed to Fordist mass production, then the effortless and almost magical flexible accumulation of toxins by the body exceeds even the most utopian beliefs in the "invisible hand" of the market. We can see toxicity in our bodies, then, as a sneaky triumph of capitalist logics at the most daily and personal level. Capitalism is not "out there," it is "within us."

While all of us, including polar bears in the Arctic, are products of this form of bodily globalization, the process is by no means equal or democratic. Indeed, the inequities of global capitalism also have become part of our bodies. The environmental justice movement, including both activists and scholars, has demonstrated that people of color are more likely to find that their neighborhoods have been chosen for toxic waste dumps. The unequal distribution along lines of class and race of hazardous workplaces, high-risk jobs, housing near manufacturing or processing plants, and toxic disposal sites means that poor people and people of color can reasonably expect to have a greater share of toxic body burden.[4] Likewise, the movement of industry to "developing" countries, differential national environmental protections, and global corporations' ability to set working and environmental conditions have meant that people in the developing world tend to find themselves in more toxic environments than do people elsewhere. Toxins themselves do not recognize national boundaries or discriminate among subjects, but corporations and governments do, and they have long endeavored to delimit some exposures and protect certain people, with varying degrees of sincerity and success. Studying toxicity can reveal how the venture of global capitalism has literally produced us and thereby incorporated us into a shared story; such study can simultaneously provide a way of tracking the deadly inequities that are integral, not incidental, to capitalism's development.

Considering toxicity allows us to bridge the analytical polarization of global and local by placing the body in the picture. Toxicity calls for new attention to the problem of scale. Are we to study a chemical, invisible to the naked eye; a body; a particular human or animal population; a geographic location of consumption and/or production; a global economic network?[5] How do we take on the challenge of connecting the intimate and personal with the global and bureaucratic? We know that capitalism is heterogeneous and contingent, yet, as anthropologist Anna Tsing has pointed out, a dichotomy between global and local tends to reappear. We regularly "invoke distinctions between local reactions and global forces, local consumption and global circulation, local resistance and global structures of capitalism. . . . Yet we know that these dichotomies . . . draw us into an imagery in which the global is homogeneous precisely because we oppose it to the heterogeneity we identify as locality."[6] "Toxin" is by definition a relational term: a chemical is categorized as a toxin because of its activity in human or animal bodies. Toxins form bonds with or alter the cells in our bodies; they become part of us and change us. The concept of toxicity ties the body to the chemical world it encounters and vice versa and can therefore be a way of considering the effects of global capitalism without losing track of globalization's contingent manifestations, its instantiation in particular times and places. The toxicity of our workplaces, our homes, and our commodities references the bodily molecular activity we experience or wish to prevent. Asking questions about the history and geography of toxicity's flow necessarily raises questions about decision making on various levels and may allow us to see the global as it works *within* national regulations, corporate priorities, advertising campaigns, and social movements.

The idea of a commodity chain, for instance, might be revised by considering toxicity in ways that bring out bodily vulnerability at all levels of the global economy, including the vulnerability of workers, consumers, and business executives. The model of a commodity chain — tracking the movement of commodities through production, distribution, sales, and consumption — has offered scholars a way to isolate particular locations of study within globalization's sprawl. Social scientists have tended to see the links in a commodity chain as economic in nature, bringing cultural analysis in only at the point of consumption. However, as Tsing has noted, all links along a commodity chain are sites of cultural production.[7] We might add to that insight the idea that all of the links can be (depending on the toxin) sites of exposure, bringing the human element of risk and vulnerability to our inquiry. Scholars have certainly already begun studying sites of production and consumption as points of exposure, but they are usually studied in isolation from each other. Considering the history of toxicity's flow may raise significant new questions about decision making and the allocation of risk at all levels of capitalist production, from the body to the highest levels of corporate organization. In particular, attention to toxicity may open the corporation to cultural analysis. High levels of production or bureaucracy, in our studies, too easily appear overrationalized or depersonalized. We tend to believe businesspeople overmuch that decisions are made rationally in order to maximize profits, as though "profit" is independent of cultural definitions and assumptions. Likewise, we tend to assume that business cultures operate dispassionately and effectively.[8] Following the toxins would not have exactly the same impact as following the money or the commodity. The boundaries of our scholarly stories may need to change to accommodate this chemical activity.

Time, like space, looks different when toxicity is considered. Globalization, as has been often noted, promises to compress time, and lessen its significance. The digital age, for example, means financial transactions across continents can be completed almost instantaneously. In the United States, we seem to live in a world in which goods are bought, consumed, and quickly discarded. While the nation relies on the past for its claim to a particular set of borders and founding myths, globalization's strongest commitment to time appears to be in a utopian futurism that escapes past limitations. Toxins belie this fantasy of time's lessening hold on us. Indeed, if one considers toxicity as part of consumption, then we need to significantly revise and extend over time our conception of the events of consumption. Long after the cigarette was purchased and has disappeared into ash, the moment of lighting the cigarette and inhaling its smoke echoes in the body when one becomes ill. Illness, including when specific environmental cause is hard to pinpoint, may be moments or decades after exposure, and it often dramatically changes one's relationship to consumption and the memories of it. How do we address this aspect of consumption that is rooted in history and memory? How does this change the experience of a "consumer culture"?

The chemical activity of toxins offers us an opportunity to reconsider questions of agency and subjectivity in relationship to the myriad possessions that capitalism has bestowed upon us. Cultural critic Bill Brown has argued that the way things constitute selves and society "is something stranger than the history of a culture of consumption."[9] While the study of a culture of consumption highlights the construction of desire for commodities, style, and identity (either condemning these practices as politically vacuous or finding contradictions and possibilities within them), Brown urges us to see commodities themselves as having agency and acting upon people. He calls upon us to explore "how inanimate objects construct human subjects, how they move them, how they threaten them, how they facilitate or threaten their relation to other subjects."[10] Of course, the meanings of commodities are culturally constructed and shift; they are not inherent in the object. That insight, however, has perhaps obscured the degree to which we confront a world saturated with commodities whose meanings are not entirely of our own individual making and that act upon us, sometimes quite apart from our "use" of them.

Seen from this angle, the proliferation of commodities has a broad impact on subjectivities, conceptions of gender and race (as well as gender and race identity formations), and constructions of social life and politics. For example, historian Lizabeth Cohen has demonstrated that twentieth-century U.S. political subjectivities are not just *about* things but are shaped and reshaped via the consumer marketplace and its reformulation of human relationships and languages of entitlements.[11] Brown writes, "The question is less about 'what things are for a given society' than what claims on your attention and on your action are made on behalf of things."[12] How toxins act upon and constitute subjects is both biological and cultural. Making toxicity an object of study in American studies allows us to consider how commodities act upon us at a molecular level in unanticipated ways. When we become ill or become aware of the threat of illness, we find new claims have been made on our attention and our action. Integrating a consideration of toxicity with studies of consumption, then, can deepen the ongoing theoretical and empirical project of understanding our world of goods.

In particular, environmental studies scholars have shown that growing awareness of toxicity sometimes challenges modernist notions of the body and shifts the political terrain. The claims made on our attention by a new awareness of toxicity are often discomfiting. "Now I'm learning more than I really want to know," Duncan writes at one point in his *National Geographic* article. Nevertheless, such knowledge — the recognition of the intimacy of our relationship with our mattress covers and carpets, our circuit boards and cigarettes — revises the notion of the body as an autonomous vessel that is relatively impermeable. Historian Linda Nash argues that modern medicine's model of the body was short lived: it emerged only with the consolidation of the medical profession in the late nineteenth century and has consistently confronted contradictions and alternative models of understanding. The modern vision of medical healing focused not on achieving a balance between the body and its environment, as had earlier models, but on ridding the body of foreign germs that threatened it from without. This was a view of the body as autonomous, clearly boundaried, and sovereign unless threatened by foreign entities.[13]

The emergence of an environmental movement focused on pesticides at midcentury signaled a challenge to this medical model of the self and generated new political responses. The publication of Rachel Carson's *Silent Spring* and the emergence of California Latino and Filipino farm workers' activism against the use of pesticides both drew national attention to environmental health concerns in the 1960s. An environmental movement developed in the 1970s that took preservation of "wilderness" and curtailing pollution as twin (if competing) concerns. In the 1980s, people of color in various places responded to the toxicity of their neighborhoods, publicizing some gross deeds of corporate irresponsibility (such as the intentional dispensing of PCBs from trucks along rural North Carolina highways) and made environmental justice part of a larger civil rights vision.[14] These movements had diverse (and sometimes incompatible) politics and not all challenged the modern notion of the autonomous body. For example, the preservation of wilderness could be motivated in part by a belief that individual autonomy could be renewed through an encounter with pristine "nature."[15]

Toxicity and the Consuming Subject

Nevertheless, the environmental movement writ large created a language with which to critique "cancer clusters" and other ways we find ourselves vulnerable to toxicity.[16]

The transformations in models of the body are far from complete, both in environmental science and in political and scholarly discourses. Despite new measurement systems noted by *National Geographic*, scientifically demonstrating the nature of bodily transformations due to toxins is still difficult. Smoking guns have proved to be the easiest to address: the statistical relevance of a cancer cluster near a toxic waste site and the demonstrable role of cigarette smoking in the etiology of lung cancer satisfied scientific criteria for proof and made political and legal claims more convincing. A deeper challenge has been to create claims within the realm of scientific uncertainty. If the molecular activity of chemicals occurs partly in combination, or through genetic mutations that occur through different, disconnected exposures over time, how do scientists determine what is a safe body burden for a particular chemical? And how do they prove disease etiologies? As environmental science and epidemiology struggle to create models that move beyond the germ-theory model of the body, political and humanities-based scholarly responses likewise hinge on shifting notions of bodily vulnerability or imperviousness. What is undeniable is that the modern medical model of the body has been shaken to its core; what model(s) of the body will replace it continues to be deeply contested.

The political ramifications of this incomplete shift are multiple and are still being played out. We can see some of the tensions in the *National Geographic* feature on toxicity. The article finely delineating Duncan's body burden is the central and longest piece in the series and is the hook that engages the readers into the topic. Pictures broaden out the scope and both precede and follow the piece about Duncan, providing viewers with an x-ray of a girl's abdomen laced with lead particles, the women from Richmond, Nicaraguan tobacco workers, and a child with birth defects attributed to Agent Orange. A short piece subtitled, "A World of Hurt," follows delineating acute toxic exposures and their effects. *National Geographic* explicitly draws a connection between Duncan and the other people pictured ("the known horrors inflicted by high doses of chemicals make the small amounts among each of us even more unsettling"), but it does not lead readers to one political response or another; the ethical relationship of our individual, or class, or national vulnerability to a larger collectivity remains open and unexplored.

It would be possible for a reader to see the pieces of the *National Geographic* spread as versions of the same story: four ways that transnationally migrant toxins can become manifest in pervious human bodies and cultures. This reading would break down the dichotomy between self and global "other" in which *National Geographic* has historically traded and invite new, transnational identifications and politics. We see just such identifications and politics emerging globally in the environmental movement, including in consumer-based movements.[17]

Another reading of the *National Geographic* articles is possible, however. The spread leads with Duncan's self-described "journey of chemical self-discovery." We learn that he lives in Berkeley, California, and travels in the capacity of his professional job as a journalist. Though he is geographically situated, he is presented as typical and representative, a U.S. everyman. He is the Emersonian self, reappearing with disturbing chemical baggage and demanding a reconsideration of individualism and autonomy. This challenge to the Emersonian self, however, stands in tension with the way Duncan serves as counterpoint to the other examples pictured: most are nonwhite, all experience more disturbing exposures, and none receive nearly as much attention as Duncan, who remains the main character. Duncan may appear as the "universal" U.S. body in contrast to "others" in an echo of *National Geographic*'s historical practice.

This sort of modernist reading of the individual body imperiled by toxins might invite a reinvigorated effort to sanitize one's own environment, before it is too late. One might respond reasonably with fear at the uncertainty of the effects of these exposures and the loss of the modernist dream of a safe body boundary. As in the politics surrounding immigration and terrorism, one might attempt to shore up modernism's crumbled defenses, despite the dubious effectiveness of the results. Nationalist solutions, such as a fence between the United States and Mexico to oppose immigration or new commodity import laws to stem the flow of toxic chemicals, do not address the global nature of the problems at hand; they offer distinctly nineteenth-century solutions to twenty-first-century problems. Likewise, utilizing class privilege to attempt an individualized quarantine through the purchase of safe food, water, and other goods denies the ways our economies and environments are connected and are at best only partially successful even for the privileged.[18] While legislation and consumer movements might play a positive and crucial role in collective solutions, they can also reinforce an individualist politics of privilege and fear. American studies scholars have particular skills at analyzing imperial and neo-imperial traditions and may apply those skills to promoting collectively successful environmental politics in a global context.

Equally compelling, however, is the charge to discuss and theorize emergent models of the body and toxicity and their epistemological and political implications. Environmental historian Michelle Murphy has found that people who experience multiple chemical sensitivity (MCS) face skepticism from doctors trained to isolate disease causalities and manifestations. Nevertheless, people with MCS rematerialize their new self-understandings in Internet chats, blogs, journals, and health food stores. Although these understandings, just as those expressed in accepted medical models, may be contradictory or problematic, they offer insight into new ways of understanding the self and society.[19] Medical sociologist Arthur Frank argues that we, as a society, need to hear the stories of ill people, precisely because so many of them are rejecting modern notions of the body and are, therefore, theorizing "post-modern times" through the telling of their own experiences. For Frank, new epistemologies and new ethics can emerge from listening to the stories of those whom he refers to as the "remission society" — the growing numbers of people who have received a life-threatening diagnosis but who negotiate with the medical system and come to know themselves in an ill and undeniably pervious and vulnerable body.[20] Environmental justice movements constitute new publics and develop new strategies in working for positive change. Just what kinds of understandings of subjectivity and politics might emerge from specific locations in this large-scale shift deserve our scholarly attention.

In short, considering toxicity calls for renewed attention to the relationships between the body and the economy and requires us to transform our way of studying the spatiality and temporality of "consumption." The ways we, as American studies scholars, narrate these relationships have possible political ramifications across issues of environment, health, and the future of the global economy. New interdisciplinary influx may be one intellectual benefit of such an endeavor, not just in the fields I cite here but also possibly in public health, epidemiology, history of medicine, economics, and geography. Such expansive study would further our time-honored tradition of shifting the object and disciplinary mix of our American studies work as required in order to respond effectively to current states of emergency.

NAN ENSTAD

Thanks to Andrew Case, Anne Enke, T. V. Reed, and the editors of this volume for helpful suggestions regarding this essay. Thanks to Elspeth Brown for organizing the American Studies Association roundtable where I presented my first take on these musings.

1. David Ewing Duncan, "The Pollution Within," *National Geographic* 210, no. 4 (October 2006): 116–43 (pictures by Peter Essick). *National Geographic* included U.S. subjects from the first days of its publication but usually in foreign settings. By the 1970s the magazine regularly reported on environmental issues. In addition, it began covering U.S. locations and included more controversial subject matter. It retained, however, a validation of its U.S. readership as rational and generous and created a humanism that rendered others "just like us," obscuring difference. Catherine A. Lutz and Jane L. Collins, *Reading National Geographic* (Chicago: University of Chicago Press, 1993), 45–46, 280.

2. As a popular magazine, *National Geographic* does not lead scientific or scholarly change but rather refracts it for a general U.S. readership. Its changing gaze is thus reflective of the larger shifting attention of scientists who have developed new technologies for measuring trace chemicals in the body, as well as scholars who study toxicity in various disciplines. For excellent analyses of this shift in attention and its implications, see the recent forum "Toxic Bodies/Toxic Environments: An Interdisciplinary Forum," edited by Jody A. Roberts and Nancy Langston, in *Environmental History* 13 (October, 2008). Their introduction is found on pages 629–35; the forum itself runs from page 629 to page 703. As Roberts and Langston put it, "Some of these tests, such as biomonitoring and body-burden analyses, highlight that we not only experience our environment in obvious ways, but that we are also united with it at the molecular level. Trace chemical found in the air, water, and soil are now being detected *within* us" (629; emphasis in original).

3. The most comprehensive history of the public health disaster of cigarettes is Allan M. Brandt's excellent book, *The Cigarette Century: The Rise, Fall, and Deadly Persistence of the Product That Defined America* (New York: Basic Books, 2007). See also Richard Kluger's Pulitzer Prize–winning, *Ashes to Ashes: America's Hundred-Year Cigarette War, the Public Health, and the Unabashed Triumph of Philip Morris* (New York: Vintage, 1996); and David Kessler, *A Question of Intent: A Great American Battle with a Deadly Industry* (New York: Public Affairs, 2001). My own book-in-progress, entitled "The Jim Crow Cigarette: Following Tobacco Road from North Carolina to China and Back," is a cultural history of a cigarette corporation, rather than a study focusing on policy, law, or public health; it therefore engages directly with questions of labor, consumption, and subjectivity in relationship to the transnational circulation of a toxic product.

4. The field of environmental justice studies is large and growing. This work takes race as a central category of analysis and is closely linked to activists who have insisted that environmental issues are closely linked to race and class inequities. Solutions, therefore, must connect environmental justice to issues of poverty and racism, including housing, occupational inequities, and urban decay. For some influential works, see Robert D. Bullard, *Dumping in Dixie: Race, Class and Environmental Quality* (Boulder, Colo.: Westview Press, 1990, 1994, 2000); Laura Pulido, *Environmentalism and Economic Justice:*

Two Chicano Struggles in the Southwest (Tucson: University of Arizona Press, 1996); Jodi Adamson, Mei Mei Evans, and Rachel Stein, *The Environmental Justice Reader: Politics, Poetics and Pedagogy* (Tucson: University of Arizona Press, 2002); David Nabuib Pellow and Robert J. Brulle, *Power, Justice and the Environment: A Critical Appraisal of the Environmental Justice Movement* (Cambridge, Mass.: MIT Press, 2005); Luke W. Cole and Sheila R. Foster, *From the Ground Up: Environmental Racism and the Rise of the Environmental Justice Movement* (New York: New York University Press, 2001).

5. For an excellent discussion of the interdisciplinary study of illness and environment, including a discussion of scale, see Gregg Mitman, Michelle Murphy, and Christopher Sellers, "Introduction: A Cloud over History," *Osiris* 19 (2004): 1–17. This volume of *Osiris* is a special issue edited by Mitman, Murphy, and Sellers and is entitled "Landscapes of Exposure: Knowledge and Illness in Modern Environments." In this volume, Nicholas B. King argued that studying the "scale politics" of various actors — the ways people employ different scales in representing an issue — may itself be a way of understanding how health and the environment are linked politically and socially. See "The Scale Politics of Emerging Diseases," 62–78.

6. Anna Lowenhaupt Tsing, *Friction: An Ethnography of Global Connection* (Princeton: Princeton University Press, 2005), 58.

7. Ibid., 51.

8. Chris Rosen and Christopher Sellers have critiqued business historians for factoring out environmental issues from their analysis because the corporations they studied considered them "externals" and unrelated to profit. Clearly, "profit" is a cultural construction that does not actually measure all costs. See "The Nature of the Firm: An Ecocultural Approach to Business History," *Business History Review* 73 (1999): 577–600. For work that sees the corporation as a cultural system that includes vulnerability, resistance, and failure, see Tsing, *Friction*. See also James Livingston, "Corporations and Cultural Studies," *Social Text* 44 (Autumn–Winter, 1995): 61–68; David W. Noble, *Death of a Nation: American Culture and the End of Exceptionalism* (Minneapolis: University of Minnesota Press, 2002). For a more broadly based consideration of the transnational flow of goods and toxins than the commodity chain model would provide, see J. R. McNeill, *Something New under the Sun: An Environmental History of the Twentieth Century World* (New York: W. W. Norton, 2000).

9. Bill Brown, *A Sense of Things: The Object Matter of American Literature* (Chicago: University of Chicago Press: 2003), 5.

10. Bill Brown, "Thing Theory," in *Things*, ed. Brown (Chicago: University of Chicago Press, 2004), 7. Brown calls for a new materialism that dovetails nicely with a resolute materialism in environmental studies, which insists that the "natural" world acts upon us. William Cronon states, "To such basic historical categories as gender, class, and race, environmental historians would add a theoretical vocabulary in which plants, animals, soils, climates, and other nonhuman entities become the coactors and codeterminants of a history not just of people but of the earth itself." See "A Place for Stories: Nature, History and Narrative," *Journal of American History* 78 (March 1992): 1349. See also Cronon, *Nature's Metropolis: Chicago and the Great West* (New York: W. W. Norton, 1991); Mitman, Murphy, and Sellers, "Introduction: A Cloud over History" 10–12; Christopher Sellers,

"Thoreau's Body: Towards an Embodied Environmental History," *Environmental History* 4, no. 4 (October 1999): Sciences Module, 493. Bruno Latour's work underwriting such materialism within science studies is cited both in environmental studies and by Brown. See Bruno Latour, "Do Scientific Objects Have a History?: Pasteur and Whitehead in a Bath of Lactic Acid," *Common Knowledge* 5 (Spring, 1996): 76–91; and Latour's provocative contribution to Brown's edited volume, *Things*, entitled "Why Has Critique Run out of Steam: From Matters of Fact to Matters of Concern," 151–73. Recently, work tracking the history of things has abounded, some of which grants agency to the object. Among the most popular and compelling of these is Michael Pollan, *The Botany of Desire: A Plant's-Eye View of the World* (New York: Random House, 2001); Michael Pollan, *The Omnivore's Dilemma: A Natural History of Four Meals* (New York: Penguin, 2006).

11. Lizabeth Cohen, *A Consumer's Republic: The Politics of Mass Consumption in Postwar America* (New York: Knopf, 2003). See also Davarian Baldwin, *Chicago's New Negroes: Modernity, Migration and Black Urban Life* (Chapel Hill: University of North Carolina Press, 2007), for his discussion of a "marketplace intellectual life" that goes beyond "consumption" in considering the impact of the proliferation of goods; and Lawrence Glickman, *Buying Power: A History of Consumer Activism in America* (Chicago: University of Chicago Press, 2009).

12. Brown, "Thing Theory," 9. See also Arjun Appadurai, *Modernity at Large: Cultural Dimensions of Globalization* (Minneapolis: University of Minnesota Press, 1996).

13. Linda Nash, *Inescapable Ecologies: A History of Environment, Disease and Knowledge* (Berkeley: University of California Press, 2006).

14. This highly abbreviated history inevitably oversimplifies the complex development of the environmental movement. For a good synthesis, see Robert Gottlieb's revision of his 1992 book, *Forcing the Spring: The Transformation of the American Environmental Movement* (Washington, D.C.: Island Press, 2005).

15. This idea has been criticized thoroughly within the environmental movement. See William Cronon's "The Trouble with Wilderness, or, Getting Back to the Wrong Nature," *Environmental History* 1, no. 1 (January 1996): 7–55.

16. Christopher Sellers traces the methods and discourse of toxicology and epidemiology used to demand regulation during the post–World War II environmental movement to the field of "Industrial Hygiene" that developed between the 1910s and the 1930s. For a fascinating analysis of this knowledge production, see his *Hazards of the Job: From Industrial Disease to Environmental Health Science* (Chapel Hill: University of North Carolina Press, 1997).

17. For example, see Paul Hawken, *Blessed Unrest: How the Largest Movement in the World Came into Being and Why No One Saw It Coming* (New York: Viking, 2007).

18. Andrew Szasz critiques such individualist politics as being an "inverted quarantine." See *Shopping Our Way to Safety: How We Changed from Protecting the Environment to Protecting Ourselves* (Minneapolis: University of Minnesota Press, 2007). Adam Rome shows such politics at work historically in *The Bulldozer in the Countryside: Urban Sprawl and the Rise of American Environmentalism* (New York: Cambridge University Press, 2001).

19. Michelle Murphy, *Sick Building Syndrome and the Problem of Uncertainty: Envi-

ronmental Politics, Technoscience, and Women Workers (Durham: Duke University Press, 2006), 154–58.

20. Arthur W. Frank, *At the Will of the Body: Reflections on Illness* (Boston: Houghton Mifflin, 1991); Frank, *The Wounded Storyteller: Body, Illness, and Ethics* (Chicago: University of Chicago Press, 1995), esp. 1–25. See also Arthur Kleinman, *The Illness Narratives: Suffering, Healing and the Human Condition* (New York: Basic Books, 1988); Cheryl Mattingly and Linda C. Garro, eds., *Narrative and the Cultural Construction of Illness and Healing* (Berkeley: University of California Press, 2000).

Past Burning

The (Post-) Traumatic Memories of (Post-) Queer Theory

CHRISTOPHER CASTIGLIA

Queer theory burns me up.

Among the incendiary elements in much contemporary queer theory, we might focus on three: first, its increasing neglect of AIDS — not only the past and continuing devastation of sexual culture in the United States but also the role that AIDS, AIDS activism, and AIDS theory played in the generation of queer theory; second, its focus on negative affect — shame, abjection, grief— to the exclusion of the affects that characterized the sexual revolution, including exuberance, defiant pride, exorbitant pleasure, giddiness, enthusiastic innocence, outrageous optimism, loyalty, and love; third, the conversion of epistemology into ontology, of history into psychic universalism, or, put simply, of loss into absence.[1] These three features are interrelated. As AIDS was erased in the dominant media, queer theory joined this forgetting, participating in the loss not only of the memories of particular gay men who died of AIDS but of rituals of memory and cultural innovation that those men pioneered. That loss could not be acknowledged in a culture of forgetting that insisted that AIDS had become "manageable" and hence less newsworthy, propelling into the vortex of American amnesia both the disease and the historical context that allowed it to reach pandemic proportions, the subcultural practices it decimated, and the cultural and activist responses it provoked.

Unable to acknowledge our profound loss in a context of cultural silence, queers generated a host of negative affects characteristic of post-traumatic disorder.[2] Queer theory's bad feelings continued to register profound loss and rage, but these were now severed from their historical object and reattached to the "queer psyche" itself. Douglas Crimp rightly contends that ambivalence was often at the heart of AIDS activism. It is equally true that such activisms, turned inward in the face of an apparently vanishing object, become reinvented as the psychic ambivalences of "queer shame."[3] As often occurs in survivors of trauma, a history of abuse becomes ritual self-abuse, the experience of helplessness in the face of the original trauma rendered legible and manageable through the representation of an inter-personal wrong as a self-contained psychic disruption. Such internalizations of trauma require a high degree of abstraction, from interpersonal to intra-psychic abuse, which in the case of AIDS was provided by queer theory and its shift from grief, which signals a loss experienced through external agency (something has been taken away from me, and I grieve) to a self-contained absence (I am abject because of some internal lack or psychic fragmenta-tion).[4] The shift from loss to absence fosters the evacuation of history from the scene of trauma.

When AIDS in the United States disappeared from queer theory, it van-ished from American studies as well because of a move toward the trans-national, the hemispheric, and the global. Although focusing attention on transnational paradigms correctly stretches our understanding of the border crossings of capital, populations, and ideology (allowing us, for instance, to understand the global spread of HIV/AIDS), it has also made local freedom struggles within the United States seem provincial and narrow, tainted with the bad smell of national exceptionalism. In constructing "identity politics" *tout court* as the leftover false consciousness of an embarrassingly naive past, much sophisticated work in American studies has inadvertently contributed to the forgetting of AIDS and to the attribution of bad feeling to those who cannot or will not forget. Too big for queer theory and too small for Ameri-can studies, AIDS — and indeed the whole history of sexual liberation strug-gles — has fallen through the cracks of institutional memory.

Some recent work — in queer theory, American studies, and gay men's cul-ture — has, however, attempted to reverse this amnesia, insisting on memory as an urgent means of creating alternative social and sexual practices in *the present*. Recognizing memory's inability to recapture a past in its own terms, yet resisting queer theory's construction of memory as shame-inducing nos-talgia, recent postqueer treatments of memory provide a more hopeful ap-proach to the inventive and collaborative efforts to inhabit "crisis" in order to produce greater freedom in the here and now.

CHRISTOPHER CASTIGLIA

The Crisis Which Is Not One

As AIDS became a matter not of institutional neglect, corporate profiteering, and public phobia but one visible only as universalized bad feeling, queer theory turned flaming activism into self-immolation. By choosing the image of scorching flesh, I mean to invoke a touchstone in trauma theory. In the story of the burning child, the father of a dead child falls asleep while a hired man sits with the corpse. As he sleeps, the father dreams that the child comes to him and calls for help, as he is burning. The father awakens to discover that in fact the hired man has dropped off to sleep, allowing a lit candle to fall onto and burn the body. For Cathy Caruth, the story is a lesson in the belatedness of trauma: one realizes that one has survived trauma only after the fact, and therefore one's experience of trauma is only ever a fragmented and ambivalent memory.[5] Caruth's insight into how trauma mingles memory and presence has important consequences for queer theory and AIDS narrative. If memory and presence are one and the same in the context of trauma, then to disavow memory, to "forget" the crisis of AIDS, is to necessarily alienate oneself from the possibility of presence as well. Hence, queer theory's repeated articulations of "absence" — the rupture of the subject, the death-driven psyche, the shame and abjection that stand as universalizing memorials of some absent satisfaction — are traces of a disavowed memory, of a historical loss and a lost history. Although queer theory can be said to be the "child" of AIDS activism, in the context of Caruth's analysis queer theory is the sleeping father, refusing to awaken — not to the original trauma of the child's death, which, like deaths from AIDS, cannot be recuperated after the fact, but to the second-order trauma of not having listened *in time* to the ethical demands of memory.

Lest we turn "trauma theory" into yet another universalizing abstraction, however, we should note that AIDS is a trauma with a difference. For Caruth, the belatedness of trauma is intrinsic to its anomalousness: because the mind has no previous story through which to make sense of an unprecedented horror, the event is internalized *as* absence, generating the fragmentation and temporal disjointedness that often characterize post-traumatic testimony.[6] With AIDS, however, the trauma comes not from the lack of stories to convert loss into narrative (the long historical span of the epidemic ensures a plethora of such stories) but from an *abundance* of memory confronting a technology of forgetting that *forces* amnesia upon those striving, in the face of deaths, to retain a continuity of cultural transmission.

The "forgetting" of AIDS may be related to its construction as a "crisis," which supposedly requires a therapeutic "working through" that often imposes a chronologically ordered, unambivalent, and conciliatory memory-narrative in place of "unhealthy" (enraged, desiring, disjointed, perverse) ones. To choose the old over the new, the disordered over the chronological, ambivalence and desire over victimization and reconciliation, interpersonal struggle over individualizing psychic "ownership" is to be "locked" in the past, doomed to "acting out" (kin to AIDS activists' "acting up") rather than the normative progression implied by "working through."[7] The therapeutic imperative to "work through" crisis often prescribes amnesia as a prophylactic against contagious and diseased memory. In a June 1995 interview with National Public Radio, gay neoconservative Gabriel Rotello insisted that the necessary cure for those "so traumatized by their past as gay men" that they cannot consent to governmental closings of bars and bathhouses should be "a complete break with the past" that would enable "a 20 to 30 year period . . . of social conservativism."[8] For Rotello, trauma, far from bringing its own forgetting, is caused by excessive memory, the "cure" for which is a prophylactic amnesia that will bring gay men into a reparative "normalcy." The highly unstable divisions Rotello asserts between sex and normalcy, traumatic memory and therapeutic forgetting, generate a crisis of social location for gay men that became a second-stage trauma.

Some gay men resisted prophylactic amnesia and normative memory, however, refusing the sexual normalization that took the AIDS crisis as its cover. As Douglas Crimp notes, "What many of us have lost is a culture of sexual possibilities: back rooms, tea rooms, bookstores, movie houses, and baths: the trucks, the pier, the ramble, the dunes. Sex was everywhere for us, and everything we wanted to venture."[9] Crimp clearly has not forgotten, nor has he saturated his memories with the shaming accusation that Rotello puts on memories of the sexual revolution. "Because this violence also desecrates the memories of our dead," Crimp argues, "we rise in anger to vindicate them. For many of us, mourning *becomes* militancy."[10] Crimp here powerfully articulates a coherent account of traumatic loss, which he places at the core of militant activism. Whereas for Rotello memory brings paralysis and amnesia healthful progress, for Crimp memory brings radical action for a nonnormative present, while amnesia brings normative paralysis.

Radical deployments of memory such as Crimp's faced two additional obstacles, however, the first of which, arising from the internalizing, individualizing, and universalizing conceptions of Freudian melancholy, becomes evident in Crimp's manifesto. Crimp begins by placing blame for traumatic loss on "ruthless interference with our bereavement," which imposed on gay memory "the violence of silence and omission almost as impossible to endure as the violence of unleashed hatred and outright murder."[11] Not long after naming the external agents of a second-stage trauma, Crimp concedes that "militancy might arise from conscious conflicts *within* mourning itself."[12] That subtle shift introduces a troubling ambivalence that gets more pronounced as the essay progresses: is the conflict *within* mourning (contained within the process of grief and, hence, an effect of gay men's psychic ambivalence) or is mourning a militant position in a *social* conflict (in which gay men continue remembering in the face of insistent forgetting)? Initially, Crimp allows both to exist simultaneously, claiming, "When, in mourning our ideal, we meet with the same opprobrium as when mourning our dead, we incur a different order of psychic distress, since the memories of our pleasures are already fraught with ambivalence."[13] As Freud noted, however, the ambivalence of melancholy leads to self-abuse on the part of the melancholic, who blames himself for actions he formerly recognized as existing outside himself. The ambivalence of melancholy, for Freud, is the result of an internalization, which renders "the ego itself . . . poor and empty" only because the *external* world was full of such poverty — the kind of "empty" opportunity of lost sex culture Crimp begins by naming — not because of an ambivalence intrinsic to melancholic desire itself.[14] Crimp becomes a Freudian melancholic, translating external forces that would "interfere" with gay memory into a loss-producing ambivalence within gay mourning itself.

The danger comes, however, when Crimp turns the resulting "poor and empty" ego into a universal queer psyche. Social conflict over the status of gay memory thus gives way to "a fundamental fact of psychic life: violence is also self-inflicted."[15] "Unconscious conflict can mean that we may make decisions — or fail to make them — whose results may be deadly too," Crimp contends, adding, "And the rage we direct against [New York City Health Commissioner] Stephen Joseph, justified as it is, may function as the very mechanism of our disavowal, whereby we convince ourselves that we are making all the decisions we need to make," blinding us to "our terror, our guilt, and our profound sadness."[16] Without denying the insight of Crimp's brilliant analysis (self-inflicted ambivalence may well account for the "wrong decisions" that lead, for instance, to the rising rate of HIV infection among young gay men), his account of ambivalence threatens to erase, through psychic universalism and internalized conflict, the possibility of social contestation over the status and public enactment of queer memory. Turning activist rage into terror, guilt, and sadness, Crimp shows how the erasure of social enactments of memory in the AIDS crisis generates the "archive of negative affect" that queer theory takes up, post-traumatically, as the universal queer psyche.

While the internalizations of conflict into psychic ambivalence run one risk, the opposite gesture — turning history into a progressive narrative with no ambivalence at all — proves equally risky. In 1988 Vito Russo assured fellow demonstrators, "Someday, the AIDS crisis will be over. Remember that. And when that day comes, when that day has come and gone, there'll be people alive on this earth — gay people and straight people, men and women, black and white — who will hear the story that once there was a terrible disease in this country and all over the world, and that a brave group of people stood up and fought and, in some cases, gave their lives, so that other people might live and be free."[17] Russo's rhetoric draws its power from a utopian prolepsis, allowing those struggling for survival against terrible odds to rest, if only momentarily, in the fictiveness of time, when a grief-stricken past will dissipate into a hagiographic and liberated future. While this promise supplies a satisfying uplift, however, it works at cross-purposes with the goal of Russo's speech, which is to inspire activism grounded urgently in the *present*. The temporal narrative that underlies Russo's stirring conclusion flattens past and future, experience and aspiration, into two-dimensional mutually exclusive sites of unalloyed grief and liberty without space for the present, where hope and despair, rage and grief, are potently mixed into an activism that, *pace* Russo's granting of advocacy to the inevitability of time, is the only means for turning rhetorical promise into lived history.

We must be cautious, then, in deploying the politics of memory to avoid giving temporality a distinctive agency, for the problem, as Russo also notes, is that while we are waiting for a redemptive future, no one in the present is listening to the testimony of the dead and struggling. Part of the problem comes from Russo's conception of what it means to "remember." In the speech, memory is a transparent relay between a factually self-evident past and a value-stable future, in which those remembering play no ethical or creative role. The problem with this account, however, is that *interest* — the fact that some go on "as though we weren't living through some sort of nightmare" while others "hear the screams of the people who are dying and their cries for help" — suggests that the present is far from a neutral space of transmission but is, rather, composed of competing claims to justice, in which memory, created or disavowed from those positions of interest, plays a crucial role.

Russo's speech provides a competing construction of AIDS, however, that works against time, frustrating the impossible displacement of the present. The first sentence of Russo's speech does not promise an end to AIDS, after all, but to *crisis*, and it is this construction of AIDS that frustrates temporal displacement. When activists named AIDS a "crisis," they identified its profoundly *traumatic* nature, meaning not only the horrors of the syndrome itself but, more especially, its existence outside and against the apparently seamless temporality of Russo's inspiring promise.[18] Trauma is defiantly countertemporal, breaking from the predictable sequencing of both memory and narrative (memory *as* narrative). Trauma survivors are often characterized as temporal stutterers, starting again and again, struggling to give chronological order to stubbornly disjointed affects and events. By insisting on AIDS as a crisis — and by calling for more experience of that crisis — we might overcome the obstacles to queer memory named earlier, insisting on the right to memory without necessitating the imposition of normative values, therapeutic chronology, or prophylactic forgetting. By calling AIDS a crisis *rather* than a trauma, moreover, we insist on its *social* location, giving us an external object on which to direct our anger and freeing us from the negative affects that we carry, like scars of past burnings, at the core of our irremediably sad and shameful selves. At the same time, we must understand queer memory as neither transparent nor recuperative but rather, as Caruth suggests, as a register of belatedness. Understanding that we are awakening too late to our responsibility to those who died from AIDS and the cultures they created may become an occasion not for self-blame but for mutual responsibility and a reinvigorated sense of postessentialist (including the "essence" of negative affect) inventive pleasure.

To call for more memory of/in crisis in the name of creativity and pleasure may seem counterintuitive, but memory and responsibility are occasions for joy and progressive invention as much as for grief. Here we can return to Caruth's analysis of the tale of the burning child. "The passing on of the child's words transmits not simply a reality that can be grasped in these words' repetition," Caruth contends, "but the ethical imperative of an awakening that has yet to occur."[19] To awaken to one's responsibility to the past is not, then, an imperative to recreate the past exactly and transparently *as it was*, but rather an invitation to ethical imagination. Awakening to a present in which one perceives "the very gap between the other's death and his own life," we inherit the opportunity for "crossing from the burning within to the burning without."[20] Following Caruth's lead, we can see that until queer theorists respond to the cry of the past — to pastness in its historical and extrasubjective specificity of loss — we will continue to misconstrue a burning without as a burning within, social inflictions of shame as internally abjecting drives, causing us to miss our present creative capability to respond to bad feeling by inventing not utopian futures or amnesic presents, but *memories*, suspended between a responsibility to the spectacular *realness* of the past and the collaborative *inventiveness* of the present that will allow for creative collaboration as an activist practice, a new mode of democratic citizenship — of citizenship *in crisis* — within the current culture of amnesia.

Queer Theory Is Burning

It is not unusual for post-traumatic survivors to enact, in the manner of Freud's melancholic, the violence of the original trauma on themselves and others. In the case of queer theory, this reenactment has taken the form of the internalization of social conflict as psychic ambivalence ("bad feelings"), requiring the translation of loss into absence that instantiates the abstracting of historical trauma characteristic of post-traumatic disorder. In locating that disorder in queer theory, however, I want to insist on its collective and historical operation, generating "antisociality" as AIDS post-trauma, rather than locating it, as queer theory often does, in the abstract and individualizing realm of "the queer psyche."

Although the abstraction represented by queer theory's negative affects threatens to obscure the social conflict at its core, it nevertheless remains tied to the fear and shame about the sexual revolution (now abstracted simply as "sex") endemic both to the initial traumatic response to AIDS and to the neoconservative assault on gay memory. This genealogy of post-traumatic abstraction stretches from Leo Bersani's 1987 proclamation that "most people don't like sex" to the Summer 2007 issue of *South Atlantic Quarterly*, "After Sex?" whose title succinctly captures the conversion of loss (to be "after" in the sense of "post-" is to have moved beyond the moment when sex was possible) into absence (to be "after sex" in the sense of looking for sex is to assume that one is in a state of desire for what one does not have); in the first account the disappearance of sex is chronological, in the second ontological, in the first sex is lost, in the second it is absent.[21]

The titles of the essays in this issue — "Starved," "Lonely," "Glad to Be Unhappy," "Queer Theory: Postmortem," "Disturbing Sexuality," "Post Sex: On

Being Too Slow, Too Stupid, Too Soon" — seem to affirm Heather Love's assertion that the archive of queer feelings is a tour de force of depressive symptoms: "nostalgia, regret, shame, despair, *resentiment*, passivity, escapism, self-hatred, withdrawal, bitterness, defeatism, and loneliness."[22] It is debatable whether this catalog of bad feelings has been, as Love claims, the primary, let alone the *only*, "corporeal and psychic"[23] response to antigay violence, including the assault on queer memory described earlier; the pride, exuberance, shameless defiance, purposefulness, enthusiasm, hilarity, joy, and love of the gay pride movement and the sexual revolution would constitute an alternative "archive." Focusing on negative feelings is not a psychic inevitability but a historical *choice*, and much queer theory since the early 1990s has privileged one set of affects over the other in ways that erase the sexual culture of the 1970s while normalizing the traumatized loss of the post-AIDS generation. Rather than understanding that discourse as a cynical participation in a bad institutionalizing bargain that grants a place at the intellectual table in return for translating pride and pleasure into constitutive and hence irremediable shame and abjection, we might understand queer theory's bad feelings as a poignant surfacing of grief without an object, that object having been made unnamable first by the conservative assault on memory, then by mainstream media's erasure of AIDS from its daily rehearsal of national crises, and finally by queer theory's own translation of historical loss into ontological absence.

One particularly sophisticated example of how queer theory produces a post-traumatic narrative that both effaces historical conflict in favor of psychic abstraction and generates negative affects that efface collaborative community can be found in the May 2006 issue of *PMLA*. A forum in that issue examines the "antisocial thesis," which asserts that queer sex epitomizes the self-shattering, temporally disorganizing, anticollective death drive that queers have historically represented within Western culture. As part of that forum, Lee Edelman and Judith Halberstam push the antisocial thesis further, expanding its political (or, conversely, antipolitical, the two terms seeming, vertiginously, to describe similar affects) efficacy (or, again, antiefficacy). For Halberstam, queer theory's archive — totalized as the "gay male archive" — proves disappointingly narrow. Focused on Proust, Warhol, Broadway musicals, and Judy Garland, gay men, according to Halberstam, have failed to notice the *Realpolitik* going on in the more radically antiracist and counternormative archive composed of *Finding Nemo*, Spongebob, and Patti Smith.[24] Leaving aside the facetious homophobia of this characterization of gay men as exclusively devoted to the dandyish affects of "fatigue, ennui, boredom, ironic distancing, indirectness, arch dismissal, insincerity, and camp" and the uncritical commercialism of Halberstam's alternative archive (radical culture via *Disney*?), what is noteworthy here is Halberstam's insistence that we broaden queer theory's affective range to include "rage, rudeness, anger, spite, impatience, intensity, mania, sincerity, earnestness, overinvestment, incivility, and brutal honesty."[25]

The affects Halberstam describes might seem at first glance incongruous. The aggressiveness of rage, rudeness, anger, spite, impatience, intensity, mania, and incivility seems to have little in common with the seemingly quieter and less antagonistic affects of sincerity, earnestness, and honesty, brutal or otherwise. Unless, that is, one considers both sets of affect in the context of trauma. These two sets of affect have consistently been used to characterize two constituencies, children and the traumatized, and most explosively so when children are traumatized by sexual abuse. In many analyses of trauma victims, affects of unusual earnest and sincere honesty (a determination to get stories "right," to provide accurate chronology, to appear more transparently sincere than artful) becomes joined to the spiteful rudeness of "acting out" in the absence of narrative credibility or accessible memory. Frustrated by their inability to provide the transparent sincerity they wish to convey, trauma survivors, like children frustrated in the desire to express their wants, "act out" through inarticulate rage, obsessive repetition, often violent and apparently spiteful incivility. As a result, trauma victims are often characterized *as* children, thereby perpetuating the sense of powerlessness it is intended to shame into "mature" civility and chronologically ordered narration.

Post-traumatic narratives, including collective ones like queer theory, therefore, often express deep ambivalences toward children and childhood, as becomes clear in Lee Edelman's response to Halberstam.[26] The most effective response in Edelman's essay comes in its affective charge, which demonstrates exactly the combination of rage and sincerity, impatience and overinvestment that Halberstam calls for. Edelman performs this affective synthesis not by refuting Halberstam's claim that gay men are not socially engaged but by lampooning those like Halberstam who, happy "to earn their applause . . . by putting the puppet of humanism through its passion play once again, . . . lead in a hymn to the Futurch even while dressed in heretical drag. Delightfully drugged by the harmony, the freedom from harm, that their harmonies promise, they induce us all to nod along, persuaded that we, like their puppet, on which most humanities teaching depends, shall also eventually overcome, for knowledge, understanding, and progress must, in the fullness of time, set us free."[27] What Edelman here mocks as "the Futurch" becomes embodied in the child and its deceptive capacity to represent a transformative future. The "good" kid, by implication, would be the one with no future, the state so often experienced by traumatized children.

Edelman betrays some rather limiting assumptions about both politics and freedom here. First, he assumes that freedom necessarily means freedom from harm, whereas political freedom arguably requires precisely such an engagement with risk, violence (psychic or otherwise), and harm. Second, Edelman suggests that freedom has a teleology (the place into which humanism will "set us free") rather than acknowledging that struggles to enact political power — struggles remarkably *similar* to the psychic forces he describes as the "death drive" — have characterized much political theory and practice, including the much-maligned humanistic ones. Finally, Edelman asserts the simultaneity of humanist politics and futurity. While Edelman cogently identifies a heteronormatively reproductive logic with a strain of political futurity, he is wrong to totalize that strain to include all political theory, just as Halberstam is wrong to reduce all gay men to a politics of style or to reduce such politics to mere ennui or apolitical indirectness. It is true that much political rhetoric, on the left and the right, focuses on enacting reform for the sake of "our children's children," but it is also true that for other political agents the focus has been not on the future but on the present ("What do we want? Health care! When do we want it? NOW!").

The shortcomings in Edelman's argument arise from an overinvested ambivalence figured by the child, an ambivalence that arises from the post-traumatic relation to a never-quite-effaced memory of the past. It bears noting here that the sexual revolution of the 1970s and the gay men who participated in it were characterized as *infantile*: narcissistic, pleasure-driven, irresponsible, in a state of perpetually arrested development. If the liberal "child" of futural democracy is the object of Edelman's critique, the child of the gay male past is the object of his suppression, an infantile uncanny, in which the "child," bifurcated, like gay culture generally, between a disavowed past and an unworthy future, has no present. Out of this ambivalence toward childhood arises a poignant melancholy about lost childhood, about lost *pastness*. In her search for an alternative queer archive, Halberstam turns to children's texts: cartoons, Disney films, and the like. There is pathos to Edelman's fucked (over) child, as if the critic is unable to leave the child behind and yet resents its company, hating it and *being* it simultaneously.

Past Burning

It is the same state of ambivalence — earnestly identificatory, ragefully anti-social — that characterizes trauma.

Post-traumatic narratives often circle around a (barely) suppressed past, so Edelman and Halberstam, for all their disagreements, share a reluctance to surrender a past that they nevertheless do not acknowledge. Both critics, in their calls for queer presence made manifest through a sincere rage and an impatient presence, echo the claims made in the years after the onset of AIDS by gay men and lesbians such as Douglas Crimp, Cindy Patton, Simon Watney, Samuel Delany, Gregg Bordowitz, Sarah Schulman, and David Wojnarowicz. Those critics, far from languishing in "fatigue, ennui, boredom, ironic distancing, indirectness, arch dismissal, insincerity, and camp" or deferring pleasure and action into a future figured as romantic childhood, deployed "rage, rudeness, anger, spite, impatience, intensity, mania, sincerity, earnestness, overinvestment, incivility, and brutal honesty" to demand an immediate end to the AIDS crisis and a return to the values of the sexual revolution. While universalizing loss into the transhistoricism of "the queer psyche" might at least generate rhetorical connections with others possessed of that psyche in the past, it has, instead, made the work of the past yet another loss among the many attributable to AIDS. Despite queer theory's persistent unremembering, however, traces of the past remain in the tones, affects, and agendas that constitute the (not quite) repressed archive of queer theorists such as Edelman and Halberstam.

Postqueer Memory and American Studies

While we might first look to queer theory for a historical and theoretical reckoning with AIDS and its past, we might also expect such an account within American studies, which has turned extraordinary critical attention to national "crises" occasioned by government neglect and social prejudice. There too, however, we find a surprising silence, although for opposite reasons. Although scholars working in American studies, historicists almost to a person, might counter the trend toward amnesia, the shift within that field toward larger conceptual frames such as the transnational or the "global" has similarly contributed to national forgetting. Rushing to represent nationalism as intrinsically synonymous with narrow provincialism or naive false consciousness, we have too often slighted the histories of resistance and renovation that have been central and continuing parts of U.S. history and culture. In particular, American studies has become increasingly resistant to "identity politics," characterized, in opposition to the large-minded

Realpolitik of global transnationalism, as a provincial leftover of a discredited past. Whether we acknowledge it or not, histories of resistance and alternative social formation, and the methodologies inspired by social justice movements, have been made to seem uncritically nostalgic and quaintly local. This reaction against the kinds of identity politics that propelled American AIDS activism in the 1980s may explain why, although AIDS is clearly a global phenomenon and American styles of AIDS activism became models around the world, this phenomenon has rarely been included in Americanists' recent turn to the transnational. In losing sight of the local and the alternative, both in our own time and in the past, we lose sight of not only the rich complexity of American life — a complexity that continues to drive innovation and counternormativity throughout the country — but also the optimism, the will to come together and make something *better*, which has a rich history in this country and without which, for all the brilliance of our critiques, we have very little to teach citizens trying to live in the present. For this reason, there is much that American studies can learn from a queer memory in crisis.

A different account of the relationship between American studies and sexual cultures in the United States, an account arising from memory in crisis, is offered by Mark Merlis's *American Studies*.[28] The novel comprises the mostly interior ruminations of Reeve, a former graduate student of an eminent American studies scholar, loosely based on F. O. Matthiessen, driven to suicide when Cold War anticommunism and homophobia led Harvard to fire him. Growing old and hungry for companionship, Reeve invites hustlers into his home, one of whom beats him so badly that he is hospitalized. As he lies in his hospital bed, Reeve remembers his mentor and the lessons he taught about American literature's "invincible city," a social utopia built on Whitmanian fraternity that Reeve translates into the post–World War II gay culture he lived in as a student in Boston. As he remembers and reflects, Reeve begins to form a poignant bond with the apparently straight, mostly inarticulate young man who occupies the other bed in his hospital room. Enabled by his memories of both an academic field and a sexual subculture, the narrator comes to find shared points of connection, shared pleasures and fears, that allow him to draw strength for his recovery and to lift himself from the isolating despair with which he begins his narration. He does so, moreover, without romanticizing the past (he is critical of the "invincible city" found both in the literature of the American Renaissance and in urban gay culture) or believing he can recapture history (he frequently comments on the partiality of his knowledge, the failure of his recollection, and his biasing ambivalence toward his memories). The gaps and ambivalences in memory do not produce greater isolation or shame for Reeve, however, but offer opportunities for collectivizing translation. A remembered moment of crisis — his recollections circle around the trauma of being beaten, a trauma that makes human collaboration and responsibility all the more necessary — becomes, in short, the opportunity for a creative construction of, if not an invincible city, at least a more generous and compassionate community within it.

American Studies is part of a growing number of cultural and critical texts that take seriously Christopher Nealon's call "to understand, through an identification with an ancestor, how history works, what it looks like, what possibilities it has offered in the past, and what those possibilities suggest about our ineffable present tense."[29] Such works constitute a postqueer turn in the study of sexuality, memory, and subculture, taking up the creative possibilities of imperfect, often painful recollection — memory in crisis — in order to translate trauma's bad feelings into more just and pleasurable social alliances. The goal of such memories is not to comfort or to recover, but radically to transform the conditions that produce loss in the first place. Memory is neither clean nor comforting but is messy business, and never more so than in crisis. Our collaborative inventions of memory must allow us, as Heather Love encourages, to "feel backward," acknowledging ambivalence, uncertainty, and impatience alongside admiration, clarity, and joy. We must reckon with the past as well as reconcile with it. Our memories, moreover, will be maddeningly general *and* local, made up of the mass cultural forms that pass, willynilly, through the individual and local filters of need, habit, and whimsy.

But above all, postqueer memory is an occasion to engage others in a collective invention of the present, of creativity and care, in the context of pleasure. For such memories to emerge, however, the inevitability of the present must first be challenged. Crisis is the social rupture out of which such memory takes material form as a new present. Perhaps this is why, as Dominick LaCapra notes, trauma victims can be reluctant to relinquish their trauma, preferring to experience what he calls the "traumatic sublime," "an uncanny source of elation or ecstasy," that generates nonessentialized collectivities.[30] The traumatic refusal of normative "demands and responsibilities of social life" may produce, LaCapra asserts, nonnormative and *pleasurable* sociabilities, which "paradoxically become the valorized or intensely cathected basis of identity for an individual or a group rather than events that pose the problematic question of identity."[31] Caruth, too, suggests the collectivizing and innovative possibility of post-traumatic memory, especially fragmentary ones, which become an invitation for others to narrate *their* experiences and hence a record of "the way we are implicated in each other's traumas."[32] Insisting that *all* memory carries elements of invention, creating "a history that is no longer straightforwardly referential," Caruth argues that such inventions are both collective and ethically charged.[33] Without denying the often deep ambivalences at the core of our relationships to the past, those living in crisis challenge the automatic linkage of ambivalence and antisocial negativity or of memory and transparent recovery, and instead suggest how ambivalence, placing gaps in the apparently seamless values of both normative humanism and queer universalism, creates opportunities for new conceptions of and *as* collective life.

Incomplete or ambivalent memories produce just such collectivizing sublimity in Alexandra Juhasz's 1995 *Video Remains*, which combines footage of the film maker's college friend Jim Lamb, who died from AIDS in 1993, with voice-overs of conversations between Juhasz and various friends about memory and film making, mortality and activism.[34] The video burns with the imperative to remember and the impossibilities of doing so in a complete, coherent, or ennobling manner. "I can't say I'm honoring peoples' memories well enough. One always fails in the face of that responsibility," Juhasz says in the voice-over, adding, "I think we need to absolve ourselves of the guilt."

Absolution is frustrated, however, by memory's incapacity to recover a lost past. Novelist Sarah Schulman (whose *People In Trouble* is another powerful example of postqueer memory) assures Juhasz, "When these people are dead, and when I am dead, these interviews will still exist, and people will be able to go back and see that . . . there was an active gay movement and an active gay community that supported people with AIDS who were abandoned by straight people and their families and their government. And that was the true dynamic, though it hasn't yet been shown." Despite this promise, the capacity of contemporary viewers to "go back" is frustrated by the fact that, as another friend states, "The video is so alive and the people are so dead." As time progresses, moreover, memories fade and commitment to activism on behalf of the sick and dying loses its urgency. "One of the things that seems to be true, I don't know about the 90s but certainly the 2000s," Alisa Lebov tells Juhasz, "is that we've almost stopped talking about [AIDS] with one another, and that's how you and I met, that's how I *know* you."

The project of responsible memory is equally frustrated by the often-ambivalent worthiness of the past and its inhabitants. Although one friend wishes to find in the memory of those who have died "all this wisdom" and "amazing poetry," Juhasz's friend Jim, whom she describes as "a crazy, lying, wild, brilliant, dynamic man" who "died in a state of unfulfilled chaos, which is how he lived," refuses the dignified profundity that memory often craves. Although Jim "wanted to be recorded speaking great insight and poetry," his incoherent and rambling narratives, often self-involved and seemingly point-less, seem "very tragic," leading Juhasz — and the viewer — to feel ambivalence toward Jim and "these video tapes that stand in for memories." The past is neither ideal nor profound, at least not entirely, nor can its recollections be complete or ever present. Realizing this, one might well have bad feelings.

Despite its ambivalence and frustration, however, *Video Remains* is strikingly, if critically, optimistic. A story told by Juhasz's hair stylist, Michael Anthony, sums up what "remains" after friends have passed. Offering to vacuum the "dust bunnies" left in the apartment after his vocal coach, a transvestite also named Alexandra, has packed to move to a hospital where s/he will die from AIDS, Alexandra tells him, he reports, "Leave them there for all the memories of all the good times we had here. Throw them in the air so the next person will remember what it was like when we had our great get-togethers and our parties and our great moments of intimate conversation and planning for other things in our lives and our goals." Memories, trans-lated into the most mundane form of everyday "remains" — dust — persist as a continual reminder to Anthony — as to the others interviewed in the video — of his love for people in the past and the choices they made, good or bad. Above all, it reminds them that "we stuck by them," that a collective ethos once existed, contrary to the present appearance of indifference.

Reiterating this point, Schulman claims, "If you suffer, and you never get accountability or justice, then you learn that it doesn't matter how you treat other people, and you learn it from the example of being the victim, and it gets extended. Now, if you get accountability and justice, then I think you can have a real healing and the suffering ends. And I think people strive for that." That striving can take the form of, in Juhasz's words, "living our lives as responsibly and responsively as we can, and continuing activism on any level, on any issue, is to me a way that we can honor those lives." To do that, we need the creativity of film makers such as Juhasz, the collaboration of friends such as Anthony, Shulman, and Lebov, and the objects of memory, however incomplete or flawed, like Jim. Together they form a postqueer memory, realistic about the materiality of loss and the persistence of ambivalence, yet aware that, without our pasts, personal and collective, we have no stories to tell. Especially as academics move beyond the collectivizing power of identity, postqueer memory of and in crisis may be one of the only means to break the hold of normative inevitability and, reckoning with the past, to engage in collective activism on behalf of "accountability and justice" and creativity on behalf of greater social pleasures for ourselves in the present.

NOTES

1. Loss, for Dominick LaCapra, is historically situated, related to specific persons in particular circumstances. Absence, on the other hand, is transcendent, transhistorical, and generic. Whereas loss can be worked through (which LaCapra likens to Freud's notion of mourning), absence can only be acted out (which he likens to melancholia). "When absence and loss are conflated," LaCapra writes, "melancholic paralysis or manic agitation may set in, and the significance or force of particular historical losses (for example, those of apartheid or the Shoah) may be obfuscated or rashly generalized" (64). See *Writing History, Writing Trauma* (Baltimore: Johns Hopkins University Press, 2001).

2. The DSM-IV describes the "essential features" of post-traumatic stress disorder as "the development of characteristic symptoms following exposure to an extreme traumatic stress or involving direct personal experience of an event that involves actual or threatened death or serious injury, or other threat to one's physical integrity; or witnessing an event that involves death, injury, or a threat to the physical integrity of another person; or learning about unexpected or violent death, serious harm, or threat of death or injury experienced by a family member or other close associate (Criterion A1). The person's response to the event must involve intense fear, helplessness, or horror (or in children, the response must involve disorganized or agitated behavior) (Criterion A2). The characteristic symptoms resulting from the exposure to the extreme trauma include persistent re-experiencing of the traumatic event (Criterion B), persistent avoidance of stimuli associated with the trauma and numbing of general responsiveness (Criterion C), and persistent symptoms of increased arousal (Criterion D)" (*Diagnostic and Statistical Manual of Mental Disorders*, 4th ed. [Washington, D.C.: American Psychiatric Association, 1994], 424). The horrifying encounter with death and dying on an unprecedented scale, combined with the anxiety of often not knowing one's own HIV status, the fear of losing one's home or job or family because of discrimination, the persistent frustration of inadequate — or no — health care, the rage at press and popular cultural misrepresentations, and the disorienting perception that AIDS is an *unreal* phenomenon, rendered invisible in mainstream culture while hypervisible to those responding to its ravages, qualify AIDS as a trauma by the DSM definition, several times over.

3. See Douglas Crimp, *Melancholia and Moralism: Essays on AIDS and Queer Politics* (Cambridge, Mass.: MIT Press, 2004). On queer shame, see Michael Warner, *The Trouble with Normal: Sex, Politics, and the Ethics of Queer Life* (New York: Free Press, 1999).

4. "Modern society is characterized by a dearth of social processes, including ritual

processes, which assist individuals during major transformations in life such as marriage, birth, or death," Dominick LaCapra writes. "One finds such processes primarily in traditional pockets of secular society which are not unaffected by more general tendencies toward the evacuation of engaging collective forms and rituals" (213). LaCapra makes the "evacuation" of mourning practices a generalized "tendency" generative of modernity rather than the direct and specified result of purposeful discursive efforts *within* modernity. There are, I would argue, no absence of rituals surrounding the heteronormative "major transformations" of marriage and birth, as there has been around the death of people with AIDS and the sexual cultures they created. Gay men, not surprisingly, function as the opposite of a "traditional pocket" as LaCapra describes it: far from being haunted by memory that they would seek to lose and the rituals for such losing (mourning) they cannot find, gay men have made abundant rituals for public mourning — not to lose but to preserve — and those rituals, and the cultural archive they represent, have been the target not of an incidental evacuation but of a deliberate assault. *Writing History, Writing Trauma* (Baltimore: Johns Hopkins University Press, 2001).

5. Cathy Caruth, *Unclaimed Experience: Trauma, Narrative, and History* (Baltimore: Johns Hopkins University Press, 1996).

6. Caruth assert that "threat is recognized as such by the mind *one moment too late*. The shock of the mind's relation to the threat of death is thus not the direct experience of the threat but precisely the *missing* of this experience, the fact that, not being experienced *in time*, it has not yet been fully known" (ibid., 62). The "historical power of the trauma is not just that the experience is repeated after its forgetting," therefore, "but that it is only in and through its inherent forgetting that it is first experienced at all" (ibid., 17).

7. The exception to this normalizing treatment of trauma can be found in Ann Cvetkovich's *An Archive of Feelings*, arguably the first work of "postqueer" memory. For Cvetkovich, trauma is "a name for experiences of socially situated political violence" (3). A queer treatment of such experiences, Cvetkovich writes, would neither "pathologize it" nor "seize control over it from the medical experts," but would "forge creative responses to it that far outstrip even the most utopian of therapeutic and political solutions" (3). Cvetkovich is not "willing to accept a desexualized or sanitized version of queer culture as the price of inclusion within the national public sphere"; instead, she "wanted the sexual cultures that AIDS threatened to be acknowledged as both an achievement and a potential loss" (5). Writing, "My desire, forged from the urgency of death, has been to keep the history of AIDS activism alive and part of the present" (6), Cvetkovich establishes her "archive" as a valuable model of postqueer memory. *An Archive of Feelings: Trauma, Sexuality, and Lesbian Public Cultures* (Durham, N.C.: Duke University Press, 2003).

8. National Public Radio, *All Things Considered*, 1 June 1995, purchased print transcript by Burrelle's Transcripts. For a fuller discussion of Rotello and other advocates for gay cultural amnesia, see my "Sex Panics, Sex Publics, Sex Memories," *boundary 2* 27, no. 2 (Summer 2000): 149–75.

9. Crimp, *Melancholia and Moralism*, 140.

10. Ibid., 137.

11. Ibid.

12. Ibid., 139.

13. Ibid., 140.

14. Sigmund Freud, "Mourning and Melancholia," in *General Psychological Theory* (New York: Simon and Schuster, 1991), 164–79.

15. Crimp, *Melancholia and Moralism*, 146.

16. Ibid., 149.

17. Vito Russo, "Why We Fight" (speech at ACT UP Demonstrations, Albany, New York, 9 May 1988, and at the Department of Health and Human Services, Washington, D.C., October 10, 1988), ⟨www.actupny.org/documents/whfight.hmtl⟩.

18. Although I am using "crisis" and "trauma" as synonyms here, there are important differences. "Crisis" removes "trauma" from the individualizing rhetoric of therapy and returns it to its social context. And "crisis" focuses on the affective response of survivors rather than on the wound inflicted by a finite historical event. I return to these important differences in my discussion of trauma theory.

19. Caruth, *Unclaimed Experience*, 112.

20. Ibid., 106.

21. Leo Bersani, "Is the Rectum a Grave?" *October* 43 (1987): 197–222; Janet Halley and Andrew Parker, eds., *After Sex? On Writing since Queer Theory* (Durham: Duke University Press, 2007).

22. Heather Love, *Feeling Backward: Loss and the Politics of Queer History* (Cambridge, Mass.: Harvard University Press, 2008), 4.

23. Ibid., 4.

24. Judith Halberstam, "The Politics of Negativity in Recent Queer Theory," *PMLA* 121, no. 3 (May 2006): 823–25.

25. Ibid., 824.

26. Lee Edelman, "Antagonism, Negativity, and the Subject of Queer Theory," *PMLA* 21, no. 3 (May 2006): 823.

27. Ibid., 821.

28. Mark Merlis, *American Studies* (New York: Penguin, 1996).

29. Christopher Nealon, *Foundlings: Lesbian and Gay Historical Emotion before Stonewall* (Durham: Duke University Press, 2001), 86.

30. LaCapra, *Writing History, Writing Trauma*, 23.

31. Ibid., 23.

32. Caruth, *Unclaimed Experience*, 24.

33. Ibid., 11.

34. Alexandra Juhasz, dir. *Video Remains*, 2005.

Paranoid Empire

Specters from Guantánamo and Abu Ghraib

ANNE McCLINTOCK

The question is still open: what is the purpose of Guantánamo Bay? Is it a prison for "terrorists"? Is it an interrogation camp for suspects? Or is it perhaps something altogether more harrowing?

By now it has been established that most of the men and, yes, the teenagers imprisoned, and many of them tortured at Guantánamo are neither terrorists nor "enemy combatants" but innocent people.[1] By now it has also been established that most of the men and, yes, the women and children imprisoned, and many of them tortured, at Abu Ghraib and other U.S. bases in Iraq and Afghanistan are likewise neither terrorists nor enemy combatants but innocent people, most often picked up in random sweeps: taxi drivers, shepherds, shopkeepers, laborers, prostitutes, relatives of possible "suspects," and in some cases children and the very elderly, people who, by the government's own admission, could not provide and have not provided "actionable intelligence."[2]

The specters from Guantánamo and Abu Ghraib place in our hands a profound and compromising question: what is the motive for torturing people whom the government and the interrogators know are innocent? This is a terrible question with terrible implications, not only for the people immiserated by ruinous U.S. occupation but also for how we understand what kind of empire it now is that extends its ghostly filaments beyond Guantánamo and Abu Ghraib throughout the shadowy, global gulag of secret interrogation prisons, "black sites," torture ships, and offshore internment camps now known to straddle the world. Simply to ask the question, "Why torture innocent people?" is to enter a dark labyrinth, a labyrinth of imperial paranoia marked on all sides by flashpoints of violence and atrocity (the massacres at Haditha, Falluja, Nisour Square, Azizabad, and Nadali, only a handful among many), a labyrinth haunted by the historical ghostings and half-concealed specters that I call "imperial déjà vu."

By now it is fair to say that the United States has come to be dominated by two grand and dangerous hallucinations: the promise of benign U.S. glo-balization and the permanent threat of the "war on terror." I have come to feel that we cannot understand the extravagance of the violence to which the U.S. government has committed itself after 9/11 — two countries invaded, thousands of innocent people imprisoned, killed, and tortured — unless we grasp a defining feature of our moment, that is, a deep and disturbing double-ness with respect to power. Taking shape around fantasies of global omnipo-tence (Operation Infinite Justice, the War to End All Evil) coinciding with nightmares of impending attack, the United States has entered the domain of paranoia: dream world and catastrophe. For it is only in paranoia that one finds simultaneously and in such condensed form both deliriums of absolute power and forebodings of perpetual threat–hence, the spectral and night-marish quality of the "war on terror," a limitless war against a limitless threat, a war vaunted by the U.S. administration to encompass all of space and per-sisting without end. But the war on terror is not a real war, for "terror" is not an identifiable enemy nor a strategic, real-world target. The war on terror is what William Gibson calls elsewhere "a consensual hallucination,"[3] and the U.S. government can fling its military might against ghostly apparitions and hallucinate a victory over evil only at the cost of catastrophic self-delusion and the infliction of great calamities elsewhere.

I have come to feel that we urgently need to make visible (the better po-litically to challenge) those established but concealed circuits of imperial vio-lence that now animate the war on terror. We need, as urgently, to illuminate the continuities that connect those circuits of imperial violence abroad with the vast, internal shadowlands of prisons and supermaxes — the modern "slave-ships on the middle passage to nowhere" — that have come to charac-terize the United States as a super-carceral state.[4]

Can we, the uneasy heirs of empire, now speak only of national things? If a long-established but primarily covert U.S. imperialism has, since 9/11, man-ifested itself more aggressively as an overt empire, does the terrain and object of intellectual inquiry, as well as the claims of political responsibility, not also extend beyond that useful fiction of the "exceptional nation" to embrace the shadowlands of empire? If so, how can we theorize the phantasmagoric, imperial violence that has come so dreadfully to constitute our kinship with the ordinary, but which also at the same moment *renders extraordinary* the ordinary bodies of ordinary people, an imperial violence that in collusion with a complicit corporate media would render itself invisible, casting states of emergency into fitful shadow and fleshly bodies into specters? For imperialism is not something that happens elsewhere, an offshore fact to be deplored but as easily ignored. Rather, the force of empire comes to reconfigure, from within, the nature and violence of the nation-state itself, giving rise to perplexing questions: who under an empire are "we," the people? And who are the ghosted, ordinary people beyond the nation-state who, in turn, constitute "us"?

We now inhabit a crisis of violence and the visible. How do we insist on seeing the violence that the imperial state attempts to render invisible, while also seeing the ordinary people afflicted by that violence? For to allow the spectral, disfigured people (especially those under torture) obliged to inhabit the haunted no-places and penumbra of empire to be made visible *as ordinary people* is to forfeit the long-held U.S. claim of moral and cultural exceptionalism, the traditional self-identity of the United States as the uniquely superior, universal standard-bearer of moral authority, a tenacious, national mythology of originary innocence now in tatters. The deeper question, however, is not only how to see but also how to theorize and oppose the violence without becoming beguiled by the seductions of spectacle alone.[5]

In the labyrinths of torture we must also find a way to speak with ghosts, for specters disturb the authority of vision and the hauntings of popular memory disrupt the great forgettings of official history.

Paranoia

Even the paranoid have enemies.

— DONALD RUMSFELD

Why paranoia? Can we fully understand the proliferating circuits of imperial violence without understanding the pervasive presence of the paranoia that has come, quite violently, to manifest itself across the political and cultural spectrum? By paranoia, I mean not simply Hofstadter's famous identification of the U.S. state's tendency toward conspiracy theories.[6] Rather, I conceive of paranoia as *an inherent contradiction with respect to power*: a double-sided phantasm that oscillates precariously between deliriums of grandeur and nightmares of perpetual threat, a deep and dangerous doubleness with respect to power that is held in unstable tension, but which, if suddenly destabilized (as after 9/11), can produce pyrotechnic displays of violence. The pertinence of understanding paranoia, I argue, lies in its peculiarly intimate and peculiarly dangerous relation to violence.[7]

Let me be clear: I do not see paranoia as a primary, structural *cause* of U.S. imperialism or as its structuring *identity*. Nor do I see the U.S. war on terror as animated by some collective, psychic agency, submerged mind, or Hegelian "cunning of reason," or by what Susan Faludi calls a national "terror dream."[8] Nor am I interested in evoking paranoia as a kind of *psychological diagnosis* of the imperial nation-state. Nations do not have "psyches" or an "unconscious"; only people do. Rather, a social entity such as an organization, state, or empire can be spoken of as "paranoid" if the dominant powers governing that entity cohere as a collective community around contradictory cultural narratives, self-mythologies, practices and identities that oscillate between delusions of inherent superiority and omnipotence and phantasms of threat and engulfment. The term "paranoia" is analytically useful here, then, not as a description of a collective national psyche or as a description of a universal pathology, but rather as an analytically strategic concept, *a way of seeing and being attentive to contradictions within power*, a way of making visible the contradictory flashpoints of violence that the state tries to conceal.

Paranoia is in this sense a *hinge phenomenon*, articulated between the ordinary person and society, between psychodynamics and sociopolitical history. Paranoia is in that sense dialectical rather than binary, for its violence erupts from the force of its multiple, cascading contradictions: the intimate memories of wounds, defeats, and humiliations condensing with cultural fantasies of aggrandizement and revenge, in such a way as to be productive at times of unspeakable violence. For how else can we understand such debauches of cruelty?

A critical question still remains: does not something terrible have to happen to ordinary people (military police, soldiers, interrogators) to instill in them, as ordinary people, in the most intimate, fleshly ways, a paranoid cast that enables them to act in obedience to the paranoid visions of a paranoid state? Perhaps we need to take a long, hard look at the simultaneously humiliating and aggrandizing rituals of militarized institutions, whereby individuals are first broken down, then reintegrated (*incorporated*) into the larger corps as a unified, obedient fighting body, the methods by which schools, the military, training camps — not to mention the paranoid image-worlds of the corporate media — instill paranoia in ordinary people and fatally conjure up collective but unstable fantasies of omnipotence.[9] In what follows, I want to trace the flashpoints of imperial paranoia into the labyrinths of torture in order to illuminate three crises that animate our moment: the crisis of violence and the visible, the crisis of imperial legitimacy, and what I call "the enemy deficit." I explore these flashpoints of imperial paranoia as they emerge in the torture at Guantánamo and Abu Ghraib. I argue that Guantánamo is the territorializing of paranoia and that torture is paranoia incarnate.

The Enemy Deficit: Making the "Barbarians" Visible

Because night is here but the barbarians have not come.
Some people arrived from the frontiers,
And they said that there are no longer any barbarians.
And now what shall become of us without any barbarians?
Those people were a kind of solution.

— C. P. CAVAFY, "Waiting for the Barbarians"

The barbarians have declared war.

— PRESIDENT GEORGE W. BUSH

C. P. Cavafy wrote "Waiting for the Barbarians" in 1927, but the poem haunts the aftermath of 9/11 with the force of an uncanny and prescient déjà vu. To what dilemma are the "barbarians" a kind of solution? Every modern empire faces an abiding crisis of legitimacy in that it flings its power over territories and peoples who have not consented to that power. Cavafy's insight is that an imperial state claims legitimacy only by evoking the threat of the barbarians. It is only the threat of the barbarians that constitutes the silhouette of the empire's borders in the first place. On the other hand, the hallucination of the barbarians disturbs the empire with perpetual nightmares of impending attack. The enemy is the abject of empire: the rejected from which we cannot part. And without the barbarians the legitimacy of empire vanishes like a disappearing phantom. Those people were a kind of solution.

With the collapse of the Soviet Union in December 1991, the grand antagonism of the United States and the USSR evaporated like a quickly fading nightmare. Where were the enemies now to justify the continuing escalation of the military colossus? "And now what shall become of us without any barbarians?" By rights, the thawing of the Cold War should have prompted an immediate downsizing of the military; any plausible external threat had simply ceased to exist. Before 9/11, General Peter Schoomaker, head of the U.S. Army, had bemoaned the enemy deficit: "It's no use having an army that did nothing but train," he said. "There's got to be a certain appetite for what the hell we exist for." Dick Cheney likewise complained: "The threats have become remote. So remote that sometimes they are difficult to discern." Secretary of State Colin Powell agreed: "Though we can still plausibly identify specific threats — North Korea, Iran, Iraq, something like that — the real threat is the unknown, the uncertain." Before becoming president, George W. Bush likewise fretted over the post–Cold War dearth of a visible enemy: "We do not know who the enemy is, but we know they are out there." The invasion of Iraq had been a long-standing goal of the U.S. administration, but there was no visible enemy with which to sell it. In 1997 a group of neocons at the Project for the New American Century produced a remarkable report in which they stated that to make such an invasion palatable would require "a catastrophic and catalyzing event — like a new Pearl Harbor."[10]

The 9/11 attacks came as a dazzling solution to both the enemy deficit and the problem of legitimacy. General Schoomaker saw the attacks as an immense boon: "There is a huge silver lining in this cloud. . . . War is a tremendous focus. . . . Now we have this focusing opportunity, and we have the fact that (terrorists) have actually attacked our homeland, which gives it some oomph." After the 2001 invasion of Afghanistan, Powell noted, "America will have a continuing interest and presence in Central Asia of a kind we could not have dreamed of before." Charles Krauthammer called for a declaration of total war. "We no longer have to search for a name for the post–Cold War era," he declared. "It will henceforth be known as the age of terrorism."[11]

On the other hand, 9/11 presented an instant dilemma. On that spectacularly memorialized day, the most powerful state in the world was brought to a catastrophic halt by the murderous temerity of nineteen young men with weapons no grander than box cutters and the will to die. For a few chaotic hours, the state was paralyzed, the Pentagon and White House all but evacuated, all ports closed, all planes grounded. The silver harbingers of calamity had appeared as if from nowhere, evading the vigilance of the world's most potent surveillance and intelligence system. The stunned impotence of the administration was all the more humiliating in that the military was in the middle of a NORAD exercise called Vigilant Warrior. Clarke described the impotent chaos at the center of power at the Pentagon and the White House:

"[This was] bigger than anything we had imagined," he recalls. "The horror, the horror."[12]

Most pertinently, the attackers having with the utmost ostentation flaunted their power to subject the United States to surprise attack and global humiliation, instantly vanished, leaving only a charred void in the realm of vision, a gaping tear in the smooth, controlled flow of the image-world, a rupture in the realm of vision to which the network cameras returned again and again with the repetitious fascination and horror of the fetish, making the attack the most recorded single event of all time. Far from being the "barbarians" they would incessantly be called, the attackers understood, with murderous precision, the logic of modernity: "All that is solid melts into air."

Although the attacks would be incessantly interpreted as "new," they were nothing of the sort. The continent had been attacked before, during the invasion of white settlers. U.S. airplanes had unleashed nuclear cataclysm on two Japanese cities. In 1998 the World Trade Center was attacked. The fiction of newness was necessary only to bolster the legitimacy of illegal forms of war. What was, however, genuinely new about the aftermath of the 9/11 attack was that control of the technologies of the image-world had swiveled in orientation: instead of the West looking at the rest of the world through the God-eye of modern visual technologies, it was as if the globe had swung on its axis and the ex-colonized world was now gazing at the West with technologies of vision believed for centuries — by the West — to be under the West's control. With the Enlightenment, seeing was made equivalent with knowing and the power to *see* became equated with the power to *dominate*. In the aftermath of 9/11, the world was no longer — and, I believe, will never again be — under Western eyes. Instead, a wounded United States was looked at, watched, and surveyed during a moment of great exposure, devastation, and loss. In short, what disappeared into the immense catastrophe of gray and crimson smoke were not only thousands of ordinary lives but also the West's privilege of being the bearers of God-vision.

Can we fully understand the extravagance of the U.S. response to the attacks without grasping the implications of this global reorientation of the privilege of vision? Was it any accident, for example, that one of the first U.S. assaults inside Iraq was on the Baghdad offices of Al Jazeera — as if to blind the insolent eye of the watching "Orient"? That 9/11 presented a trauma in the realm of vision (the *visibility* of the United States to attack and the *invisibility* of the enemy) is testified by the images of "shadowy," "invisible," and "unseen" enemies that quickly proliferated: Attorney General Gonzalez complained, "We face an enemy that lies in the shadows." President Bush stated, "This is a conflict with opponents who believe they are invisible." Krauthammer warned: "This is going to be a long twilight struggle: dirty and dangerous." And Seymour Hersh summed it up: "The Al Qaeda terrorists were there to be seen, but there was no system for seeing them."[13] In short, this would be a war not only over oil, water, and the resources of globalization but for control of the global image and data worlds.

The suicide attackers, deliberately flying passenger planes into buildings as they did, instantly obliterated themselves in the fiery cataclysm, removing their bodies from the realm of visible retribution and thereby removing all means for the Bush administration to be seen to recuperate its wounded potency. The state was faced with an immediate dilemma: how to *embody* the invisible enemy and *be visibly seen* to punish it? The U.S. state had to turn ordinary people into enemy bodies and put them on display for retaliation. In the humiliated aftermath of 9/11, the Bush administration set out to embody the enemy in three ways. First, the enemy was *individualized* as a recognizable *face* — the epic, male, archenemy Bin Laden, a strategically disastrous tactic, for the administration could not put Bin Laden on display, either dead or alive. Second, the dispersed forces of al Qaeda, traversing as they do over sixty countries, were *nationalized*, equated with two nation-states. The invasion of Afghanistan was justified by identifying Afghanistan as a nation-state that had given sanctuary to al Qaeda, which would present a critical contradiction, for the men later imprisoned at Guantánamo were defined as lying outside the protection of the Geneva Conventions on precisely contradictory grounds that Afghanistan was a failed nonstate. Iraq presented an even deeper problem: there was no casus belli for the invasion and (following the lessons of Vietnam) the illegitimate war would need to be kept as invisible as possible from public scrutiny. As conservative commentator David Brooks asked: "How are we going to wage war anymore, with everyone watching?"[14]

The third solution was to produce the enemy *as bodies* under U.S. supervision, subjecting them to dreadful revenge in the labyrinths of torture. The prisoners' confessions under torture were confessions not to anything they had done, or to any information they had, but to the absolute power of their torturers and of the United States. Their confessions would be made visible and fixed in the act of photography.

Pornography: Photography and Forgetting

> The camera relieves us of the burden of memory.
> It surveys us like God, and it surveys for us. Yet no other god has
> been so cynical, for the camera records in order to forget.
> — JOHN BERGER, *About Looking*

> Spectacle is a form of camouflage.
> — JARED SEXTON & STEVE MARINOT

I have become preoccupied and perplexed by the persistent presence of photography in the scene, or should we say the obscene, of torture. I am concerned, however, less with what the photos appear to reveal than with what lies half-hidden in broad daylight in the shadows and fringes beyond them. I am preoccupied, in other words, not by the seduction of the spectacle but rather by what the photos conceal, what they allow us to forget. What do the photographs from Abu Ghraib record — in order to forget? How does spectacle become a form of camouflage?

In February 2004, the revelation of the photographs from Abu Ghraib faced the U.S. administration with a potential political debacle. We now know that over sixteen thousand photographs were taken, of which fewer than two hundred were leaked to the public.[15] Only a handful have entered public circulation, and of that handful only two have achieved iconic status: one of an Iraqi prisoner standing on a box with electric wires attached to his genitals, toes, and fingers, and one of prison guard Lynndie England holding a wounded Iraqi prisoner on a tie-down strap.

Should we not from the outset ask why so many modern states have recorded in such detail their own atrocities (the Nazis, the Khmer Rouge, apartheid South Africa, Saddam Hussein, and now the United States)? Do they not do so to cloak themselves in the semblance of disinterested rationality, recording their debauches of cruelty as an abstract calculus of cause and effect, no more than the punishment of the enemy on behalf of the security of the public?

Susan Sontag reminds us that "cameras define reality in the two ways essential to the workings of an advanced industrial society: as a spectacle (for the masses) and as an object of surveillance."[16] John Berger has likewise noted the state's early interest in photography as an instrument of surveillance: "Within a mere 30 years of its invention as a gadget for an elite, photography was being used for police filing, war reporting, military reconnaissance."[17]

At Abu Ghraib, I argue, U.S. military intelligence, the CIA, the contractors, and the interrogators photographed the prisoners as part of a performance of bureaucratic rationalization: to make the prisoners *legible* as enemies, thereby putatively "legitimizing" the occupation. At the same time, the photographs served as a means of perfecting the torture by using the visual archive of cruelty to ever-refine, in retrospect, techniques for breaking people down (dubbed by the ghastly euphemism "enhanced interrogation measures"). The photos were also used to humiliate and intimidate the prisoners, and, when shown outside the prison, were used to terrorize the prisoners' families and communities. In some cases, they were used to blackmail prisoners into becoming infiltrators of the resistance. Finally, subjecting the prisoners to constant photographic surveillance became in itself a form of torment; many of the prisoners so photographed fell into deep depression and some became suicidal.

Then something extraordinary happened at Abu Ghraib. In February 2004 the two generally distinct functions of the camera (as an instrument of state surveillance and as a means of private spectacle for the masses) collided. This collision — taking place as it did in the digital space of the Internet — threatened to plunge the administration into crisis. In Iraq and Afghanistan, as consumer capital made the digital camera available to ordinary people on a scale never before possible, the recording of atrocity became not simply a function of the state but also a means of personal aggrandizement for the soldiers. Throughout the "theater of war," U.S. soldiers, military police, and guards took thousands of photographs, certainly as personal trophies but also, I propose, as a means of fixing *as spectacle*, in the photographs' promise of permanence, the soldiers' unstable moments of power. The camera became a technology of witnessing, a *ritual of recognition* of the soldiers' absolute dominion over their prisoners. But because this dominion was borrowed and phantasmagoric, it could not be sustained and was therefore destined to recur for ritualistic repetition. The photographic moment had to be endlessly repeated: the photographs handed around to other soldiers, used as computer wallpaper, and sent back home. But in the process, the photographs became public, and in becoming public, they suddenly exposed to the glare of international scrutiny the atrocities of U.S. violence. Yet the crisis was averted. How?

As the Abu Ghraib scandal reverberated, two master narratives were mobilized to contain the debacle. First, the classic (centuries-old) imperial "bad apple" narrative: the notion that the macabre cruelties were merely the isolated, late-night shenanigans of a few, undersupervised, Robotripping, trailer-trash guards.[18] The bad-apple story allowed the scandal to be contained as aberrant, certainly, but isolated; as deviant, yes, but unrepresentative; as morally repellant, no doubt, but unofficial and un-American. Three investigations concurred that the abuse was merely "the disgraceful conduct by a few American troops, who dishonored our country and disregarded our values." James Schlesinger, former secretary of defense, dismissed Abu Ghraib as "*Animal House* on the night shift."[19] That much is now familiar. What we still need to grasp is the astonishing pervasiveness with which the bad-apple story morphed into a second master narrative: the "pornography made them do it" story. Critic after critic, on both sides of the political spectrum, saw the military police (MPs) as inspired to their nightly theatrics of torment not by the White House chain of command but by pornography.

Let a few examples suffice. Celebrity preacher Charles Colson argued before the Family Research Council that the guards had been corrupted by a "steady diet of pornography." As it happens, Colson is the "father" of the "faith-based prison" idea and a central figure in the theo-con movement behind the contracting firm Blackwater. Robert Knight of the Culture and Family Institute (also associated with Blackwater) claimed that gay porn gave soldiers the "idea to engage in sadomasochistic activity." Rush Limbaugh saw nothing in the photos to be steamed up about; they were just "standard good old American pornography." The photos were quickly mobilized for a Christian supremacist, right-wing agenda as cultural pundits hijacked the imperial war beyond the United States and directed it into the "culture wars" within the United States, averting the public gaze away from the calamitous scenes of *imperial misrule* unfolding in Iraq, which fell once more under the administration of forgetting, and pointing the media spotlight instead at the familiar cultural bogeymen of *gender misrule* inside the United States. Pornography, S/M, gays, women in the military, feminists, dominatrices, and drugs were all named as culprits, with women singled out for special opprobrium and judicial censure. Maureen Dowd called her column "Torture Chicks Gone Wild."[20]

More tragically complicit in this regard, however, were critics in the liberal middle — Slavoj Zizek, Arthur Danto, Katherine Viner, Rochelle Gurstein, and even Susan Sontag, to mention only a few — who likewise argued that it was pornography and the culture of S/M that made the guards do it. Even as sophisticated a reader of images as Sontag, for one, saw the relation between porn and torture as one of explicit causality and mimetic iteration: "How much of the sexual tortures inflicted on the inmates of Abu Ghraib," she wondered, "was *inspired* by the vast repertoire of pornographic imagery on the Internet . . . which ordinary people try to *emulate*?"[21] Zizek argued that the abuses were incited by a culture of gay s/m going back to Mapplethorpe.

Upon the merest scrutiny, the "porn made them do it" argument fissures into a welter of contradictions, particularly striking with respect to gender agency, causality, and conditions of production and consumption. Most of the images leaked to the public were not in fact pornographic or even sexual in the first place. Yet Sontag writes, "Most of the torture photographs have a sexual theme." A moment's scrutiny of the photos shows this is not the case. Sontag continues, "Pictures of prisoners bound in painful positions, or made to stand with outstretched arms, are infrequent."[22] Again, a brief scrutiny shows this is not the case.

The critics' responses are in fact rife with startlingly contradictory perceptions of *gender agency*: was it men abusing women or women abusing men that was the problem? Was it gay porn or straight porn? Rochelle Gurstein denounced the photos as yet more evidence of standard male subjugation of women in porn ("pathetic" Lynndie England, she declares, is the new Linda Lovelace).[23] In striking contrast, Arthur Danto, in an astounding piece in *Artforum*, saw the same images as pornographic but for precisely the *opposite* reason. Danto is most incensed not by the torture of Iraqis but by the evidence that the photos offer of a long, and to him deplorable, history of "males in a posture of humiliation before women."[24] Contradictions of *causality* also abound. The standard condemnation of s/m is that it mimics and replicates patriarchal state power in the private sexual realm through a relation of mimetic causality (monkey see, monkey do).[25] In denunciations of the Abu Ghraib photos, the causal flow is reversed, as patriarchal, state power is viewed as mimicking and replicating private sexual rituals (torturer see, torturer do). All told, the vast majority of the images from Abu Ghraib are not standard pornography at all, not at the descriptive level of the imagery itself or in their conditions of production, consumption, or distribution.

A double strategy was mobilized: of conflation and occlusion. Conflating torture with porn *banalized the torture*, underplaying the extremity of the atrocities slowly being divulged not only at Abu Ghraib but also at Guantánamo and in Afghanistan. At the same time, conflating porn with torture once more *monsterized pornography* as an ahistorical, unchanging, universal realm of inherent violence and torture, which it demonstrably is not. But porn is our normal monster, the monster we know how to hate. Porn is the sexual abject, "something rejected from which one does not part."[26] As our normal monster, porn serves as a screen onto which are projected a host of gender anxieties (about violence against women, gender subversion, women's sexual agency, nonprocreative sexuality, among them) that can then be condemned without exploring the deeper sources of gender violence. At the same time, condemning the porn as *images* made it far easier to screen out the far worse *events* emerging at Abu Ghraib.

Paradoxically, sexualizing the atrocities made it easier to dismiss them. The outcry over the photos as sexual images eclipsed the evidence of the actual torture of prisoners (including women and children) who were raped, stripped, sexually assaulted and humiliated, forced to stir vats of feces until they passed out, and forced to witness the torture of others: women forced to watch men being abused and men forced to watch women being abused. The pornography argument turned the question of torture abroad back to a question about *us* in the United States: *our* morality, *our* corrupt sexualities, *our* loss of international credibility, *our* gender misrule. In the storm of moral agitation about *our* pornography and *our* loss of the moral high ground, the terrible sufferings of ordinary, innocent people in two occupied and devastated countries were thrown into shadow. In the floodlit glare of the media, Abu Ghraib rose up as an isolated, monstrous event, looming horrifyingly but exceptional, and casting into ever-deeper darkness the systematic culture of imperial violence that existed long before and extends well beyond Abu Ghraib.

By focusing on pornography (which is generally discussed — mistakenly, I believe — as an issue primarily of gender and sexuality alone), questions of race and imperialism also fell into shadow, cloaked by the corporate media culture of amnesia and the administration of forgetting. The specific techniques used at Abu Ghraib are not new (some go back to the Inquisition); they are continuous with a long imperial archive of colonial and racist cruelty. They belong to a well-established, imperial regime of discipline and punishment in which colonized people were for centuries depicted by the West as historically "primitive," as animalized, as sexually deviant: the men feminized, homosexualized, or hypersexualized; and the women figured as sexually lascivious (it is no accident that the one photo from Abu Ghraib of a woman is of a prostitute), a long-standing and tenacious imperial narrative of racial "degeneration" that, at the very moment of its redeployment, was once more elided in the storm of moral agitation about pornography. Photography records in order to forget. Spectacle becomes a form of camouflage.

Most culpably, equating torture with porn allows us to *look away* and not ask questions: disturbing questions about the long, continuing history of U.S. torture, questions about current military policy, questions about why people torture in the first place, and, most harrowingly, why the U.S. government tortures people who are innocent and who, being innocent, have no information to surrender that can halt their agonies.

What then are the imperial circuits that we need to illuminate in order politically to challenge? First, there is the *vertical* chain of command: from Bush and Cheney, through Rumsfeld's secret Special Access Program, through the private contractors from Titan, who were all over Abu Ghraib, down to the guards.[27] Second, there are the *horizontal* circuits of global continuities: the torture, murder, and rape that are widespread throughout Iraq and Afghanistan, extending to the gulag of secret prisons and interrogation centers around the world. Third, we need to see the *historical* continuities of torture that haunt U.S. history from its inception: the torture of American Indians; slavery; lynching; torture in the Philippines, Vietnam, and Central America in the 1980s. Finally, we need to make visible the continuities of imperial torture with the carceral violence in the national prison system and the rituals of military training.[28] The Abu Ghraib atrocities were not isolated or exceptional; they were typical, systematic, and widespread. Abu Ghraib was only one (accidentally illuminated) site along a vast, concealed network of paranoid violence, including Guantánamo Bay. In the Abu Ghraib photos, these circuits of violence were forgotten at the very moment of their revelation.

So if porn did not produce the torture, what did?

Guantánamo Bay: Paranoia Territorialized

Alive in the grave.
— MAHER ARAR (a Canadian deported by the United
States to Syria, where he was tortured)

Let me return to the two questions with which I began: What is the purpose of Guantánamo Bay? Why torture ordinary people whom the interrogators know to be innocent and who have no information to confess to halt their torment?

Who are the men held in Guantánamo? The administration has called them "all masterminds," "among the most dangerous, best trained, vicious killers on the face of the earth," "the worst of the worst," "the worst of a very bad lot," "very dangerous people who would gnaw hydraulic lines in the back of a C-17 to bring it down," legally summed up as "unlawful combatants" who "do not have any rights."[29]

On the contrary, the majority of the men held at Guantánamo were arbitrarily detained. As early as 2002, Michael Dunlavey, head of interrogations at Guantánamo, himself complained that he was receiving only what he called "Mickey Mouse" prisoners.[30] Only 8 percent of the prisoners have been classified by the Pentagon as al Qaeda. In 2004 the *New York Times* conducted an extensive investigation that yielded the consensus that of nearly seven hundred men held at Guantánamo, "only a relative handful" could yield any information at all. Only 5 percent were "scooped up" on anything that could be called a battlefield. In a majority of cases they were not even picked up by the U.S. military but by the Northern Alliance, the Pakistani military and intelligence, frequently handed over for bounties (U.S.$5,000 to $10,000), sometimes betrayed by neighbors or by people simply seeking remuneration. Some of the early prisoners were juveniles; one was an Afghan man 101 years old. Overwhelming evidence now exists that the vast majority of those detained at Guantánamo are there not because of anything they have done but simply because of where they were. Why, then, imprison and torture them?

In an Associated Press photograph taken at Guantánamo on 11 January 2002, U.S. officers bend over their prisoners in a scene of power so absolute it stops short only at death. What is striking about this scene is that it appears at first not to be a scene of violence at all. There are no weapons or floggings, no rackings or mutilations, no visible agony or fright. There is an aura of calm and ordered *hyperrationality*: an excess of geometrically ordered space, equivalence, and repetition. The officers bend over their charges with a formality that might almost be solicitude. The prisoners do not appear to be suffering: they kneel quietly; they might even be praying. Peering at this scene as we do from the outside, through the single, blurred frame of the wire-mesh, it is not immediately obvious that we are privy to a scene of torture. The airy, open enclosure does not, despite the kennel-like cages and razor wire, seem to belong in the visual archive of torture. Nonetheless, torture is in progress. We are witness here to a new regime of torture: the breaking down of the self through radical sensory deprivation, disorientation, and extreme stress — torture administered without visible trace or touch. The U.S.

Prisoners held at Camp X-Ray, Guantánamo Naval Base, 11 January 2002.
(Associated Press/U.S. Navy, Shane T. McCoy)

administration even has a name for it: they call it "touchless" torture. One can say that the camps at Guantánamo were built to perfect it. Look closer at the image and you will see that the men are wearing blackened ski-goggles, thermal mittens, ear muffs, and surgical masks. There is a terrible tension here between the bright *visibility* of the *scene* and the unseeable darkness of the prisoners' torment, the *invisible obscene* of their suffering. They cannot see, touch, taste, move, or breathe properly. Their suffering has been composed with the utmost rationalized calculation, so that it is invisible, with no traces left on the body. The *hypervisibility* of the men as *bodies* is staged as precisely equivalent to their *invisibility* as *human beings*. Look at the blurred wire that frames the image: the frame of vision is here exactly equivalent to the frame of carceral power. At Guantánamo the long Western regime of super-vision finds its apotheosis. Not for nothing was the first camp called Camp X-Ray.

If any image should become paradigmatic of postmodern imperialism, surely it is this one. The men are reduced to zombies, unpeopled bodies, dead men walking, bodies as imperial property. This image is hypermodern and yet, alongside it, unbidden, the history of American slavery rises up — imperial déjà vu. When each new prisoner is brought off the plane, his ear muff is lifted and a U.S. marine says in his ear, "You are now the property of the U.S. Marine Corp."[31] Called "packages" by the Marines, these men are unpeopled bodies, reduced to subhuman status, mere property of the state. Is this not why the state has gone to such lengths to prevent them from committing suicide: to show that John Locke's Enlightenment dictum, "Each man has a property in his own person," does not apply to them; that their bodies belong not to them but to the absolute, supralegal power of the United States? When some prisoners did commit suicide, the commander at Guantánamo called it a "unilateral declaration of war."[32] If embodying the invisible enemy is the only act that legitimizes imperial violence, then the men's removal of their bodies through suicide robs the empire of its only rationale.

Guantánamo perfects touchless torture as a clinical calculus of cause and effect: the violence staged as a purely rational effect of the danger of an enemy made hypervisible in orange clothes and mesh cages. Hence the double function of the orange clothes: on the one hand, orange signifies danger to Western viewers; on the other hand, in the Muslim world, men wear orange clothes before execution. Many of the prisoners arriving at Guantánamo believed the orange suits signaled their imminent death.

Guantánamo is a geography of paranoia, where the United States' absolute dominion over the enemy is territorialized and made visible (fantasies of omnipotence); at the same time, these orange-suited men, caged, shackled, and transported round on trolleys present a phantasmagoria of immense global danger. If producing the enemy is the only act that legitimizes imperial violence, then the torture of the prisoners is necessary *not* to provide information, *not* to prevent future acts of violence, *not* for reasons of national security, but to *display* the bodies of the enemy and keep these bodies under hypersurveillance in see-through cages and mesh cells. At the same time, the prisoners are conjured into legal ghosts. Guantánamo is a historical experiment in supralegal violence, an attempt to bypass the Constitution and ransack the ancient right of habeas corpus, inventing new rules of domination, exclusion, and obliteration. In other words, Guantánamo embodies less the unleashing of a wild anarchy but rather something more ominous: the meticulous setting up of a parallel, ritualized (if cynically controlled) *theater of judicial semblance*, an attempt to theatrically display state violence as legitimate — a perverse Alice-through-the-looking-glass simulacrum of legality where none exists.

Most harrowingly, I believe, Guantánamo is a torture laboratory, an unspeakable experiment in touchless torture, an experiment in perfecting ever more sophisticated techniques for breaking human beings down.

Abu Ghraib: Cascades of Paranoia

In the summer of 2003, a memo was dispatched from U.S. military intelligence at Combined Joint Task Force 7 Headquarters as an "ALCON" (to all concerned): "The gloves are coming off, gentlemen, regarding these detainees. Colonel Bolz has made it clear we want these individuals broken."[33] In early 2004, General Geoffrey Miller, former commander of Guantánamo, was sent to Abu Ghraib to "Gitmoize" the prison, and it was only after Miller's arrival that the atrocities began. It cannot be stressed enough that according to Red Cross reports, statements by military intelligence, and testimony at the Abu Ghraib trials, up to 90 percent of all the prisoners at Abu Ghraib were arrested by mistake or had no intelligence-gathering value whatsoever. Indeed, *all* of the victims in the notorious photos were innocent. So if neither porn nor extracting intelligence motivated the macabre cruelties, what did?

By fall 2003, the war in Iraq was imploding. Bin Laden was still at large, al Qaeda was expanding, and the U.S. military was unable to penetrate the swelling resistance. The military felt increasingly humiliated and was desperate for results. In October 2003, Operation Iron Hammer was launched. Paranoid megalomania merged with fears of engulfment as soldiers began arresting huge numbers of ordinary Iraqi civilians in "cordon and capture" sweeps. Thousands of Iraqis were pulled randomly off the streets, out of their homes, shops, and fields. In short order, Abu Ghraib was filled to overcapacity with six thousand to seven thousand prisoners, many of whom were women and children, a fact the administration has assiduously kept hidden.[34] Why, indeed, were such lengths taken to conceal the presence of women and children? Disclosing the fact that women were imprisoned, raped, and tortured would have ruptured the questionable legitimacy of the occupation in two ways. First, the Bush administration insisted on referring to the prisoners as "terrorists," as "al Qaeda," but al Qaeda does not have female members. Second, the imperial "rescue myth" used for centuries to rationalize imperial invasion as a benevolent act of saving women of color from colonized men could not be upheld if the United States itself was revealed to be torturing captive women.

By 2004 Abu Ghraib was a vast fortress with five separate complexes. Saddam had kept thirty thousand prisoners there: there were rape rooms, torture chambers, gallows rooms. By all accounts, conditions were horrific.[35] Overseen by Janet Karpinski, who had no foreign-language skills and no corrections experience, the place was massively underequipped. There was no centralized management, no procedures for processing prisoners, no standard procedures for discipline. Conditions for the prisoners were appalling: they were filthy, often stripped naked (a violation of the Geneva Conventions), or dressed in ragged prison garb, blankets, or hospital gowns. Food was poor; sanitation, medical attention, and electricity, barely existent. Death after death was described as due to "natural causes."

Abu Ghraib was located in the hostile Sunni triangle, where despite the grandiose names of the camps — Camp Victory and Camp Vigilance — the U.S. soldiers were under constant mortar attack. Everyone, "prisoners, soldiers, officers — all — were frightened by the violence."[36] The usual prisoner-to-guard ratio in the United States is 4:1; at Guantánamo it is 1:1; at Abu Ghraib it was 75:1. Most of the MPs lived in filthy conditions, many of them sleeping in jail cells themselves. They were exhausted, frightened, under-supervised, and in some cases very depressed and traumatized.

Is this not precisely the climate of paranoia? At Abu Ghraib, a terrible doubleness reigned with respect to power: fear and impotence oscillating dangerously alongside omnipotence. On the one hand, the MPs lived in daily frustration and impotence. Young people in an utterly foreign world, they were vastly outnumbered by the unruly prisoners with whom they shared no language. They were also at the bottom of a long chain of command, their superiors on occasion firing shots at their feet in order to frighten them into producing "results." On the other hand, these disoriented and frightened MPs were given power over the desperate, unruly prisoners under their control. For the MPs, the enemies beyond the walls were also terrifyingly invisible. Hydrue S. Joyner, for one, expressed his anger and impotence: "If it's my time to go, I at least want to face the enemy head on."[37] Where the soldiers and MPs did face the "enemy" head-on was in the dark, wet, filthy corridors, showers, and cells of their own torture world, the world of paranoid power that Charles Graner called "Bizarro World."[38]

I make this point not to exonerate the MPs but rather to argue that torture emerges at the flashpoint of a long cascade of paranoia, overdetermined by a complex of conditions: most fundamentally, *imperial competition* for control over the diminishing resources of globalization (oil, land, water, and labor); by the *political interests* of an aggrieved group of neoconservatives in the White House; a conglomerate of *corporate interests* (oil, energy, construction, security, and the "new economy" of private contractors); *competing powers within the United States* (not least, fissures between the military, FBI, the CIA and, later, the judiciary) — in other words, a set of overdetermined conditions cascading down through the chain of command from Bush, Cheney, Rumsfeld, the CIA, and military intelligence and erupting in the paranoid culture of fear and megalomania that engulfed the MPs. External conditions for torture at Abu Ghraib were governed and choreographed by a long chain of political and military command that authorized the violence from the highest quarters. Moreover, the torture techniques inflicted on the prisoners did not originate at Abu Ghraib but have established precedents in U.S. history in the Philippines, Vietnam, and Central America.

Torturing as Paranoia Incarnate

Has the Bureau created new men who can pass without
disquiet between the unclean and the clean?
— J. M. COETZEE, *Waiting for the Barbarians*

A profound and disturbing question remains: Does not something terrible have to happen to those ordinary people at the bottom of the chain of command to motivate them *personally* to actually carry out acts of torture? Is it not precisely the conditions of paranoia experienced at the most intimate, fleshly level — oscillations between humiliation, vulnerability and engulfment and fantasies of almost godlike potency — that provided the emotional climate for the MPs' participation?

If any specific cultural texts helped choreograph the tortures, two are indisputable and neither is pornographic. The first is a lamentable academic book by the anthropologist Raphael Patai that circulated widely through the neocon establishment shortly before the invasion in 2003. The second is the CIA interrogation manual, *The Kubark Manual*, first drafted in 1963, which draws on postwar research into the psychology of human behavior as a comprehensive theory of interrogation. The manual emphasizes "methods of inducing regression of the personality to whatever earlier or weaker level is required for the dissolution of resistance and the inculcation of dependence."[39] The methods are designed to provoke feelings in the victim of "being cut off from the known . . ., plunged into the strange. . . . Control of the source's environment permits the interrogator to determine his diet, sleep patterns, and other fundamentals. Manipulating these into irregularities, so that the subject becomes disoriented, is very likely to create feelings of fear and helplessness."[40]

Torture techniques widely practiced throughout Iraq, Afghanistan, and at Guantánamo follow the *Kubark Manual* and the SERE (Survival, Evasion, Resistance and Escape) program in inducing a radical dissolution of the self through hoodings, sensory deprivation, sleep disruption, extreme cold or heat, rape, sexual humiliation, and extreme "stress positions." A widespread form of torture, called "the Palestinian" because of its use in Israeli prisons, involves shackling people's hands behind their backs and suspending them with the full weight of their bodies hanging from dislocated shoulders, often for hours or nights in writhing, screaming agony. Prisoners are forced to wear female underwear over their faces, are called by animal names and forced to crawl and bark like dogs, and forced to defecate and urinate on themselves. The most extreme and successful method is the near-death torture of "waterboarding."

But were not the conditions advocated by the *Kubark Manual* (shock, disorientation, fear, loss of self, and willingness to surrender) also precisely the paranoid conditions of the MPs' "Bizarro World," conditions where they were "cut off from the known . . . plunged into the strange," conditions designed to produce "a kind of psychological shock," to disorient and frighten and thereby induce radical submission? Then, given brief, godlike power over the prisoners, would not these scared, frustrated, and angry MPs, paranoid and dangerously wounded people as they were, become capable, in turn, of mercilessly wounding and humiliating others? To ask these questions is not to exonerate the MPs; rather, it is to account both for their complicity and for the wider, imperial conditions that shaped a pervasive climate of military paranoia.

Charles Graner, in particular, is the embodiment of paranoia. Among the MPs, he was the ringleader and master of ceremonies. Sergeant Ivan Frederick testified that he saw Graner write the words "Po White Trash" on the back of a Hummer. Frederick also testified that the other MPs "saw Graner as God."[41] At night Graner organized theme parties, one of which he called "Naked Chem-Light Tuesday."[42] At one party, Graner pulled down his shorts, poured a Chem-Light onto his penis, and walked around showing everyone his glowing phallus.[43] Is this not the oscillation of paranoia perfectly captured as spectacle: a "Po White Trash" God with an incandescent penis?

Graner took hundreds if not thousands of photographs. According to Frederick, Graner "always talked about Desert Storm and the things he saw and did and he had no way to prove these things happened, so this time around, he said, he was going to take pictures to take home as proof." If Graner's prowess in Desert Storm was invisible, now, in the photos he incessantly took, his precarious masculinity could be magnified and witnessed in visible rituals of recognition, his oscillating paranoia (Po White Trash / God with a glowing penis) momentarily fixed in the scene of omnipotence. The photos promised to capture and fix in their glossy surface Graner's fleeting moments of grandeur—hence, their proliferation. Graner flaunted the photos, passing them around to other MPs and sent them home. For Graner, the photographs had *exhibition value*, as evidence of his all-too-transient moments of exaggerated power.

Graner also made Lynndie England visible. Revealed at the trials as deeply insecure, depressed, and unable to fully grasp what was going on, England saw Graner as a glamorous "outlaw."[44] For England, posing for photos proved her love. For Graner, making England pose in his depraved theatrics flaunted his power to make her "do things." In the notorious photo of England holding a prisoner on a tie-down strap, Graner had choreographed the scenario, dragging the prisoner from the cell then placing the strap in England's reluctant hand. Photographing the scene bore double witness: to Graner's gender power over England and to his racial power over a humiliated Iraqi prisoner. He e-mailed the photo home: "Look what I made Lynndie do."[45]

In sum, torture is ultimately not the extraction of information from terrorists; it is a diabolical manifestation of paranoia, the determination to break down the tortured person's being and force him to "confess," not to crimes he has committed, which mostly he has not, or to provide actionable intelligence, which mostly he does not have, but rather to confess to one thing alone — the godlike domination of the torturer and, by extension, the vindication of the United States as global superpower.

I can find no more eloquent expression of this motive for torture than the words of Tony Lagouranis, a torturer himself:

One other change happened, in parallel with our increasing torture: we moved from seeking intelligence, our original justification, to seeking confessions. It was as if the domination we exercised over our prisoners was not complete until they admitted what they had done. This was the most frightening change that came over us, because it signaled a shift from torture for an intelligence purpose to torture for the sole purpose of controlling another. . . . Those [9/11] attacks . . . made us want to respond in kind. Suddenly, their defeat was not enough. Standard military operations using high-tech weaponry and the utter obliteration of the enemy via cruise missiles and five-thousand pound bombs was not enough. They should be made to feel the same pain we felt and America, the mightiest power in history, should be able to dominate this enemy utterly and tyrannically. It came to be perceived as our right, due to us as a hegemonic power. So we suddenly had no problem absolute tyrannical power in the hands of army specialists. They would show each terrorist the face of America, and they would dominate the terrorists' very souls. . . . That's the kind of victory many Americans want. . . . This kind of dominance requires evil. The prisoner will not break unless he believes the potential for escalation is endless and the only way to convince him of that is to be the embodiment of evil. For a truly evil person, the rules of civilization do not apply, and any course of action is possible. The prisoner who faces an evil captor is transported to a totally alien world that makes no sense and that he finds impossible to fathom. This is where true terror and panic set in. . . . Who are we? We are a nation that overwhelmingly supports torture. This is what we want. This puts me beyond despair.[46]

Torturers are thieves of the soul. The tortured person is slowly unraveled, a person unmade, a body unpeopled, a person forced, unspeakably, to inhabit the wounded carapace of a body once tenanted by life but refused that final, sacred right to die; the solitary self watching itself dissolve from the tiny, unhallowed corner of its cell, knowing that its self has irretrievably gone but its body is still not allowed to die.

In an Associated Press photograph taken at Abu Ghraib on 2 April 2005, a prisoner extends his hand beyond the edges of his cage in an unforgettable invitation to be witnessed as human — to have his humanity returned. I want to close with this hand, this gesture that reaches beyond the cage of torture, this hand held out to us not only as an invitation to compassion, which is

Man in cage cell on outskirts of Abu Ghraib, 2 April 2005.
(Associated Press/John Moore)

necessary but not sufficient, but as an invitation to political action. If we are told in due course that the war in Iraq has been "won" (one can recall Agricola's famous description of the Roman empire: "They create a desolation, and call it peace") and if the prison at Guantánamo is eventually shut down, it is urgent that we keep in mind that the United States is now building a much bigger, far more secret, multimillion-dollar prison complex at Bagram Air Base in Afghanistan.[47] Who, indeed, are the people that this immense carceral complex is designed to encage? As Barack Obama commits himself to continuing the war on terror, only relocating its center in Afghanistan, there is grave risk that the circuits of imperial violence and the consequent sufferings of thousands of ordinary people will fall ever deeper into shadow. This hand from the cage of torture reaches out to us as an invitation: for outrage at images alone cannot challenge imperial power, only collective action can.

NOTES

An earlier version of this article was published in *Small Axe* 13, no. 1 (2009): 75–89. I wish to thank Rob Nixon for his unstintingly generous help in the writing of this article.

Paranoid Empire

1. I am deeply indebted to the following indispensable books: Tara McKelvey, *Monstering: Inside America's Policy of Secret Interrogations and Torture in the Terror War* (New York: Carroll and Graf, 2007); Mark Danner, *Torture and Truth: America, Abu Ghraib and the War on Terror* (New York: New York Review of Books, 2004); Seymour M. Hersh, *Chain of Command: The Road from 9/11 to Abu Ghraib* (New York: HarperCollins, 2004); S. G. Mestrovic, *The Trials of Abu Ghraib: An Expert Witness Account of Shame and Horror* (London: Paradigm, 2007); Alfred W. McCoy, *A Question of Torture: CIA Interrogation, from the Cold War to the War on Terror* (New York: Metropolitan, 2006); Steven Strasser, ed., *The Abu Ghraib Investigations: The Official Reports of the Independent Panel and the Pentagon on the Shocking Prisoner Abuse in Iraq* (New York: Public Affairs, 2004); Andy Worthington, *The Guantanamo Files: The Stories of the 774 Detainees in America's Illegal Prison* (London: Pluto, 2007); Clive Stafford Smith, *Eight O'Clock Ferry to the Windward Side: Seeking Justice in Guantánamo Bay* (New York: Nation Books, 2007); Michael Ratner and Ellen Ray, *Guantánamo: What the World Should Know* (White River Junction, Vt.: Chelsea Green, 2004); Clive Stafford Smith, *Bad Men: Guantanamo Bay and the Secret Prisons* (London: Weidenfeld and Nicolson, 2007); and Joseph Margulies, *Guantánamo and the Abuse of Presidential Power* (New York: Simon and Schuster, 2006). Philip Gourevitch and Erroll Morris, *Standard Operating Procedure* (New York: Penguin, 2008), and Jane Mayer, *The Dark Side* (New York: Doubleday, 2008), both appeared after this article had been completed.

2. No engagement with the issue of U.S. torture would be complete without an acknowledgment of the exemplary and indispensible interventions of the Center for Constitutional Rights and all the other lawyers and human rights activists globally who have been working tirelessly to challenge the abuses.

3. See William Gibson, *Neuromancer* (New York: Ace Books, 2000), 51.

4. Christian Parenti, *Lockdown America: Police and Prisons in the Age of Crisis* (New York: Verso, 1999), 170. On the issue of the super-carceral state, see also Ruth Wilson Gilmore, *Golden Gulag: Prisons, Surplus, Crisis and Opposition in Globalizing California* (Berkeley: University of California Press, 2007); and Michelle Brown, "'Setting the Conditions' for Abu Ghraib: The Prison Nation Abroad," *American Quarterly* 57, no. 3 (2005): 973–98.

5. For a brilliant analysis of the role of spectacle, see Retort (Iian A. Boal, T. J. Clark, Joseph Matthews, and Michael Watts), *Afflicted Powers: Capital and Spectacle in a New Age of War* (New York: Verso, 2005).

6. Richard Hofstadter, *The Paranoid Style in American Politics and Other Essays* (New York: Random House, 1967).

7. Paranoia has been an aspect of U.S. political life at least since the Great Depression. See Andrew Bacevich, *The New American Militarism: How Americans Are Seduced by War* (Oxford: Oxford University Press, 2005); and Michael S. Sherry, *In the Shadow of War: The United States since the 1930s* (New Haven: Yale University Press, 1995). According to Bacevich, Sherry's *In the Shadow of War* tells a narrative that spans six decades, revealing a pervasive American sense of vulnerability, anxiety, and impotence, alongside a "relentless process of militarization" (Bacevich, 5). As Bacevich tells it, "The new American militarism made its appearance in reaction to the 1960s and especially to Vietnam, evolving

over a period of decades, rather than being spontaneously induced by a particular event such as the terrorist attacks of September 11, 2001" (6). This overdetermined atmosphere of vulnerability and humiliation was compensated with fantasies of grand militarism (especially after Vietnam) — 9/11 only made spectacularly visible the "new" American militarism long in the making. Bacevich continues: "For Americans who came of age in the 1960s and 1970s — that is to say, for the generation that today dominates national life — Vietnam was a defining event, the Great Contradiction that demolished existing myths about America's claim to be a uniquely benign great power and fueled suspicions that other myths might also be false" (34).

8. Susan Faludi, *The Terror Dream: Fear and Fantasy in Post-9/11 America* (New York: Metropolitan, 2007). While I am a great admirer of Faludi's work, in a forthcoming essay I express my reservations about her analysis of the "terror dream."

9. See especially Bacevich, *The New American Militarism*; and Todd Ensign, *America's Military Today: The Challenge of Militarism* (New York: New Press, 2004).

10. General Peter Schoomaker, quoted in "Wars 'Useful,' Says U.S. Army Chief," BBC News, 22 January 2004; Dick Cheney, quoted in Howard Zinn, *The Twentieth Century: A People's History* (New York: Harper Collins, 1998), 422; Colin Powell, quoted in James David Meernik, *The Political Use of Military Force in U.S. Foreign Policy* (New York: Ashgate, 2004), 65; George W. Bush, quoted in Frances Fitzgerald, "George Bush and the World," *New York Times Book Review*, 26 September 2002; Project for the New American Century, *Rebuilding America's Defenses: Strategy, Forces and Resources for a New Century* (Washington, D.C.: Project for the New American Century, 2000), 51.

11. Schoomaker, "Wars 'Useful'"; Richard A. Clarke, *Against All Enemies: Inside America's War on Terror* (New York: Free Press, 2004), 26; Colin Powell, quoted in Vernon Loch, "Footprints in Steppes of Central Asia," *Washington Post*, 9 February 2002; Charles Krauthammer, "This Isn't a 'Legal' Matter, This Is War," *Seattle Times*, 13 September 2001.

12. Clarke, *Against All Enemies*, 17.

13. Alberto Gonzalez, quoted in Hersh, *Chain of Command*, 5; George W. Bush, radio address, 15 September 2001; Charles Krauthammer, "A Humanitarian War," *Jewish World Review*, 12 October 2001, 25; Hersh, *Chain of Command*, 88.

14. Cited in David Levi Strauss, "Breakdown in the Gray Room: Recent Turns in the Image War," in *Abu Ghraib: The Politics of Torture*, Terra Nova Series (Berkeley: North Atlantic, 2004), 96.

15. Mestrovic, *The Trials of Abu Ghraib*, 3.

16. Susan Sontag, *On Photography* (1973; repr., New York: Picador, 2001), 178.

17. John Berger, *About Looking* (New York: Pantheon, 1980), 52.

18. The "bad apple" narrative is a classic, long-standing defense deployed by countries accused of torture — Britain used it in Kenya during the Mau-Mau revolt, for example.

19. President Bush, cited in Danner, *Torture and Truth*, 27; James Schlesinger, quoted in Julian Borger, "Pentagon Blamed over Jail 'Sadism,'" *Guardian*, 25 August 2004.

20. Charles Colson, quoted in Susie Linfield, "The Dance of Civilizations: The West, the East, and Abu Ghraib," *Dissent* 52, no. 1 (Winter 2005): 47; Robert Knight, "Iraq Scandal Is 'Perfect Storm' of American Culture," ⟨www.worldnetdaily.com/news/artcile.asp?ARTICLE_ID=38462⟩, posted 12 May 2004; Rush Limbaugh, quoted in

Eric Boehlert, "Rush's Forced Conscripts," Salon.com, 30 August 2008; Maureen Dowd, "Torture Chicks Gone Wild," *New York Times*, 30 January 2005. For more on Blackwater, see Jeremy Scahill's indispensable *Blackwater: The Rise of the World's Most Powerful Mercenary Army* (New York: Nation Books, 2008).

21. Susan Sontag, "Regarding the Torture of Others," *New York Times*, 23 May 2004 (emphasis added). See also Slavoj Zizek, "Between Two Deaths: The Culture of Torture," *London Review of Books*, 3 June 2004, 12; Arthur Danto, "American Self-Consciousness in Politics and Art," *Artforum*, September 2004, ⟨http://artforum.com/inprint/id=7391&pagenum=2⟩; Katherine Viner, "The Sexual Sadism of Our Culture in Peace and War," *Guardian*, 22 May 2004; Rochelle Gurstein, "On the Triumph of the Pornographic Imagination," *New Republic Online*, 15 May 2005, ⟨http://209.212.93.14/doc.mhtml?i=w050516&s=gurstein051805⟩.

22. Sontag, "Regarding the Torture of Others."

23. Gurstein, "Pornographic Imagination."

24. Danto, "American Self-Consciousness," 3.

25. For a retort to this conventional condemnation of S/M, see Anne McClintock, "Maid to Order: S/M and Gender Power," in *Dirty Looks: Women, Pornography, Power*, ed. Pamela Church Gibson and Roma Gibson (London: BF, 1993), 28–43.

26. Julia Kristeva, *Powers of Horror: An Essay on Abjection*, trans. Leon S. Roudiez (New York: Columbia University Press, 1982), 4.

27. See especially Scahill, *Blackwater*.

28. See especially McCoy, *A Question of Torture*.

29. The most comprehensive and brilliant account of Guantanamo is Worthington's *The Guantanamo Files*. See also Stafford Smith's two incisive books on the subject, *Eight O'Clock Ferry* and *Bad Men*.

30. Joseph Margulies, *Guantánamo and the Abuse of Presidential Power* (New York: Simon and Schuster, 2006), 65.

31. Ibid., 64.

32. Ibid.

33. McCoy, *A Question of Torture*, 131.

34. See McKelvey, *Monstering*, 194–208; and Mestrovic, *The Trials of Abu Ghraib*, 100.

35. These horrific conditions are documented in McKelvey, *Monstering*, 87–163, and Mestrovic, *The Trials of Abu Ghraib*, 34–72; and illustrated in Errol Morris's 2008 documentary, *Standard Operating Procedure*.

36. McKelvey, *Monstering*, 70.

37. Hydrue S. Joyner, quoted in ibid., 90.

38. David S. Cloud, "Private Found Guilty in Abu Ghraib Abuse," *New York Times*, 27 September, 2005.

39. *The Kubark Manual*, quoted in Danner, *Torture and Truth*, 17. See also Margulies's analysis of the role of the *Kubark Manual*, in *Guantánamo and the Abuse of Presidential Power*, 33–43.

40. Danner, *Torture and Truth*, 15.

41. Cloud, "Private Found Guilty."

42. Chem-Lights, light sticks filled with chemicals that glow for hours, were widely used to rape male prisoners in Afghanistan and Iraq and at Guantánamo.

43. McKelvey, *Monstering*, 88.

44. Mestrovic, *The Trials of Abu Ghraib*, 165.

45. McKelvey, *Monstering*, 100.

46. Tony Lagouranis and Allen Mikaelian, *Fear Up Harsh: An Army Interrogator's Dark Journey through Iraq* (New York: NAL Caliber, 2007), 247.

47. Cited in Noam Chomsky, *The New Military Humanism: Lessons from Kosovo* (Monroe, Maine: Common Courage Press, 1999), 16.

Taking the Measure of the Black Atlantic

KENNETH W. WARREN

The continuing prominence of "Black Atlantic" as a key term in the lexicon of black literary and cultural studies and beyond derives largely from the success of Paul Gilroy's 1993 book, *The Black Atlantic: Modernity and Double Consciousness* in which Gilroy set out to break what he saw as the virtual stranglehold of a United States–centered black studies regime on the field of black cultural study. Gilroy sought to shift the focus of scholarly analysis from cultural practices within U.S. national boundaries to a consideration of routes of transit connecting the United States, the Caribbean, Europe, and Africa in an attempt "to transcend both the structures of the nation state and the constraints of ethnicity and national particularity."[1] The proliferation of works of literary and cultural study referencing the Black Atlantic or the middle passage since the publication of *The Black Atlantic* attests to the exceptional appeal of Gilroy's intervention.[2] "Black Atlantic" is by now such a household word (in a striking variety of fields, including diaspora, postcolonial, and African American studies) that some apology or explanation seems almost de rigueur for anyone about to undertake a study of black cultural and aesthetic practices that does not look beyond U.S. national boundaries.

That the same can now also be said for American studies points out the revisionist power of the questions of scale and scope raised by Black Atlantic inquiry. As this volume suggests, for some time now the aim of American studies has been the critique of American studies — a critique that Black Atlantic theorizing has conducted primarily along the dimension of space in hopes that undermining the determinate function of national boundaries would both challenge and rebuild the field's very foundations. Yet, if its contestation of U.S. national coherency has left the object of inquiry for

American studies floating uncertainly in oceanic waters, Black Atlanticism itself has also come under criticism for having reinforced rather than transcended the boundaries it found so troubling. It comes as no surprise that we are already seeing the phenomenon of the "beyond" creeping into Black Atlantic inquiry.[3]

Among the questions to be raised about the Black Atlantic are whether and how it can establish warrants for an identity of blackness not only across those spaces the concept hopes to encompass but also across the various writers and texts from different historical moments that appear in Gilroy's landmark text. What kind of time frame could include in a single analytic unit, as Gilroy wants to, both Phillis Wheatley and Richard Wright? Are the 1830s Baltimore shipyards where Frederick Douglass learned to read and became acquainted with the literature of abolition similar enough to the Baltimore shipyards of the turn of the twenty-first century, whose evisceration by neoliberal economic policy was so poignantly depicted in the HBO television series, *The Wire*, to warrant being encompassed within the same Black Atlantic schema? At the end of the day, can the Black Atlantic dispense with the history it finds so confining?

The long fetch of the Atlantic world goes back well before the publication of Gilroy's book. It was primarily historians and not literary scholars who had recognized and explored the usefulness of the transatlantic slave trade and of Atlantic crossings generally as means of reorienting study of the seventeenth, eighteenth, and early nineteenth centuries. One could go all the way back to Eric Williams's *Capitalism and Slavery* published in 1944 to track this trend, but for our purposes it is really the 1970s and the decade immediately following that warrant notice. Historians of the Atlantic world were rethinking both their object and method of study. As Nicholas Canny has noted, attempts to break with teleological approaches to American history had led to the production of social histories stressing the interrelatedness of England and America during the early modern period. Canny writes that "by the close of the 1970s it became widely accepted that what had previously been described as American colonial history should now be described as the history of colonial British America," which is to say that rather than approaching this early period solely in terms of its status as a precursor to an eventually autonomous American nation, historians of colonial America began to "see their subject as one that might be more readily integrated with the contemporaneous social history of early modern England or continental Europe than with the subsequent history of the United States."[4]

Canny's argument for including the slave trade and intercultural exchange within the field of "colonial North American" redefines the subject of inquiry by asking new methodological questions about its temporal dimension (not just a "precursor" to the "subsequent history" of the U.S. nation but "contemporaneous" with early modern England and continental Europe). Treating the Atlantic world as a historical period restores a temporal dimension to what had been studied primarily as a spatial or geographic unit of study. The method follows the object in that defining the subjects of the Atlantic world as Afro-British means that these writers are approached not through the eventual teleology of U.S. history and literature but rather through the conflicted self-understandings of these individuals in their own historical moment. A single spatiotemporal location is insufficient for subjects and objects of the Atlantic world. Thus, today we might ask whether the black slave Olaudah Equiano is an Afro-British subject, a proto–African American, a diasporic African, a transnational early American, or a peregrinating colonial? In other words, does Equiano inhabit the same time frame as Gustavus Vassa? Such questions stem from changes that reflect a richer texture of historical analysis and more complex apprehensions of time.

Yet, despite these benefits, the new social history did not attend sufficiently to the intercultural exchanges among peoples across the Atlantic; nor did it pay sufficient attention to the slave trade. As a consequence, according to Canny, "historians began to lose faith in the colonial British America model . . . [and] became increasingly insistent that the history of British North America be studied within an Atlantic context" — a turn that "had been advocated by J. H. Elliot in 1970 and had been exemplified in Philip Curtin, *The Atlantic Slave Trade*, and in almost all books, whether by Europeans or Americans, concerned with trade its several manifestations." Prompted by this work, "historians thus began loosely to employ terms such as 'Atlantic history' and 'the Atlantic world' to describe their concerns."[5]

Although Gilroy's *Black Atlantic* is somewhat sparing in its acknowledgment of this preceding and ongoing historical scholarship, the book does stand in part as an attempt to build on "the suggestion that cultural historians could take the Atlantic as one single, complex unit of analysis in their discussions of the modern world and use it to produce an explicitly transnational and intercultural perspective."[6] Gilroy's crucial move in *The Black Atlantic*, though, is not merely to privilege cultural over social or demographic history but also to place matters of aesthetics, ethics, and interpretation at the center of his cultural concerns. The import of this shift for subsequent critical engagement with the concept of a Black Atlantic can be better explained after touching briefly on some of the other objectives that shape Gilroy's argument, which include locating the horror of slavery and the middle passage inside, rather than outside, the logic of enlightenment; positing nondiscursive expressive modes — music in particular — as transformative political expression; and attempting to short-circuit the essentialist-social constructivist binary that had become an impasse for scholars seeking to account for black identity. Gilroy attempts to achieve this final objective by insisting on "the plural richness of black cultures in different parts of the world in counterpoint to their common sensibilities — both those residually inherited from Africa and those generated from the special bitterness of new world slavery."[7]

Gilroy's assertion of both plural and common sensibilities among slaves and their descendants in the West (as well as among those subject to the slave system on the African continent) operates as something of what can be termed, perhaps oxymoronically, as an "experiential essentialism" through which he hopes both to register the specificities of lived historical conditions and to overcome the differences among such conditions as being enslaved, being a second-class citizen in a society that has outlawed slavery, and being a relatively well-off citizen of color in a society that recognizes and protects ones political and civil rights but has not yet made bigotry and prejudice nonfactors in day-to-day life. This is to say that, while at first glance Gilroy seems to be doing no more than remarking how the conditions of life created by the plantation system in the Americas, along with the trade in human bodies needed to sustain it, may have led to the production and appreciation of similar expressive objects and forms by geographically dispersed populations, it turns out, on further examination, that he is making a methodological assertion that allows him to presume as a basis for cultural analysis a shared sensibility among people across time and place.[8] As Jonathan Elmer notes, Gilroy's aim is to resist "what seemed to him an unnecessarily constrained historicism."[9] The Black Atlantic for Gilroy is not a historical moment.

As a result, Gilroy's notion of a Black Atlantic has worked to untether the notion of an Atlantic world from its mooring in the early modern period, thus making it available as a transtemporal concept. Tellingly, not only are most of the figures in Gilroy's study from the nineteenth and twentieth centuries, but the subtitle of Gilroy's book includes the term "double consciousness" — an idea that does not crop up until the end of the nineteenth century when Du Bois proposes it as a not unproblematic figure for understanding the condition of being black in the twentieth century. The emphases for Gilroy are philosophical, political, aesthetic, and exegetical with a decided emphasis on the last two terms. That is, Gilroy's analysis locates the heart of the black Atlantic in nonverbal expressive forms whose meanings are most accurately teased out by critics who presume to stand in the dualistic position described by Du Bois's evocative figure of speech.

Against Gilroy, however, there is another significant strand of thinking about the idea of a Black Atlantic that runs more congruently with the historicist scholarship treating the Atlantic world as a designation of a historical period. Examples of this work include, first, Adam Potkay and Sandra Burr's *Black Atlantic Writers of the 18th Century*, which focuses on the works of James Albert Ukawsaw Gronniosaw, John Marrant, Quobna Ottobah Cugoano, and Olaudah Equiano, and, second, Vincent Carretta's *Unchained Voices: Anthology of Black Authors in the English Speaking World of the 18th Century*, which brings together works by fourteen black British and American writers, including Phillis Wheatley, Benjamin Banneker, Briton Hammon, Jupiter Hammon, Francis Williams, Johnson Green, Belinda, George Liele, David George, Boston King, Venture Smith, and Ignatius Sancho. According to Jeannine Delombard, the Black Atlantic in these works demands "a turning back of the clock" to this earlier period as locus of attention for scholarly study.[10] The result of this turning is not to stress lines of continuity from past to present so much as to place these earlier writers in relation to one another. Wilfred Samuels has argued that the scholarship on these writers, of which the work of Vince Carretta is representative, insists that "all African or Creole Black authors (Phillis Wheatley and Briton Hammon, for examples) publishing in North America before the official separation of the thirteenth colonies from Britain in 1783 [must be viewed as] Afro-British writers, though several, including Wheatley, Belinda, Johnson Green, Benjamin Banneker, and Venture Smith, accepted with varying degrees of enthusiasm, the new status of being African Americans."[11] Carretta's more recent volume, coedited with Phillip Gould, also "aims to situate early black writing in its own historical terms."[12] To be sure, this insistence does not foreclose seeing these writers as precursors to the black writers who follow, but it does give priority to getting at how these individuals understood themselves within their own historical moment, absent the knowledge of the direction events would take in the future. On one view, then, "the Black Atlantic" denotes a concept or mode of identification that can be applied across time and place, while on another view the term designates a structure of identification and activity within a discrete historical period. To put the matter somewhat differently, from the first perspective, Richard Wright counts as a Black Atlantic writer; from the second, he does not.

In recent years the first perspective has been the favored one in the on-going production of Black Atlantic scholarship, but as Elmer notes, the intention of those scholars who take this line may not be to leave history behind but instead to rethink the way we conjoin "then and now." Elmer writes, "As Gilroy surely knew, our revision of modernity in terms of a Black Atlantic is a history of — and for — the present."[13] Indeed, as an example of this revisionist spirit, Ian Baucom's *Specters of the Atlantic: Finance Capital, Slavery, and the Philosophy of History* seeks to abolish the difference between history and the present by regarding the slave past as part of our contemporaneity. According to Baucom, we inhabit "a long twentieth century" that "runs from the mid-eighteenth century through the 'present' . . . conjoins the British and U.S. cycles in a single Atlantic cycle of accumulation, enshrines commodity capital at its nineteenth century midpoint, and enthrones speculative epistemologies and value forms at either end of its long durée."[14] From this perspective, the atrocities of the slave past, such as the murder of 132 enslaved Africans who in 1781 were thrown overboard from the slave ship *Zong* — the incident that stands at the heart of Baucom's study — still require redress or redemption in the present in part because such atrocities are seen as being of a piece with racial disparities in economic and social well-being that still exist within Western societies and between Western nations and nonwhite nations. That is, much of what anchors the unapologetic presentism of the dominant trend in Black Atlantic literary studies is the persistence of racial disparity into the present and a belief that attending to the injustices betokened by this disparity demands acknowledging the continuity between now and 1781.

Black Atlanticism, then, has sought bridges between a methodological challenge to conceptual limitations in the domain of intellectual inquiry and a politics focused on redressing present-day inequality. The outcome has been to orient political and analytical investigation away from national identity and the nation-state, by insisting on a persistent yet surreptitious reinscription of racial domination within the West's putative commitment to inequality and by replacing an understanding of history that treats the past as an object of inquiry with an account of history as a terrain of struggle. The brace of questions centered on the problem of what we can know of the past is thus superseded by the Benjaminian question of what we owe the past.

Yet the emergence of work in the relatively short durée of *The Black Atlantic* gesturing to a "beyond" (see note 2) suggests that the terms of Black Atlantic intervention are already undergoing critique. Instructively, some of the essays in Goebel and Schabio's *Beyond the Black Atlantic* assert, contra Gilroy, the importance of "national and ethnic specificity."[15] Indeed, a moment when the response to economic global crisis has been to augment the role of state power in the world's largest economies, and when the reins of power in the United States are in the hands of an African American president — a situation that the young black boys in Richard Wright's 1940 novel *Native Son* could only comprehend as "playing white" — and when it is far from clear that a black president betokens fundamental political transformation, might be a moment when the possible usefulness of the Black Atlantic as history is thrown into relief while its promise as a guide for future inquiry remains at best an open question.

NOTES

1. Paul Gilroy, *The Black Atlantic: Modernity and Double Consciousness* (Cambridge, Mass.: Harvard University Press, 1993), 19.

2. A partial list of recent titles would include Gesa Mackentun, *Fictions of the Black Atlantic in American Foundational Literature* (New York: Routledge, 2004); Lars Eckstein, *Re-Membering the Black Atlantic: On the Poetics and Politics of Literary Memory* (Amsterdam: Rodopi, 2006); Walter Goebel and Saskia Schabio, eds., *Beyond the Black Atlantic: Relocating Modernization and Technology* (New York: Routledge, 2006); J. Lorand Matory, *Black Atlantic Religion: Tradition, Transnationalism, and Matriarchy in the Afro-Brazilian Candomble* (Princeton: Princeton University Press, 2005).

3. See, for instance, Goebel and Schabio, *Beyond the Black Atlantic*.

4. Nicholas Canny, "Writing Atlantic History; or, Reconfiguring the History of Colonial British America," in "The Nation and Beyond: Transnational Perspectives on United States History: A Special Issue," *Journal of American History* 86, no. 3 (December 1999): 1096.

5. Ibid., 1105.

6. Gilroy, *The Black Atlantic*, 15.

7. Ibid., 81.

8. See ibid., 79–81.

9. Jonathan Elmer, *On Lingering and Being Last: Race and Sovereignty in the New World* (New York: Fordham University Press, 2008), 163.

10. Jeannine Marie Delombard, "Turning Back the Clock: Black Atlantic Literary Studies," *New England Quarterly* 75, no. 4 (December 2002): 648.

11. Wilfred Samuels, "Enlightened Black Voices: Witnesses and Participants," *Eighteenth-Century Studies* 31, no. 2 (1998): 241.

KENNETH W. WARREN

12. Vincent Carretta and Philip Gould, eds., *"Genius in Bondage": Literature of the Early Black Atlantic* (Lexington: University of Kentucky Press, 2001), 11.

13. Elmer, *On Lingering and Being Last*, 167.

14. Ian Baucom, *Specters of the Atlantic: Finance Capital, Slavery, and the Philosophy of History* (Durham: Duke University Press, 2005) 30–31.

15. Walker Goebel and Saskia Schabio, "Introduction: Relocating Modernization and Technology," in Goebel and Schabio, *Beyond the Black Atlantic*, 4.

Cicero's Ghost

The Atlantic, the Enemy, and the Laws of War

IAN BAUCOM

Against "an unjust enemy," Immanuel Kant asserts in a startling passage of *The Metaphysics of Morals*, "the rights of a state . . . are unlimited in quantity or degree."[1] The claim startles because in the immediately preceding passages of his text, in an extended section on "International Right," Kant has been working to ameliorate his prior citation of Cicero's famously bleak assertion "inter arma, silent leges" (in times of war, the laws are silent) by deducing a silent law resilient within the classical wartime silencing of the law, a set of wartime rights, restrictions, and principles that would grant "states . . . the possibility of abandoning" a purely anomic "state of nature in their external relations and [even in a state of war] of entering a state of right" with one another. Holding forth that possibility of mutually recognized right — between states — in wartime, Kant nevertheless insists that the universal he wishes to affirm has its condition of exception, a condition triggered when a "state" finds (or elects) itself ranged against an enemy of a particular, troubling, law-annulling sort: an "unjust enemy." Having indicated that the simple existence of an enemy of this sort might evacuate the rule of law it is his fundamental purpose to affirm, Kant's succeeding task is to identify who this aberrant, law-annulling foe might be. Who, he thus asks, is this "unjust enemy"? Who is this figure to whom the laws of war, by the procedures of their own immanent reasoning, fail, legally, to apply? "Someone," he answers, "whose publicly expressed will, whether expressed in word or in deed, displays a maxim which would make peace among nations impossible and would lead to a perpetual state of nature if it were made into a general rule."[2]

To begin an essay within a volume that takes as it central problematic "the object of study in American studies" with a relatively obscure dilemma internal to Kant's late Enlightenment theory of international law seems, to put it simply, perverse. And, indeed, when I first came across this passage in the *Metaphysics*, I did not conceive of it as having any particularly "American" bearing. The problem (of the "unjust enemy") seemed, rather, akin to the type of problem in the generalized field of political theory or political theology that Giorgio Agamben has raised with reference to the figures of "homo sacer" and the concept of "bare life." What, I began to wonder, might the relation be between Agamben's "homo sacer" and Kant's "unjust enemy"? As history reminds us, however, theoretical dilemmas arise because of, and within, the discrete historical moment in which they appear. Or that, at least, is how I have come to understand the emergence of Kant's "unjust enemy" within his moment of Enlightenment war making and its pertinence to the moment contemporaneous with this volume's articulation and design, a moment still-recently conceived in some quarters of state-making power as inaugurating a new, global, "American Century," a moment in which a text seeking to further the radical renovation of American studies aptly takes as its title "States of Emergency," a moment in which emergencies and exceptions have been not just the names for a theoretical conundrum but for a condition of ruinous, global and historical fact.

Or let me put it this way. Who, from the perspective of such a moment (or from the vantage of the Enlightenment moment of Kant's writing) are the historical correlatives of the "unjust enemy"? Why, in the late eighteenth century, does this figure appear to haunt a project of international law that takes as its ambitious goal the establishment of a condition of "cosmopolitan right" and "perpetual peace"? What role has the unjust enemy been made to fill in the long modern history of law-making and law-preserving violence? What connections might the unjust enemy, and the exceptional legal space surrounding this figure, have to those accounts of the states of exception through which writers like Giorgio Agamben have been attempting to make sense of our contemporary experiences of law, violence, and sovereignty? What lines might there be running back from the appearance of this figure in Kant's late eighteenth-century text to earlier attempts to formulate a law of war and forward to the reappearance of the unjust enemy in the guise of the Bush administration's unprivileged belligerent and unlawful enemy?

Given the subtitle of this essay, it will, perhaps, come as no surprise that I have come to understand the genealogy of this figure to be crucially

Atlantic. More specifically, I argue, it is in the native Americans of the "new World" and the "Caapmen," "Hottentoos," and other indigenes of the South African Cape that both Kant's "unjust enemy" and the prisoners now indefinitely detained in Guantánamo Bay, Cuba, find their haunting legal and discursive precedent. Kant's Hobbesianism certainly points in that direction. For whoever else his unjust enemy might be, it is clear from the answer he provides to his own question that this figure is an analogue of sorts to Thomas Hobbes's *homo homini lupus*, a belated Enlightenment double of the man-who-is-a-wolf-to-man, that Hobbesian man purportedly unwilling to abandon the state of nature and war of all against all. If, on Agamben's reading of Hobbes, we should see in this wolfish, outlaw figure a modern reanimation of the Indo-European type of the "wargus," a lupine figure traceable, in its turn, to the paradoxical Roman type of "homo sacer" in whose dual capture and exclusion by the law Agamben finds the secret to his concept of the political, then Karl Schmitt's reading of Hobbes suggests that we should pay rather closer attention to Hobbes's explicit willingness to identify the state of nature not with a moment exceptionally virtual within Roman religious and constitutional law but with the "short, nasty, brutish" way of life he saw explicitly embodied by the indigenous inhabitants of the Americas — the key exemplars, in his work, of a people living in the state of nature.

At issue in these two competing appraisals of Hobbes, I am suggesting, are not only two variant accounts of the origins of "the man who is a wolf to man" but two variant genealogies of the unjust enemy. Where a reading along Agamben's line would find in the unlawful combatant, the unjust enemy, the man who is a wolf to man one serial incarnation after another of the original Roman type of "homo sacer," a reading paying closer attention to the floating presence of America in Hobbes's writings and to the development, contemporaneous with Hobbes's career, of a body of international law that explicitly exempted the "free" "conflict zones" of the Americas and Africa from the normative regulations of the laws of war, implies that in Hobbes's man who is a wolf to man, Kant's unjust enemy, and the Bush administration's unlawful combatant, we find something not simply reducible to Agamben's "homo sacer," but, rather, the trace of a figure entering modern legal and political discourse from the circum-Atlantic war-making projects of the European imperial powers and the states of exception written into their international laws of war. Or, to put things more simply: in answering the questions, "Who is the unjust enemy"? "What are the origins of this figure?" is it to ancient Rome or to the Atlantic world of the late sixteenth through mid seventeenth centuries that we should be looking?

If my answer to these questions, as I have already begun to imply, is the Atlantic, then, in light of the full title of this essay, the subsidiary query certainly arises: what does Cicero (one of the key sources of Agamben's account of the extended historical unfolding of the "state of exception" as global rule) have to do not only with late Renaissance humanist law and Kant's *Metaphysics* but with those "unlawful combatants" languishing in the United States' Cuban holding cells? In what respect might this Roman ghost be said — then, as now, if not, perhaps, in the way that Agamben has argued — to be haunting the long modern history of the Atlantic and its discourses of enmity?

BY INITIAL way of answer, let me shift register and scenes, away from the European and American outposts of the Atlantic triangle to a third corner of the Atlantic, the southern tip of Africa, where on the nineteenth of March 1660, nine years after having set sail from the Netherlands to establish a fort and gardens at the Cape of Good Hope, Commander Jan van Riebeeck sent a letter to the Council of Seventeen (the governors of the Dutch East India Company) announcing the successful conclusion to a "war" in which he and his garrison had been embroiled against the "Hottentoos" and "Caapmen" living in the area around the company's settlement. Van Riebeeck's antagonists in this conflict had been, he wrote, an assortment of "tobacco thieves," "beach rangers and brigands," who, the winter before, had "suddenly" "attack[ed] us . . . on all sides."[3] In response to this attack, Van Riebeeck issued a proclamation giving "full permission" to "everyone to seize or shoot them [the Caapmen] wherever they are found," issued a bounty of twenty guilders for any "of these robbers" if taken alive, ten if dead, and "half price for women and children."[4] Summarizing the outcome of this war, Van Riebeeck announced that his decisions had achieved the desired effect of "impressing" his foes "with a proper panic" and "terror" and led them to abandon their hostilities.[5] Recapitulating one particularly gratifying incident in which a certain Corporal Giers, having killed two of these "brigands," captured another and then executed him, carrying to Van Riebeeck the "upper lip" of the men he had slain as proof of his actions, the commander explained to the Council of Seventeen the utter legality of all the steps he had taken in licensing, and rewarding, the slaughter of men, women, and children "wherever they are found": "In consequence of the war made against us they had completely forfeited their rights and . . . we were not inclined to restore them, as the country had become the property of the Company by the sword and the rights of war."[6]

What rights-canceling "rights of war," one might ask, did Van Riebeeck have in mind, and was he legally correct to claim them? In the event, he was—or, at least, arguably so: first, by the doctrine of "reprisals" which, according to the existing law of war, enabled the delegation of the punitive rights (and *in situ* personality) of a sovereign state to a private entity, such as the company and its representatives; And, second, by the productive vagueness in the definition of sovereign personhood provided by Hugo Grotius (former legal counsel to the company and author of the seminal 1625 volume, *The Rights of War and Peace*), a definition that in designating as sovereign "that power . . . whose actions are not subject to the control of any other power" reads uncannily like Schmitt's theory of sovereignty *avant la lettre*.[7] Most crucially however, Van Riebeeck's claim to possess a law-sanctioned power of violence found authentication in the global "right of punishment" on which Grotius and a fellow company of late Renaissance humanist jurists had staked their claim to have defined for the European powers global jurisdiction over the "law of nature" (which meant in practice, jurisdiction over any territory beyond the boundaries of the European state-system). As Grotius quite unambiguously put it, "Those who are possessed of a sovereign power have a right to exact punishment not only for injuries affecting immediately themselves or their own subjects, but for gross violations of the law of nature and of nations, done to other states and subjects. . . . Upon this principle there can be no hesitation in pronouncing all wars to be just, that are made upon pirates, general robbers, and enemies of the human race. . . . [It is] a right resulting entirely from the law of nature."[8]

Key to this assertion was not only the contention that any individual "sovereign power" possessed global jurisdiction over the "law of nature" but the question of what precisely might constitute a punishable "violation *of* the law of nature" (emphasis added). Grotius's answer is contained in the elaboration he provides to the general "principle" he is insisting on. Primary among the grossest violations of the law of nature are piracy and general robbery, though why either should constitute not simply a civil crime but an affront to the law of nature is not yet clear, so, in a subsequent portion of his text, Grotius explains his reasoning by drawing a distinction not, as one might expect, between the types of *action* committed by pirates and robbers and those acts consistent with the law of nature but between the *forms of social organization* characteristic of the state, on one hand, and piracy on the other:

"A state, though it may commit some act of aggression, or injustice, does not thereby lose its political capacity, *nor can a band of pirates or robbers ever become a state.* . . . For with the latter the commission of crime is the sole bond of union."[9] The pirate or the general robber, Grotius argues, violates the law of nature not in consequence of any discrete act of theft or violence but by a prior and continuing refusal to enter into the political, law-and-contract bound community of a commonwealth. To refuse the bond of union provided by the European state form is to violate the law of nature, to become an enemy of the human race, and so, in Grotius's opinion, to forfeit all right and become subject to sovereign punishment. Or, to put things in terms directly relevant to Van Riebeeck's actions, purely by virtue of their apparent form of social organization, by virtue of appearing to him in the guise of "brigands" or "beach rangers," the "Caapmen" and "Hottentoos," they could be said to be living in violation of that *law* of nature which demanded that they abandon the *state of nature* and consent to their sovereign governance and so (quite apart from and prior to any act of belligerence on their part) had "forfeited their rights" and rendered themselves punishable.

Nor was this opinion exclusive to Grotius and his fellow humanist jurists — it is central to Hobbes's own understanding of the complex interplay between the "state" and the "law" of nature, organizational, in fact, to his account of the ways in which the fundamental legal obligation of those living within the otherwise lawless anarchy of the state of nature is that they abandon that condition and enter into life within the commonwealth. Precisely because his first "right" of nature (which affirms "the liberty every man hath . . . for the preservation of his own nature") exists in irreconcilable tension with the warlike *condition* of the state of nature in which no man can guarantee his own preservation, the first "law" of nature is that man must abandon the insecurity of the war of all against all and enter into the protection of a commonwealth under the sovereign command of an overawing power. In anticipating or mirroring Hobbes's arguments, Grotius and his fellow humanists were not, therefore, so much inventing a law of nature that they held pirates, robbers, brigands, and other "such men" to be violating, as asserting its pertinence not only to the philosophical but also to the juridical domain, rendering violations of this law explicitly, legally, actionable, defining the failure to belong to a recognizable sovereign state as an offense punishable under the now twinned laws of nature and of war. And while the generic examples Grotius cites of these stateless "enemies of the human race" are those of the pirate and the robber, the historical example provided by Van Riebeeck's actions at the Cape suggests that the real enemies subject to this universally asserted right of punishment were the indigenous peoples of the expanding, formal, and informal European empires.

One problem, however, remained. For in affirming the right of punishment on which Van Riebeeck can be seen to have been relying, Grotius had put himself in a paradoxical position. Where in one section of his text he explicitly endorses the right of "a sovereign power" to wage war against precisely the type of foe the commander represented himself to be confronting (robbers, brigands, beach-rangers as he variously calls them), elsewhere in his text Grotius seems to insist upon the precise opposite.

> To what kind of war such an appellation ["just"] most duly belongs will be best understood by considering the definition, which the Roman Lawyers have given of a PUBLIC or NATIONAL enemy. "Those, *says Pomponius*, are PUBLIC and LAWFUL ENEMIES, with whose STATE our own is engaged in war: but enemies of every other description, come under the denomination of pirates and robbers.... So that by the opinion of the Roman Lawyers it is evident, that no war is considered lawful, regular, and formal, except that which is begun and carried on by the sovereign power of each country.[10]

Grotius was not alone among the sixteenth- and seventeenth-century humanist jurists from whom the modern law of war derives in arguing thus. "War," Alberico Gentili had previously insisted in his 1588 *De Iure Belli*, "derives its name from the fact that there is a contest for victory between two equal parties, and for that reason it was first called *duellem*, 'a contest of two.' . . . In the same way we have *perduellem*, 'war,' *duelles* and *perduelles*, 'enemies,' whom we now call *hostes*. . . . In fact, *hostire* means 'to make equal' . . . therefore *hostis* is a person with whom war is waged and who is the equal of his opponent." Thus, he concluded, any definition of war as "'armed force against a foreign prince or people,' is shown to be incorrect by the fact that it applies the term 'war' also to the violence of private individuals and of brigands."[11]

Licensed by the right of punishment to wage war against pirates, robbers, and brigands "wherever they are found," while restricted from identifying "war" against "such men" as "war" in any just and proper sense, the humanist law of war thus found itself at an apparent impasse, one motivated by the twin, but conflicting, historical pressures to which Grotius, Gentili, and their intellectual companions were responding. For if the impulse to define war as a contest between formally equal sovereign counterparts had been motivated by the need to resolve Europe's otherwise irresolvable wars of religion, and if the humanist key to solving that puzzle had been, as Schmitt and others have argued, to have derived, from the sovereign equality of belligerent state actors, the concept of the "just enemy" (*justis hostis*) with whom a peace treaty could be concluded, the historical moment in which that legal puzzle was solved was also one in which the continental powers were embarking on an intensified global round of empire building and imperial war making against an array of "peoples" whom they were distinctly disinclined to recognize as sovereign, much less equal, much less just.[12] To balance the twin imperatives of crafting a law of war that would strengthen the sovereignty of European states without necessitating a recognition of the sovereignty of the extra-European peoples on whom they were waging war, a second key figure was thus required, one to set alongside but as a negative double to the "hostis," one, that is, to set *within* the law of war as legally *outside* the law of war: the figure of the "unjust enemy," against whom one could legally wage war, but to whom, as Van Riebeeck had contended, the rights of war did not apply.

It was in inventing this figure that the canon of Roman legal discourse enters the Atlantic imperial scene as a vital supplement to the natural law theory on which the humanists had otherwise relied. Most useful of all were Cicero's speeches and writings, specifically the *Philippics*. For in that series of speeches denouncing the rebellious Mark Antony and asserting for the Roman people the right to make war against this "bandit" and his "villainous band of brigands," while simultaneously denying that this stateless man deserved any reciprocal recognition as a legitimate "public enemy," Cicero had identified the very legal figure the humanists were searching for: a nonsovereign foe against whom a sovereign state could go to war while excepting that enemy from the rights and protections stipulated by the laws of war. The crucial passage appears in the fourth *Philippic*, and while it possesses little of the burnished rhetorical luster of Cicero's grim "inter arma silent leges" (when arms speak, the law is silent), it is one which, through its repeated use and reuse by the sixteenth- and seventeenth-century founders of modern international law, has exerted an immense influence on the modern law of war, and — in consequence of that law's unfolding over the past four centuries — on those broadly imperial and specifically Atlantic discourses of sovereignty, exceptionality, and enmity that are my primary subject.

The passage reads so: "Your ancestors, Men of Rome, had to deal with an enemy who possessed a Commonwealth, a Senate-House, a treasury, a consensus of like-minded citizens, one with whom a treaty of peace could be concluded if events took that turn. This enemy of yours is attacking your commonwealth, but he himself has none. He is eager to destroy the Senate, the council of the world, but he himself has no public council. . . . As for a united citizenry, how can he have that when no community calls him citizen? How can peace be made with an adversary whose cruelty taxes belief and whose good faith is nonexistent. So, Men of Rome, the whole conflict lies between the Roman People, the conqueror of all nations, and an assassin, a bandit, a Spartacus . . . [and his] villainous band of brigands."[13] Given the dilemma they were confronting — the urgent need to define, and find classical warrant for, an unjust enemy against whom a sovereign state could legitimately and unreservedly wage war without, thereby, recognizing that foe as reciprocally sovereign — it is little wonder that the humanist jurists would have seized on this passage and cited it over and again. Grotius cites it. Gentili cites it at the close of a lengthy chapter on the unprotected place of "brigands" in the law of war, as does Richard Zouche, Gentili's successor as professor of law at Oxford, in what might be the clearest exposition of the uses to which Cicero was put in resolving the legal paradox confronting the humanists. Concluding a section of his 1650 *Exposition of Fecial Law and Procedure*, in which he distinguishes between the two types of "enemies" with whom a state might find itself at war, "some of whom are of a worse and others of a better condition," Zouche identifies the latter as "lawful enemies . . . to whom are due all the rights of war" and then, quoting Cicero, clarifies who such a lawful enemy might be: "one who has a State, Senate, Treasury, citizens consenting and agreeing and some method of making peace."[14] Against these licit, protected foes, he posed all those other enemies "of the worse condition . . . [those] to whom the laws of war do not apply" — "robbers" "brigands" "pirates," or, as his group name for this second type of belligerent, this less and worse than an enemy, "inimici," those who are "inimical" — and inimical in a particular sense: inimical by virtue of failing to possess a state, senate, and treasury; inimical, as Grotius elsewhere makes clear, by virtue of having violated Hobbes first "law of nature"; inimical by virtue of having refused to abandon the insecurity of the state of nature for the wealth of life under the overawing power of a sovereign state; inimical, in Hobbes terms, by virtue of not having abandoned a condition in which "there is no place for industry . . . no culture of the earth, no navigation, no use of the commodities that might be imported by sea, no commodious building. . . . no arts, no letters, no society, and which is worst of all, continual fear and danger of violent death, and the life of man, solitary, poor, nasty, brutish and short." Life, "solitary, poor, nasty, brutish, and short," may be the most famous item of this litany of scandals, but as the preceding elements of Hobbes's charge sheet make clear, and as the humanist jurists of the late sixteenth and early seventeenth century chose, by criminalizing, to emphasize, the true outrage of the unjust enemy was to exist outside the state form, and, by existing so, to refuse, in exchange for subordination to the ever-accumulating power of the commonwealth, to enter into a life of ever-accumulating industry, cultivation, and commodity exchange, life under the dual, reciprocal sovereignty of state and treasury, violence and money.

IF VAN RIEBEECK could find in his adversaries, in the "brigands and robbers" he reported to the Council of Seventeen, precisely such an unlawful, unprotected, rightless enemy, then he is certainly not the last to have done so. Over the intervening centuries this inimical enemy of the state, this strange hybrid of modern imperial history, humanist jurisprudence and ancient Roman law, this frightful admixture of Hobbes's *homo homini lupus*, Grotius's and Gentili's "pirate" or "brigand," Zouche's homo inimicus, and Cicero's man without a state, has recurred as a haunting figure in the legal and philosophical discourses and war-making projects circulating and crisscrossing the Atlantic and the globe, resurfacing not only in the guise of Kant's unjust enemy but, in the same period of his writing, in the form of the Breton insurrectionists against Republican rule, whom Napoleon had proclaimed as "bandits" unprotected by the laws of war and who Honore de Balzac, in his novel of the Chouan revolt, characterized, with perhaps greater historical warrant than he realized, as appearing on the European scene as a type of "American redskin, or some savage from the Cape of Good Hope." Balzac was not alone among his historical contemporaries in drawing that exact parallel. Walter Scott, in *Waverley* indulged it too, troping the highland insurrectionists against the English crown as "an invasion of African negroes, or Esquimaux Indians." And Kant, too, allowed himself the same comparison, if through a more extended and indirect simile. I have already cited his explicitly Hobbesian definition of the unjust enemy as one "whose publicly expressed will, whether expressed in word or in deed, displays a maxim which would make peace among nations impossible and would lead to a perpetual state of nature if it were made into a general rule."[15] To that anterior philosophical model for his own homo inimicus (against whom, he insists, "the rights of the state are unlimited"), Kant, in the *Metaphysics of Morals*, adds a secondarily borrowed (but still thoroughly Hobbesian) anthropological double: the "Hottentots" of the Cape and "most native American nations."

It is only fair to note that in the section of the text (on "Cosmopolitan Right"), in which Kant turns his attention to the indigenous subjects of the Atlantic world, his apparent intention is to limit the implications of what his immediately preceding discussion of the "unjust enemy" has just licensed (by means of an extended meditation on the ways in which his theory of law might or might not apply to the inhabitants of the Cape and the Americas). The sum effect of that meditation, however, is to draw these "lawless" people within a cosmopolitan theory of "right" only at the cost of exposing them to a now universally warranted license of violence Hobbes had reserved for the overawing power of the national state but which Kant now awards to the international agents and sovereign representatives of the cosmopolitan ideal.

Kant's thoughts on this matter, in their mix of clarity and torturous self-hesitation, are worth citing at length:

> [A]ll nations are *originally* members of a community of the land. But this is not a *legal community* of possession [*communio*] and utilization of the land, nor a community of ownership. It is a community of reciprocal action [*commercium*], which is physically possible, and each member of it accordingly has constant relations with all the others. Each may *offer* to have commerce with the rest, and they all have a right to make such overtures without being treated by foreigners as enemies. This right, in so far as it affords the prospect that all nations may unite for the purpose of creating certain universal laws to regulate the intercourse they may have with one another, may be termed *cosmopolitan* [*ius cosmopoliticum*].
>
> . . . With the art of navigation, [the oceans] constitute the greatest natural incentive to international commerce, and the greater the number of neighbouring coastlines there are . . . the livelier this commerce will be. Yet these visits to foreign shores . . . can also occasion evil and violence in one part of the globe with ensuing repercussions which are felt everywhere else. But although such abuses are possible, they do not deprive the world's citizens of the right to *attempt* to enter into a community with everyone else and to *visit* all regions of the earth with this intention.
>
> . . . [O]ne might ask whether a nation may establish a *settlement alongside another nation [accolatus]* in newly discovered regions, or

whether it may take possession of land in the vicinity of a nation which
has already settled in the same area, even without the latter's consent.
The answer is that the right to do so is incontestable. . . . But if the
nations involved are pastoral or hunting peoples (like the Hottentots,
the Tunguses, and most native American nations) who rely upon large
tracts of wasteland for their sustenance, settlements should not be
established by violence, but only by treaty. . . . Nevertheless, there are
plausible enough arguments for the use of violence on the grounds that
it is in the best interest of the world as a whole. . . . But all these supposedly good intentions cannot wash away the stain of injustice from the
means which are used to implement them. Yet one might object that
the whole world would perhaps still be in a lawless condition if men
had any such compunction about using violence when they first created
a law-governed state. But this can as little annul the above condition
of right as can the plea of political revolutionaries that the people are
entitled to reform constitutions by force if they become corrupt.[16]

In summary terms, Kant's fundamental argument is that a global right to
commerce is not only irrefutable but foundational to the emergence of an
international (indeed "universal") legal order. Moreover, he contends, this
cosmopolitan right to commerce and this universal international law extend
(via a right to settlement and regardless of indigenous "consent") into those
regions of the earth inhabited by peoples ("like the Hottentots") living in a
"lawless condition." It is on this point, though, that he runs into difficulties.
For while it is also his argument that these "lawless" people should be made
to enter into a universal cosmopolitanism only "by treaty," it is a condition
of their Hobbesian lawlessness that they are incapable of regarding treaties
as instruments possessing binding contractual force. Hence, simultaneous
to his proposition that international law (and cosmopolitan right) should
be extended by treaty rather than by violence, we have his contention that
the "consent" of the lawless is not, in fact, necessary (indeed, in a strictly
legal and philosophical sense, it is impossible). Hence also, we have Kant's
ensuing, troubled set of arguments and counterarguments against and for
the use of violence in subordinating such lawless people to law (in the interest of extending the operating spheres of global commerce). At the last, Kant
finds himself at an impasse. Clearly wishing to express both a moral repug-
nance for (and refusal of) violence as a means of establishing, globally, the
condition of cosmopolitan right, and, at the same time, compelled, by the

Hobbesian logic of his own arguments, to acknowledge violence as the only copula between "a lawless condition" and "a law-governed state," he seems at once to wish to deny and to find no way to avoid entertaining the efficacy of a recourse to what more recent theoretical discourse calls "constituting violence."

And while, in the last sentence I have cited, Kant can find a way to reject such constituting violence in the national arena (on the grounds that, however corrupt, constituted power can at least be said already to exist within the national state), all his express moral qualms cannot allow him to explain how global commerce, international law, and cosmopolitan right can come into existence without it. It is his good fortune that he does not have to provide that explanation here. For he has, in fact, done so earlier in his text, in his discussion of the "unjust enemy," which comes to his aid and solves his dilemma in much the same fashion that that figure had solved the dilemmas of Kant's mid-seventeenth-century intellectual predecessors. For precisely to the extent that "lawless people" (like the Hottentots and the native inhabitants of the Americas) can be said to be living in a state of nature, living, that is, in a condition of the stateless, acommercial, acontractual "war of all against all," they can be said, (as a pure fact of their apparent form of social organization and their exteriority to the realm of "public contract") to represent "a threat to the freedom" "of all nations" to pursue their cosmopolitan right. Accordingly, in this situation, and this situation only, Kant's text endorses a recourse to "constituting violence" or, as he puts it, affirms that against such "unjust enemies" "all nations" have the right to "unite" and "make them to accept a new constitution."[17]

IF THOSE FINAL WORDS seem uncannily pertinent to our own moment, then, in moving toward a close, I want very briefly to consider how that Kantian formula (or, more accurately, that Kantian reformulation of a mid-seventeenth-century Hobbesian law of war developed by the late Renaissance theorists of the "international") has been not merely apposite but crucial to that global theory and project of war with whose consequences we are still living; crucial to a global "security" discourse that, in providing theoretical license for such war, claimed philosophical dignity for itself by claiming direct lineal descent from Hobbes and Kant. By way of example, let me turn to a text published by Thomas P. M. Barnett, following his period as director of the "New Rules Sets Project": a collaborative venture jointly sponsored by the Naval War College and the investment consulting firm Cantor Fitzgerald. The centerpiece of Barnett's argument is a map that was published, with a short accompanying essay, in the March 2003 issue of *Esquire* magazine under the title: "The Pentagon's New Map." (Lest his readers miss the urgent historical pertinence of that map, Barnett's opening sentences read: "Let me tell you why military engagement with Saddam Hussein's regime in Baghdad is not only necessary and inevitable, but good . . . a historical tipping point . . . the moment when Washington takes real ownership of strategic security in the age of globalization.") Subsequently expanded and published in book form, Barnett's article had a fairly straightforward argument: the contemporary world is divisible in two, though not in the terms that Samuel Huntington divides it. Instead of being antagonistically counterposed on civilizational lines, the two worlds of the global present, Barnett argues, split off from one another as zones of security and insecurity: zones in which stable, state-governed polities have realized Kant's "dream of perpetual peace" and zones in which stateless, rogue-state, or failed-state polities are condemned to Hobbes's "state of nature." Isomorphic to this political distinction, Barnett continues, is an economic distinction: in the global security zone, flows of capital and energy proceed unimpeded; in the zone of insecurity, finance capital is absent, energy is frequently abundant as a natural resource but unavailable to industry, and financial contracts are radically unenforceable, where they can be said to exist at all. The security zone, in short, is characterized by stable state structures, the thick presence of political and economic "rule sets," and its concomitant integration into networks of global capital (particularly global finance-capital); the insecurity zone is characterized by the absence of all three: states, rules, and investment capital. From these arguments, Barnett draws his fundamental conclusion: the boundary between the zones of security and insecurity, between the regions of capital flow and the dearth of capital, between the world that has achieved the dream of "perpetual peace" and the world living in a Hobbesian "state of nature" is not simply a new name for the borderline between the "developed" and "underdeveloped" worlds.[18] It is, instead, the new borderland of global war, the conflict zone along whose curving global line the wars of the twenty-first century will and should be fought: not defensively, but preemptively, in order to "shrink the gap," or, as he puts it, to move the territories within this insecurity zone "from Hobbes to Kant."[19] That task, he finally insists, should not however be left to the U.S. military alone. Rather the project of global war in the twenty-first century must become the shared project of the Pentagon and a multinational finance capital industry working in combination as a new "Global Leviathan" to secure for the planet as a whole, a Kantian "perpetual peace" whose unfolding moment of arrival will be marked, and measured by the cross-planetary extension of political, legal, and economic "rule sets."

The key argument central to the mid-seventeenth-century law of war (and central again, in overtly Hobbesian terms, to Kant's own theory of international and cosmopolitan right) thus returns as key to Barnett's new map of capital, law, and war. In response to the appearance of a "predatory" people living in a putatively real state of nature on the boundaries and beyond the outposts of stable nation states and the circulating flow of capital — people living in that "lawless condition in which man is a wolf to man" (*homo homini lupus*), the condition of human life one of a perpetual war of all against all, and the pursuit of commerce impossible in the absence of an overawing, law-and-contract-securing power — sovereign power can again extend itself as a law-constituting power of violence and, in so extending law and violence, extend the flow of global capital. And it is not at all an accident that at precisely the moment in which this Hobbesian-Kantian map of war should re-emerge, or that at the very frontier of its Gulf war testing ground, so too should the figure of the inimicus return to the law-suspending center of the law of war: now in the form of the "unlawful enemy combatant" identified in President Bush's October 2001 order of war and subsequently written into U.S. law by the Military Commissions Act of 2006 — a figure, once again, distinguishable from the "lawful enemies" of the imperial state by the failure to "belong to a State party"; a figure, once again, inimical, rightless, legally exceptional, and languishing indefinitely, but by law, within yet another of the Atlantic's legally free and empty zones; a melancholy successor figure in the long line of "Caapmen," "Hottentoos," "brigands," "inimici," and "unjust enemies," against whom the imperial state has held its own "rights" to be "unlimited."

IF THE INIMICUS and the unjust enemy have returned, so too have Cicero and his *Philippics*, now as a centerpiece of Agamben's *State of Exception*. What the figure of "homo sacer" has been to Agamben's prior elaboration of bare life, the Roman institution of the "iustitium" is to this more recent work. Encompassing "a suspension not only of the administration of justice but of the law as such," and articulating "the state of exception in its paradigmatic form," the mechanisms, effects, and contemporary pertinence of the iustitium are best grasped, Agamben argues, if we take as its "exemplary case

... the one Cicero describes in *Philippics* 5.12."[20] Agamben's purpose in turning to this speech is to isolate three key features of Roman constitutional law which he understands to have underpinned the classical origins of the state of exception and to govern its modern rearticulation. In the Roman tradition he argues these three features of the state of exception are the *senatus consultum ultimum* (the consultation through which the Senate was empowered to suspend the normal operations of law); the declaration of *tumultus* (a "state of disorder and unrest"); and the iustitium (or suspension of the law) itself. "The *consultum*," as Agamben puts it, "presupposes the tumultus, and the *tumultus* is the *sole cause* of the *iustitium*."[21]

I note this, because in order in order to insist on these three features of the iustitium, Agamben must set aside a fourth feature of the Roman legal tradition, one that is also present in Cicero but does not fully fit into his genealogy of the passage from the Roman to the modern. Agamben's omission of this feature of law from *his* turn to Cicero, I believe, is symptomatic of a *type* of suppression consistent throughout Agamben's work: an omission whose effect is to locate exclusively within the domain of the constitutional the critique of sovereign violence it is Agamben's purpose to articulate. Or let me put it this way: just as it has been my suggestion that the modern genealogy and trajectory of Hobbes's *homo homini lupus* owes less to the *philological* descent of Agamben's "homo sacer" from ancient Rome to Guantánamo than to the strategic adaptation of Roman law by the sixteenth- and seventeenth-century humanist architects of modern international law, so too is it my sense that the Roman institution of the iustitium impinges upon contemporary manifestations of the state of exception not, as Agamben suggests, as the pure ground of an unbroken constitutional line coming to us under the Euro-American banner of the *translatio imperii et studii*, but as an emblem of the production of the constitutional by the international, the national by the imperial, the laws of the commonwealth by the law-constituting violence of the colony. Which is another way of saying that if we are to understand how Cicero's ghost, and the ghost of the Roman iustitium (like the ghost of the inimical) might continue to haunt our present we might need to begin by looking outside the constitutional and within the imperial rather than the other way around. We need to postulate that it is the practices of imperial war that generate an emergency of the constitution, not an emergency of the constitution that permits the practice of war.

That, at least, seems to be Cicero's argument as he develops it across the course of the *Philippics*. It is the case, as Agamben argues, that tumult precedes the consultum ultimum and that the consultum ultimum licenses the iustitium. Integral to tumult, consultum, and iustitium, as Cicero makes clear, however, is *bellum*, war: though not just any kind of war but, rather, a type of war that arises upon and as an effect of the appearance on the imperial horizon of an inimical foe. That seems to be the clear conclusion of the speech Cicero delivered on the Senate floor, subsequently recorded as *Philippic* 8. "Let us examine the point at issue," he declared. "Certain persons thought that the name of war ought not to be in the motion (debated the previous day). They preferred to call it 'tumult,' showing their ignorance not only of facts but of words. For while a war can exist without a tumult, a tumult cannot exist without a war. . . . What else is a tumult but a commotion so serious that fear beyond the ordinary arises from it — that being the origin of the word tumult. Accordingly our ancestors spoke of an Italian tumult (because it took place within our own borders) and a Gallic tumult (because it was next door to Italy), and of no other tumult whatsoever. And that a tumult is something more serious than a war can be inferred from the fact that exemptions are valid in a war but not in a tumult. Hence, as I have just observed there may be war without tumult, but no tumult without war."[22]

But what is the form of war "more serious" than ordinary war, war with tumult, tumultuous war? Cicero identifies two examples: one Italian (in brief, a civil war) and the other Gallic (an anti-insurrectionary imperial war). Common to both the Italian and the Gallic tumult (and the extraordinary, exceptional form of "war-worse-than-war" they occasion) is a distinction in the form of the enemy with whom Rome finds itself confronted, the form of enemy Cicero identifies in Mark Antony: the enemy with whom one cannot conclude a peace treaty; the enemy who commands no senate, treasure, citizens agreeing and consenting; the enemy who does not represent a sovereign state; the unjust enemy, the inimicus, as Cicero also, finally, calls Mark Antony.[23]

If, as Agamben argues, we might find in this series of speeches and declarations not only the iustitium in its exemplary form but also, in that example, the authentic paradigm of the modern state of exception, then, I am suggesting that to the chain tumult, consultum, iustitium, we must add the preceding and animating figure of the inimicus: the unjust enemy whose appearance triggers that "fear beyond the ordinary" whose twin effects are war worse than war and the suspension of the constitutional order. Key to both is the unjust enemy, the crisis figure looming up on the imperial frontier who throws the empire into exceptional war and the constitution into arrest.

It is *this* figure — whose Ciceronian avatar is Mark Antony but whose true Roman prototypes, as Richard Zouche suggested in his reading of Cicero, are the "brigands ... who infested Cisalpine Gaul," and who Jan van Riebeeck, Zouche's exact contemporary, found in the "Hottentoos" of the Cape — that I understand to have been haunting an Atlantic modernity's laws of war and projects of empire making. Most recently conjured back into existence as the "unprivileged belligerent" and "unlawful combatant," looming into the present not through an unbroken intraconstitutional line of inheritance but from the legally free and empty zones of the imperial frontier, it is this figure, this *homo inimicus* (and not Agamben's *homo sacer*) that I understand to provide the paradigm for our contemporaneity's global, war-making states of exception — and so, too, to provide a reconsidered "American studies" with renewed engagement with the *state of emergency* "as task."

NOTES

Portions of this essay are included in Ian Baucom and Mary Poovey, "Financing Enlightenment," in *Mediating Enlightenment: Past and Present*, ed. Clifford Siskin and William Warner (Chicago: University of Chicago Press, forthcoming).

1. Immanuel Kant, *Political Writings*, ed. H. S. Reiss (Cambridge: Cambridge University Press, 1970), 170.

2. Ibid., 170.

3. Jan Van Riebeeck, *Precis of the Archives of the Cape of Good Hope: Letters Dispatched from the Cape, 1652–1662*, ed. H. C. V. Liebrandt (Cape Town: W. A. Richards and Sons, 1897), 134, 135.

4. Ibid.

5. Ibid., 21.

6. Ibid., 166.

7. Hugo Grotius, *The Rights of War and Peace*, trans. A. C. Campbell, vols. 1–3 (Washington, D.C.: M. Walter Dunne, 1901), 1:62.

8. Ibid., 2:247.

9. Ibid., 3:315 (emphasis added).

10. Ibid., 3:314–315.

11. Alberico Gentili, *De Iure Belli Libri Tres*, trans. John C. Rolfe (Oxford: Clarendon Press, 1933), 2:12.

12. Carl Schmitt, *The Nomos of the Earth in the International Law of the Ius Publicum Europaeum*, trans. G. L. Ulmen (New York: Telos Press, 2003), esp. 153.

13. Cicero *Philippics*, ed. and trans. D. R. Shackleton Bailey (Chapel Hill: University of North Carolina Press, 1986), 143–45.

14. Richard Zouche, *An Exposition of Fecial Law and Procedure, or of Law between Nations, and Questions concerning the Same*, trans. J. L. Brierly (Washington, D.C.: Carnegie Institute, 1902) 37–38.

15. Kant, *Political Writings*, 170.

16. Ibid., 172–73.

17. Ibid., 170.

18. Thomas P. M. Barnett, *The Pentagon's New Map: War and Peace in the Twenty-first Century* (New York: G. P. Putnam's Sons, 2004), 161.

19. Ibid., 166.

20. Giorgio Agamben, *State of Exception*, trans. Kevin Attell (Chicago: University of Chicago Press, 2005), 41, 45.

21. Ibid., 46 (emphasis added).

22. Cicero, *Philippics*, 215. Agamben, to be fair, addresses this very passage, but he does so in order to sunder the connection between war and tumult Cicero appears to be insisting on: "All evidence suggests that this passage does not mean that tumult is a special or stronger form of war . . . instead, at the very moment of affirming a connection between war and tumult, it places an irreducible tension between them. . . . Tumult is not 'sudden war,' but the *magna trepidation* that it produces in Rome" (Agamben, *State of Exception*, 42). Separating what Cicero thus seems to link, Agamben can then go on, in the succeeding pages of his text, to remove bellum from the chain of operations resulting in the "authentic genealogical paradigm in Roman law . . . for the modern state of exception," and so conclude, as I have noted previously, "the consultum presupposes the tumultus, and the tumultus is the *sole cause* of the iustitium" (ibid., 46, emphasis added). The question I am raising is whether it is the case that "all evidence suggests that this passage does not mean that tumult is a special or a stronger form of war"? Cicero's full argument, I am suggesting (particularly his elaboration of "tumult" as something both "more serious than war" and productive of a war without "exemptions") makes that reading difficult to sustain. (The exemptions to which Cicero refers are those freeing certain patricians and select others from obligatory military service during the course of a regular war [his "war without tumult"], exemptions not valid in the case of that form of war "more serious" than ordinary war [the war *with* tumult]).

23. The entire course of the preceding speeches leading up to the war declaration in *Philippics* 8 is governed by Cicero's gradual rhetorical development of this point. While he begins by speaking of Marc Antony as an "enemy," conferring on him the proper name of the licit public foe, from *Philippic* 4 onward Cicero begins to move away from that term, to qualify or undercut it, adding to the name *hostis* (enemy), the epithets *latronem* (bandit), *parricidam* (traitor) (4.5), *percussore* (assassin), and *Spartaco* (Spartacus) (4.15) until, at last, he arrives at that definition of Marc Antony as the stateless, treasury-less, senate-less foe Gentili, Grotius, and Zouche picked up on. And then, in his ensuing speech, *Philippic* 5, Cicero rechristens Antony as "inimicus" (5.3), and with that definition in place, with that less-and-worse-than-an-enemy identified on the imperial horizon, he demands "that a state of tumult be decreed, suspension of business proclaimed, military cloaks donned, and a levy held with no exemptions in Rome and in the whole of Italy . . . [to] crush the madness of a felonious gladiator . . . [who] has taken up arms against the Commonwealth."

World History according to Katrina

WAI CHEE DIMOCK

How does Hurricane Katrina change our understanding of the United States, the lengths and widths of its history, as well as its place in the life of the planet? As a catastrophe that casts into doubt the efficacy and security of the nation, what alternatives does it suggest, what other forms of shelter does it point to, what ways does it organize human beings into meaningful groups? And how might these nonstandard groupings help us rethink the contours of the humanities, in relation to both world literature, a field already well developed, and world history, a field that perhaps still needs to be imagined, needs to be fleshed out?[1]

The nation-state seems "unbundled" by the hurricane in ways both large and small — not only as a system of defense but also as psychological insurance, political membership, and academic field. I want to use these unbundlings as an occasion to think about the circumference of our work: in terms of time frame and in terms of geographical borders. And, on both fronts, it seems crucial to ask three interrelated questions. Given the failure of the nation-state to defend its borders against a phenomenon such as Katrina, what adjustments need to be made to some of its prerogatives, including the claim of sovereignty? If it turns out that national sovereignty, in the twenty-first century, is no longer plausible across the board, what exceptions might be made, and in what contexts? And what chances are there that these shifts would reorient the practice of democracy itself, taking it out of its customary mold and freeing it to experiment with new questions, including the long-term relation between human welfare and the world's climate?

It is instructive to begin with an essay on Katrina by Michael Ignatieff, published on 25 September 2005, in the *New York Times Magazine*. "When the levees broke, the contract of American citizenship failed," Ignatieff says.

The breach is not just in the physical structures, or in New Orleans as a physical city, but in something even more consequential, namely, the integrity of the United States as a nation, its ability to *be* sovereign. According to Ignatieff, the most "basic term" of this sovereignty is "protection: helping citizens to protect their families and possessions from forces beyond their control."[2] And, just as the nation is defined by its power to protect, citizens are defined by their right to demand that protection. They are "entitled to this because they are Americans."[3]

Nationality, in other words, ought to be synonymous with a guaranteed safety, an insulation from any harm that arises. It ought to be our bulwark against the storm. And the tragedy of Katrina is that it seems to have thrown that bulwark into question. Ignatieff summarizes the problem as follows: "In America, a levee defends a foundational moral intuition: all lives are worth protecting and, because this is America, worth protecting at the highest standard. This principle was betrayed by the Army Corps of Engineers, by the state and local officials who knew the levees needed repair and did nothing, and by Congress, which allowed the president to cut appropriations for levee renewal."[4]

According to this analysis, the problem is that the sovereignty of the nation has not been sovereign enough. The United States ought to have been an invincible line of defense, and it was not. The remedy, then, is also fairly simple: that line has to be firmed up, made invincible once again. The narrative that Ignatieff constructs begins and ends with the levees for this reason, because the nation-state is broken and then mended on their backs. But to see the problem as solely a problem of the levees is already to predetermine the solution, making Katrina an event internal to the United States, an engineering failure, something that can be fixed without changing our basic sense of what the sovereign nation amounts to, what it is equipped (or not equipped) to do, and the extent of protection it is able to offer its citizens.

Nonsovereign History

As must be clear, I find this approach unduly limiting. I would like to explore a larger set of analytic coordinates than those suggested by Ignatieff, and to do so in a slightly roundabout fashion — by way of a debate that casts doubt on the sovereign claim of the nation, especially its adequacy as a unit of time, a debate that has galvanized historians no less than literary scholars. James Sheehan, in his 2006 presidential address to the American Historical Association, specifically raises this as an issue. It would "be foolish to deny the importance of states," Sheehan says. "But the state was not and is not history's natural telos. The emergence of states was neither inevitable nor uniform nor irreversible."[5] Even though national chronology might look like the only chronology there is, a self-evident way of measuring time, we pay a steep price when we reify it and routinize it, allowing ourselves no other frame of reference. "Modern historiography is inextricably linked with the modern nation," Thomas Bender writes. "This has both given focus to historical inquiry and won for it a place in civic life. But it has also been disabling, silencing stories both smaller and larger than the nation."[6] As a unit of time, the nation tends to work as a pair of evidentiary shutters, blocking out all those phenomena that do not fit into its intervals, reducing to nonevents all those processes either too large or too small to show up on its watch. Prasenjit Duara, historian of China — a country with a long record of just such disappearing acts — urges us to "rescue history from the nation" for just that reason.[7] To make sovereign borders the gatekeeper for data gathering is to make it a foregone conclusion that the form of the nation is the only form that matters.[8] It is to take that form and reproduce it in the form of the discipline, "naturalizing the nation-state as the skin that contains the experience of the past."[9]

That skin is very much the skin for those for us who call ourselves Americanists. To be sure, much of our work is critical of the nation. Still, the very existence of an "Americanist" field implicitly (and sometimes explicitly) reinforces the idea that an autonomous body of evidence can be derived from the United States, with clear dividing lines that separate it from other bodies of evidence. Neither American history nor American literature would have been a field without this assumption. Territorial sovereignty is foundational to both in this sense: not only does it produce a database that legitimizes the field; it also institutes a cutoff line for what falls outside. As Anthony Giddens observes in a different context, "Sovereignty provides an ordering principle for what is 'internal' to states and what is 'external' to them."[10] The concept of "off limits" inversely defines the borders of a political jurisdiction; it also inversely defines the borders of a field of knowledge.[11]

This conflation of nation and field leads to a research agenda almost tautological: to study the United States, we need go no further than the United States. This makes things easier, though not everyone would agree that such a tautology is in fact valid, a good approximation of the forces that shape the world. Janice Radway, in her presidential address to the American Studies Association in 1998, makes a point of invoking this model — and rejecting it.

In language strikingly similar to Duara's, she cautions us against any conception of the field as being like the territorial nation, lined with a skin: "Far from being conceived on the model of a container — that is, as a particular kind of hollowed out object with evident edges or skin enclosing certain organically uniform contents — territories and geographies need to be reconceived as spatially-situated and intricately intertwined networks of social relationships."[12]

Radway's challenge to the "container" model turns the study of the United States from a closed space to an open network, with no sovereign borders, nothing that will keep it defensibly separated from the rest of the world. What does this mean in practice? Well, for one thing, we cannot say, with any degree of finality, that anything is "extraneous," because extraneousness is not an attribute that is cut-and-dried, antecedently given. It is a happenstance, a contextual variable, changing with the array of forces that happen to be in play and with their different modes of interaction. This lack of intrinsic separation suggests that the analytic domain is always going to be heuristically stretched beyond any set of prescribed coordinates. The study of the United States can never be tautologically identical to the borders of the United States, because it can never keep the "outside" a permanent outside, externalized by fixed borders. The field then, according to Radway, can bear no resemblance to the territorial form of the nation. The nation is sovereign, or imagines itself to be. The field can have no such pretension.

What does it mean to write a history that is nonsovereign, with the seemingly extraneous being always ready, at a moment's notice, to morph into the unextraneous? I would like to come back to Katrina as a test case and explore two instances of this dynamic, when a seemingly secure jurisdiction suddenly bursts at the seams, becoming a kind of flooded container, flooded by an outside that refuses to stay out. To explore these two scenarios, I first follow the unconventional coverage of Katrina by a local newspaper, the *New Orleans Times-Picayune*. The *Times-Picayune* received the Pulitzer Prize for this report, so the importance of its work has been recognized. But the history that it gives us *is* a nonsovereign history, not only because the initiative is coming from the ground up, from a local newspaper, not reflecting a national consensus, but also because this initiative produces a database that in no way matches the official borders of the United States. Nonsovereign history is offbeat, off-key, off-center. Its unorthodox paths jump from the micro to the macro, and bypass the default center, going over and under the jurisdiction of the nation. Its scale is both smaller and larger: operating subnationally on the one hand, as a grass-roots phenomenon, and transnationally on the other hand, as a cross-border phenomenon, and, in this way, bringing into relief a practice of democracy significantly different from the nation-bound variety, at once dispersed and energized by a multicentric network.

Cross-Stitching Time

What the *New Orleans Times-Picayune* does, specifically, is to send its own staff writer, John McQuaid, to a different country — the Netherlands — in order to broaden the evidentiary base, gathering information wherever relevant, tracing a series of zigzags between two continents, two analytic poles. These zigzags generate a cross-stitching of time, necessary because the United States is not the only country having to deal with storms and the flooding that comes with those storms. The Netherlands, throughout its history, has been facing this problem, and its collective decisions shed light on the United States for just that reason. What we eventually see, in the robustness and thoroughness of the Dutch response, is an alternative timeline, a trajectory of action at once local and national, an instance of democratic politics that would have been helpful if it had indeed "flooded" the United States, if its crosscurrents had indeed permeated these shores.

"The North Sea's furious winters can kick up storm surges more than 13 feet high — a lethal threat to a country where millions live below sea level, some as much as 22 feet down," John McQuaid notes.[13] On 1 February 1953, the Netherlands was hit by a North Sea storm that lasted 33 hours. The storm surge — water pushed to the shore by the winds — was 150 inches higher than the normal sea level. The dikes collapsed in more than 450 places. Over 1,800 people died; some 4,000 buildings were swept away or badly damaged.[14] Out of a population of around 12 million, 100,000 had to evacuate. Twice as many people were killed by the flood as by the German bombing of Rotterdam in 1940.

The scale of the destruction is very much comparable to New Orleans, and the preceding circumstances are also quite similar. Simon Rozendaal, a Dutch journalist writing in the *Wall Street Journal*, comments expressly on this: "As in the American Gulf states, the Dutch levee system had been neglected. It was not long after World War II: the Netherlands had just lost its colony, Indonesia; and the Cold War diverted money and attention."[15] Local disasters are, in this sense, the almost predictable side effects of global geopolitics. They are part of a larger distributive pattern — a pattern of unequal protection that Ulrich Beck calls the global "risk society" — with the risk falling on the least privileged, and being maximized at just those points where the resources have been most depleted.[16] This was true of the Netherlands; it was true of New Orleans. In both cases, the military budget was funded at the expense of domestic infrastructures, paving the way for their eventual breakdown. The Lake Pontchartrain and Vicinity Hurricane Protection project, a public works project aimed at building up levees and protecting pumping stations on the east bank of the Mississippi in Orleans, St. Bernard, St. Charles, and Jefferson parishes, received less than 20 percent of the funding requested by the Army Corps of Engineers. This was not a secret; it was already public knowledge back in 2004. The *Philadelphia Inquirer* had run a story about this, reporting that it "appears that the money has been moved in the president's budget to handle homeland security and the war in Iraq."[17]

The *Philadelphia Inquirer* and the *New Orleans Times-Picayune* are helpless witnesses — to an unequal distribution of risk that is the norm rather than the exception. In the unfolding catastrophe, they have the status of a tragic chorus. They come bearing knowledge, and they go nowhere. They, along with various science magazines, have been writing reports for years — useless reports — about various warning signs: the erosion of the wetlands, the subsidence of the soil, and the presence of dangerous chemicals as well as dangerous artificial waterways such as the MRGO (the Mississippi River Gulf Outlet), which greatly increase the power of the storm surge. These warnings had absolutely no effect on government policies: this was true not only in the United States but also in the Netherlands. Six months before the 1953 disaster, the Dutch engineer Johan van Veen had calculated that the storm surge could rise up to thirteen feet relative to the sinking coast. The Dutch meteorological service made the same prediction, but only three of the one thousand water boards, which managed the dikes, had a subscription to this service.[18] In the case of New Orleans, the warnings had come from FEMA's own modeling of a hypothetical Hurricane Pam in 2004, and from dire forecasts appearing in *Scientific American*, *National Geographic*, *Popular Mechanics*, the *Times-Picayune*, the *Houston Chronicle*, and the *New York Times,* as well as on the Public Broadcasting Service science program, *Nova*.[19] But all this information came to nothing. It was not able to percolate to a higher level, not able to lead to the dismantling of the MRGO, for instance, or to secure proper funding for these domestic projects. And it most certainly was not able to reverse the unequal protection endemic in this country. Parallel to the physical levees that are in disrepair, there seems to be an invisible system of levees that work all too well: shutting out all local input, turning public policy into a closed-door affair, a strictly bureaucratic decision.

Dutch Delta Works

So far, then, a cross-stitching of time seems to show only the same pattern: a common hazard, and a common failure of the democratic process itself, a kind of blockage between available information and government action. But here the symmetry ends. Flood protection in the Netherlands after 1953 diverges sharply from the United States, suggesting also that the Dutch democracy is now structurally very different from its American counterpart. It is this alternative thread of time that the *New Orleans Times-Picayune* tries to highlight by sending its staff reporter there.

Before 1953, the Dutch had tried to protect their settlements by canals lined with dikes, essentially the same as the levee system in south Louisiana. The 1953 flood revealed a major flaw in that strategy, a flaw that would now prove fatal for New Orleans. Levee-lined canals, it turns out, are fundamentally unsafe: during severe storms, they would themselves become deadly passageways, allowing the churning ocean to penetrate far inland. After Katrina, a team of Dutch engineers went to New Orleans to study the failed system, and they repeated their previous reservations about the overreliance on levees. The Dutch engineer Jurgen Battjes points out, "The region's levee-lined canals were conduits for Katrina's storm surge to pour into the heart of the city. From the east, water flowed into the Intercoastal Waterway and Industrial Canal, where floodwalls were topped and then collapsed, flooding the Lower Ninth Ward, St. Bernard Parish and eastern New Orleans. From Lake Pontchartrain, it flowed into the 17th Street and London Avenue drainage canals, which were breached, flooding central New Orleans."[20]

The Dutch Delta Works (Deltawerken), begun shortly after 1953, adopted a different strategy. Rather than building higher and stronger dikes along the canals, as they had always done, the Dutch opted instead to construct giant barriers across all ocean inlets, sealing off the estuaries and turning them into giant freshwater lakes. The first (in the Hollandse IJssel) went into operation in 1958. This was followed by the damming of the Veerse Gat and the Zandkreek in 1961 and the Haringvliet and the Brouwershavensche Gat in 1971 and 1972. These closures blocked off the invading ocean, but they also destroyed the unique ecosystem of the estuaries, a unique mix of fresh water and sea water and the breeding ground for many species of North Sea fish.

Environmentalists as well as mussel and oyster fishermen fiercely opposed the plan for just that reason.[21]

From the 1970s on, then, the philosophy behind the Delta Works would undergo yet another shift, this time taking into account a twofold understanding of "protection," equalizing it across the entire habitat, and respecting the input from local communities. The goal was not only to protect southwestern Holland against the storm surge of the North Sea but also to protect the existing ecosystem of the river estuaries. The enormous Oosterscheldt Barrier was the result. One of the most spectacular feats of hydraulic engineering in the world, this barrier is 5.6 miles long, with sixty-two movable flood gates, each the size of a twelve-story apartment building. This was followed by the equally immense Maeslant Barrier, which opened in 1997. These massive but also flexible gates, kept closed only during severe storms, are the outcomes of active intervention by the Dutch citizenry. They are designed to give the Netherlands a macropolicy that reflects local input, a level of protection adequate to a flood that would come once every ten thousand years.[22]

The technology is certainly impressive, but even more so is the broad-based democratic process that puts it to work. Flood protection in the Netherlands — as government policy and as community effort — is accompanied by public debate every step of the way. It was this local input that led to the change in direction in the 1970s. And it was this local input, multiplied manifold, that made it possible for this small nation to commit itself to these vast expenditures and to plan ahead in terms of a statistical time frame of ten thousand years. More recently, in preparation for the sea-level rise that is a foreseeable though not-yet-realized consequence of global warming, the Netherlands has planned still further ahead, implementing a new policy called "Make Room for the River," moving populations away from some areas that, in the future, will most certainly be flooded.[23] Democracy, in the Dutch context, means at least three things: public information available to everyone; local input having a direct impact on policy decisions; and a political will to limit vulnerability across the board, extending protection to populations both human and not human, both currently voting and not yet born.

Against the meticulous details as well as the long-term planning of that democratic culture, what happens in the United States must be called something else. To begin with, the New Orleans levees were designed to protect only against a storm that would come once every fifty years — in other words, only against a Category 3 hurricane. And even this modest level of protection was not always maintained, as Ivor van Heerden, deputy director of the Louisiana State University Hurricane Center, points out.[24] In its self-study released on 1 June 2006, the Army Corps of Engineers admits to this, accepting blame not only for the flawed design and construction of the levees but also for its underestimation of hurricane strength based on outdated standards.[25] This is a problem it has known for some time. "It's possible to protect New Orleans from a Category 5 hurricane," Al Naomi, senior project manager for the corps, told the *Philadelphia Inquirer* on 8 October 2004. "But we've got to start. To do nothing is tantamount to negligence." The corps submitted a proposal that year to Congress requesting $4 million to fund a preliminary study. Congress tabled the proposal, never bringing it on the floor, citing budgetary constraints resulting from the Iraq War.[26]

Unlike the robust input from Dutch communities, decisions in the United States were made — or not made — behind closed doors, by a legislative body acting only out of fiscal concerns, without ever opening up its reasoning to public scrutiny. Still, even if that public scrutiny had taken place, it is not clear that the Dutch time scale of the "10,000-year flood" would have been adopted. Long-term planning has never had much of a place on the federal, state, or municipal agenda: ten thousand years seem almost unimaginable. As the *Washington Post* reports, "In 1982, the Orleans Levee District urged the Corps to 'lower its design standards to provide more realistic hurricane protection.' The levee district, stocked with political appointees, could spend freely on private investigators, riverboat gambling, and a $2.4 million Mardi Gras foundation. But it said it could not afford its share of protection from a 200-year storm, suggesting that 100-year protection would be fine."[27] This strange sense of proportions might turn out to be one of the most destructive effects of the time scale of a young nation, one that allows neither a long past nor a long future to interfere with the short but oversized centrality of the present. What does it mean never to think of time except in single and double digits? And how might these single and double digits affect a nation's ability to deal with events such as hurricanes, whose potential for harm outstrips those digits by many orders of magnitude? A nonsovereign history of Katrina shows that, beyond the broken levees, what needs to be mended is the democratic process itself and its need for a reference frame beyond the geography and chronology of the nation. The example of the Netherlands is *not* extraneous to the United States for just that reason. Indeed, it is by not externalizing this body of evidence — not blocking it out, not seeing it as foreign or exotic — that we can begin to circumvent the short timeline of the United States, embracing a democratic practice not necessarily nation-centered, but taking its circumference from the world.

The World's Water

That circumference, in turn, radically changes the way we think about causality: the web that articulates it, the claims that can be pressed, and the responses needed as a result. The implications are far-reaching, because to draw a larger input circle around the nation is also to draw a larger circle of accountability, to give a broad interpretation to the harm that it might have perpetrated at a distance, harm that might seem extraneous from one point of view. How, for instance, can we make a nation face up to the death and destruction that it is causing hundreds and thousands of civilians, thousands of miles away, on a different continent? Justice looks very different when it is framed in this way, seen as extended rather than encapsulated. Rather than being a problem of crime and punishment contained within a single nation, it becomes another instance of the flooded container: flooded, in this case, by the causal web that links it, against the illusion of sovereignty, to crosscurrents affecting the entire planet, a seascape turbulent and borderless.

World history and world literature have much to contribute to this enlarged sense of justice, for crucial to these fields are just such crosscurrents, a permeable continuum with multiple sources, multiple centers, oceanic rather than territorial. Hurricanes are very much part of this seascape: they are indexes to the hydrology of the world as a whole. Generated by air-sea interaction, this hydrology can be adequately studied only through "multi-basin indices," which is to say, by comparing data from the North Pacific, Indian, Southwest Pacific, and North Atlantic Oceans. Not only are hurricanes waterborne disasters; they are disasters unique to warm water: as long as the sea surface temperature remains below 26.5 degrees Celsius (80 degrees Fahrenheit), no hurricane will form. When oceans get heated up, they fuel a convection process that transforms cold-core tropical depressions into hot-core cyclones. Katrina itself strengthened to a Category 5 hurricane when it was passing over the Gulf of Mexico, where the surface waters were unusually warm, about 2 degrees Fahrenheit warmer than normal for that time of year.[28]

Sea surface temperature is the single-most important factor in hurricane formation. By looking at these data, MIT climatologist Kerry Emanuel was able to predict what was to come. On 31 July 2005, one month before Katrina, Emanuel published his research in the online edition of the journal *Nature*. Tracking hurricanes by their "power dissipation index" (a combination of the lifetime of storms and their intensity), Emanuel shows that "this index has increased markedly since the mid-1970s," an upward trend strongly correlated with the rise in the sea surface temperature. Both the duration of hurricanes and their wind speeds have "doubled in the past 30 years" as the Pacific and the Atlantic have warmed by 1 degree Fahrenheit between 1970 and 2004. Because changing ocean temperatures are themselves indices to climate change, Emanuel sees the increasingly destructive hurricanes as "at least partly anthropogenic." He predicts "a substantial increase in hurricane-related losses in the 21st century."[29]

Emanuel's study was corroborated almost immediately in a parallel study by a team from the Georgia Institute of Technology, reported in *Science* on 16 September 2005. By looking at "the number of tropical cyclones and cyclone days as well as tropical cyclone intensity over the past 35 years, in an environment of increasing sea surface temperature," this study finds that "hurricanes in the strongest categories (4 + 5) have almost doubled in number. . . . These changes occur in all of the ocean basins." How to explain this across-the-board jump? J. B. Webster, speaking for the Georgia Tech team, is even less ambiguous in seeing a strong correlation between the rising ocean temperatures and the rising concentrations of atmospheric carbon dioxide — chief of the greenhouse gases — though they concede that "attribution of 30-year trends to global warming would require a longer global data record and, especially, a deeper understanding of the role of hurricanes in the general circulation of the atmosphere and ocean."[30]

Whether or not hurricanes can be directly traced to global warming,[31] what seems clear is that the database needs to be planetary in scope, studying all the oceans in conjunction. When studied in conjunction, they point to a changing world, becoming daily less hospitable, looking less and less like the planet that has supported our species and other species. We take it so much for granted that we never notice that its features have grown ominous. Of the weapons of mass destruction already lined up, the most deadly will probably come not in the form of hurricanes, but as a hydrology simpler, less of a spectacle, though infinitely more catastrophic: namely, the rising sea levels due to the melting of the Arctic and Antarctic ice sheets.

In its 2001 Report, the UN's Intergovernmental Panel on Climate Change (IPCC) predicted that sea-level rise in the twenty-first century will proceed "at an average rate of 2.2 to 4.4 times the rate over the 20th century," while singling out the West Antarctic ice sheet as especially worrisome, because it "contains enough ice to raise sea level by 6 meters."[32] Meanwhile, seismic stations revealed a significant increase in "icequakes," caused by ice sheets breaking loose and lurching forward; the annual number of these icequakes registering 4.6 or greater on the Richter scale doubled from seven to fourteen in the late 1990s; it doubled again by 2005.[33] Satellite measurements of the earth's gravitational field showed a loss of fifty cubic miles of ice in Greenland in 2005, matched by a similar loss in West Antarctica.[34] The new IPCC report, issued in February 2007, stuck to a more conservative figure for the sea-level rise (7.8 inches to 2 feet by the century's end), but the human cost is staggering even at this rate.[35] The World Bank estimates, for instance, that even a three-foot rise in sea level would turn at least sixty million people into refugees.[36]

What would the United States look like? The fate of New Orleans would have been sealed long before then, as would the fate of many other coastal cities. Al Gore, in *An Inconvenient Truth*, gives us a computer projection of what would be left of Florida if the sea level were to increase by eighteen to twenty feet; it is a horrendous image. The century ahead will most certainly be dominated by this advancing seascape as the earth continues to heat up. Sovereign borders will be so diluted — literally — that they will be small comfort for U.S. citizens; even the world's largest military budget will not yield a credible line of defense. Yet the irony is that, while the nation can provide no long-term protection, it is quite capable of action that has the potential for long-term harm. The balance between human history and nonhuman processes, always problematic, is now weighted more and more in the latter's direction, with a growing gap between the kind of habitat the human species has depended on and the kind of habitat the planet is becoming. The United States is ill prepared for this development, though there are signs now that the tide might be turning, that climate change might be reeducating all of us in the primacy of the planet over the sovereignty of any nation. At this critical moment, it is especially important for the humanities to rethink its space and time coordinates, to take up questions that might once seem far removed — coming not only from hitherto extraneous fields such as earth and planetary sciences but also from hitherto extraneous populations, not traditionally included in the discipline.

WAI CHEE DIMOCK

Arctic Timeline

One such population is the Inuit living in the Arctic Circle. It is here that global warming is felt most directly and most severely, because the threshold for catastrophic change is much lower at the two poles: the difference of one or two degrees can have drastic consequences for the glaciers and the ice sheets. When it comes to climate change, the Arctic is ahead of the rest of the world: it has a timeline of its own. In December 1995 the IPCC issued a landmark report noting this uneven development. This was reaffirmed in 2004 by the eight-nation Arctic Climate Impact Assessment, which concluded that the Arctic is experiencing "some of the most rapid and severe climate change on earth."[37] In *An Inconvenient Truth*, this is dramatized as the plight of the polar bear; and what makes the world unlivable for the polar bear also makes it unrecognizable for the Inuit. They have a word for it, *uggianaqtuq*, referring to the weather, a "familiar friend now behaving strangely."[38] In November 2000 the Inuit released a forty-five-minute video to document this fatal alienation. Entitled *Sila Alangotok: Inuit Observations on Climate Change*, it offers an extensive record of melting ice, eroding coastlines, and the appearance of wildlife never seen before, including the Pacific salmon and the robin.[39] It is this unrecognizability of the world, the unrecognizability of their habitat, that makes it necessary for the Inuit Circumpolar Conference (a federation made up 150,000 native peoples in Canada, Greenland, and Russia, as well as the United States) to seek legal action against the world's foremost emitter of greenhouse gases.

This is not easy to do. Currently, the infrastructure for transnational legal action is still very sketchy. Just as we do not have the legal instrumentalities to prosecute nations for the long-distance military harm they incur, we also do not have the legal instrumentalities to prosecute nations for the long-distance environmental harm they perpetrate. We do, of course, have courts that operate on a transnational level. There are four of these at the moment: the International Court of Justice at the Hague; the International Criminal Court, also at the Hague; the Court of Justice of the European Communities at Luxembourg; and the European Court of Human Rights at Strasbourg. The first of these, the International Court of Justice, created in 1945, will hear only cases brought before it by nation-states.[40] The other three courts do, in fact, hear cases brought by nonstate actors,[41] but the grievance of the Inuit does not rise to the level of the International Criminal Court, and, not being a member of the European Union, its case also cannot be heard in the two European courts. However, with the help of environmental groups such as Earth Justice and the Center for International Environmental Law, the Inuit were able to file a petition against the Bush administration with the Inter-American Commission on Human Rights on 7 December 2005, "seeking relief from violations resulting from global warming caused by acts and omissions of the United States."[42]

Almost all the deteriorating conditions of the Arctic can be traced to climate change, not only changes in the "quality, quantity and timing of snowfall" but also the destruction of coastal communities through the increasingly erratic behavior of water in all its forms:

> Permafrost, which holds together unstable underground gravel and inhibits water drainage, is melting at an alarming rate, causing slumping, landslides, severe erosion and loss of ground moisture, wetlands and lakes. The loss of sea ice, which dampens the impact of storm on coastal areas, has resulted in increasingly violent storms hitting the coastline, exacerbating erosion and flooding. Erosion in turn exposes coastal permafrost to warmer air and water, resulting in faster permafrost melts. These transformations have had a devastating impact on some coastal communities, particularly in Alaska and the Canadian Beaufort Sea Region....
>
> Other factors have also affected water levels. Changes in precipitation and temperature have led to sudden spring thaws that release large amounts of water, flooding rivers and eroding their streambeds. Yet, after spring floods, rivers and lakes are left with unusually low levels of water, further diminished by increased evaporation during the longer summer. These changes affect the availability and quality of natural drinking water sources. The fish stocks upon which Inuit rely are profoundly affected by changing water levels. Fish sometimes cannot reach their spawning grounds, their eggs are exposed or washed ashore, or northward moving species compete with the native stocks for ecological niches.[43]

Violent storms, floods, soil erosion, loss of wetlands — these are problems we associate with New Orleans and the Gulf of Mexico. It should not come as too much of a surprise, though, to see them also played out, thousands of miles away, in the Arctic Ocean, because there is no dividing line separating these two bodies of water. This single, crisscrossing, and already-damaged hydrology makes it clear that climate, geology, and human and nonhuman life are all complexly intertwined, part of the same fluid continuum. The catastrophe, already writ large in this seemingly remote part of the world, is closer to us than we think. Sheila Watt-Cloutier, chair of the Inuit Circumpolar Conference, received the UN Lifetime Achievement Award for Human Development[44] and, along with Al Gore, was nominated for the 2007 Nobel Peace Prize.[45] The Inter-American Commission on Human Rights began its hearings on climate change in March 2007.[46] While the commission has no power of enforcement, a finding in favor of the Inuit could be the basis for future lawsuits in U.S. federal courts. World history here takes on its exemplary form, calling our attention to the tangled fate of the planet and urging us toward an enlarged sense of democracy, an enlarged sense of justice. This enlargement can begin only with local knowledge, with micro-evidence and bottom-up chronologies. If these space and time coordinates look unfamiliar, perhaps the study of the United States needs to become unfamiliar to itself in just this way.

NOTES

An earlier version of this essay appeared in *differences* 19, no. 2 (2008): 35–53. This essay benefited enormously from discussions at the "States of Emergency" conference and from careful readings by Russ Castronovo, Susan Gillman, Rob Nixon, and Lloyd Pratt — exemplary colleagues.

1. For two efforts in this direction, one general and one specific, see John McNeill and William McNeill, *The Human Web: A Bird's-Eye View of World History* (New York: Norton, 2003), and Linda Colley, *The Ordeal of Elizabeth Marsh: A Woman in World History* (New York: Pantheon, 2007).

2. Michael Ignatieff, "The Broken Contract," *New York Times Magazine*, 25 September 2005, ⟨http://nytimes.com/2005/09/25/magazine/25wwln.html?scp=1&sq=&st=nyt⟩.

3. Ibid.

4. Ibid.

5. James J. Sheehan, "Presidential Address: The Problem of Sovereignty in European History" (speech at the annual meeting of the American Historical Association, Philadelphia, 3 January 2006), reprinted in *American Historical Review* 111 (February 2006): 1–15, quotation from 1–2. For other well-known critiques of the nation-state, see Ernest Gellner, *Nations and Nationalism* (Oxford: Oxford University Press, 1983); Eric Hobsbawn, *Nations and Nationalism since 1780* (Cambridge: Cambridge University Press, 1990); Ernest Renan, "What Is a Nation?" in *Nation and Narration*, ed. Homi K. Bhabha (New York: Routledge, 1990), 8–22.

6. Thomas Bender, preface to *Rethinking American History in a Global Age* (Berkeley: University of California Press, 2002), vii.

7. Prasenjit Duara, *Rescuing History from the Nation: Questioning Narratives of Modern China* (Chicago: University of Chicago Press, 1995).

8. For an important critique of the nation form, see Etienne Balibar, "Racism and Nationalism," and "The Nation Form: History and Ideology," both in Etienne Balibar and Immanuel Wallerstein, *Race, Nation, Class: Ambiguous Identities* (London: Verso, 1991), 37–68, 86–106.

9. Prasenjit Duara, "Transnationalism and the Challenge to National Histories," in Bender, *Rethinking American History*, 25–46, quotation from 25.

10. Anthony Giddens, *The Nation-State and Violence* (Berkeley: University of California Press, 1987), 281.

11. For a sustained argument linking sovereignty to the conditions of knowledge, see Jens Bartelson, *A Genealogy of Sovereignty* (Cambridge: Cambridge University Press, 1995).

12. Janice Radway, "What's in a Name? Presidential Address to the American Studies Association," 20 November 1998, *American Quarterly* 51 (March 1999): 1–32, quotation from 15.

13. John McQuaid, "Beating back the Sea: How the Dutch Fight to Save Their Low-Lying Land," *Times-Picayune*, 13 November 2005. Available online at the Pulitzer website, ⟨http://www.pulitzer.org/year/2006/public-service/works/neworleansps12.html⟩.

14. Molly Moore, "Rethinking Defenses against Sea's Power," *Washington Post*, 8 September 2005, A22, ⟨http://www.washingtonpost.com/wp-dyn/content/article/2005/09/07/AR2005090724OO.html⟩.

15. Simon Rozendaal, "Katrina, Juliana, and Wilhelmina," *Wall Street Journal*, 7 September 2005, A16. Rozendaal is science writer for the Dutch news-magazine, *Elsevier*.

16. Ulrich Beck, *Risk Society: Toward a New Modernity* (London: Sage Publications, 1992). See also Richard D. Bullard, ed., *Unequal Protection: Environmental Justice and Communities of Color* (San Francisco: Sierra Club Books, 1994); Jeanne X. Kasperson and Roger Kasperson, eds., *Global Environmental Risk* (Tokyo: United Nations University Press, 2001); Susan L. Cutter, *Hazards, Vulnerability, and Environmental Justice* (London: Earthscan, 2006).

17. Michael Eric Dyson, *Come Hell or High Water: Hurricane Katrina and the Color of Disaster* (New York: Basic Civitas, 2006), 81.

18. Rozendaal, "Katrina, Juliana, and Wilhelmina."

19. Dyson, *Come Hell or High Water*, 77–86.

20. McQuaid, "Beating Back the Sea."

21. "The Dutch Struggle against the Waters," information supplied by the Dutch Ministerie van Buitelandse Zaken. Available online at ⟨http://www.hollandring.com⟩.

22. Ibid. See also, "How the Netherlands Prepared for a 10,000-Year Disastrous Flood," ⟨http://www.larouchepub.com/eiw/public/2005/2005_30-39.pdf/43-47_38_ecodutch.pdf⟩.

23. Joel Palca, "In a Strategic Reversal, Dutch Embrace Floods," NPR *Morning Edition*, 22 January 2008.

24. According to van Heerden, the levees could actually offer protection only against a Category 2 storm, with wind speeds of up to 110 miles an hour. See "Levees Rebuilt Just in Time, but Doubts Remain," *New York Times*, 25 May 2006, ⟨http://www.nytimes.com/2006/us/25/usflood/html⟩. See also Ivor van Heerden, *The Storm: What Went Wrong*

during Hurricane Katrina; Inside Story from a Louisiana Scientist (New York: Viking, 2006).

25. John Schwartz, "Army Builders Accept Blame over Flooding," *New York Times*, 2 June 2006, ⟨http://www.nytimes.com/2006/06/02/us/nationalspecial/02corps.html⟩.

26. Paul Nussbaum, "New Orleans' Growing Danger," *Philadelphia Inquirer*, 4 October 2004, ⟨http://hurricane.lus.edu/in_the_news/phillyinquirer100804.htm⟩.

27. "The Slow Drowning of New Orleans," *Washington Post*, 9 October 2005, A01, ⟨http://www.washingtonpost.com/wp-dyn/content/article/2005/10/08/AR2005100801458⟩.

28. "Was Katrina's Power a Product of Global Warming?," ⟨http://pewclimate.org⟩. Katrina weakened to category 4 shortly before landfall in Louisiana and Mississippi.

29. Kerry Emanuel, "Increasing Destructiveness of Tropical Cyclones over the Past 30 Years," *Nature* advance online publication, 31 July 2005, ⟨http://www.nature.com/nature/journal/vaop/ncurrent/full/nature03906.html⟩.

30. P. J. Webster et al., "Changes in Tropical Cyclone Number, Duration, and Intensity in a Warming Environment," *Science*, 16 September 2005, ⟨http://www.sciencemag.org/cgi/content/full/309/5742/1844⟩.

31. Scientists who disagree with Emanuel and Webster think that the more destructive hurricanes are caused, not by global warming, but by a natural cycle called "multi-decadal oscillations." For a summary and documentation of the debate, see the "Global Warming and Hurricanes" website of the Geophysical Fluid Dynamics Laboratory, at the National Oceanic and Atmospheric Administration, ⟨http://www.gfdl.noaa.gov/tk/glob_warm_hurr.html⟩.

32. J. H. Houghton et al., eds., *Climate Change 2001: The Scientific Basis; Contribution of Working Group to the Third Assessment Report of the Intergovernmental Panel on Climate Change* (New York: Cambridge University Press, 2001), 642.

33. Jim Hansen, "The Threat to the Planet," *New York Review of Books*, 13 July 2006, 12–16, quotation from 13.

34. Ibid., 13.

35. *Climate Change 2007: The Physical Science Basis; Summary for Policy Makers. Contribution of Working Group I to the Fourth Assessment Report of the Intergovernmental Panel on Climate Change*, ⟨http://www.usgcrp.gov/usgcrp/links/ipcc.htm#4wg1⟩. For a good summary of the report, see Bill McKibben, "Warning on Warming," *New York Review of Books*, 15 March 2007, 44–45.

36. Juliet Eilperin, "Clues to Rising Seas Are Hidden in Polar Ice," *Washington Post*, 16 July 2007.

37. *Arctic Climate Assessment Report* (Cambridge: Cambridge University Press, 2004), abstract.

38. "The Inuit, First Witnesses of Climate Change," a UNESCO report, ⟨http://portal.unesco.org⟩.

39. A BBC report gives a good account of the video. See "Climate Change in the Canadian Arctic," ⟨http://bbc.co.uk/worldservice/sci_tech/highlights/010510_canadianarctic.shtml⟩. See also "Responding to the Global Climate Change: The Perspective of the Inuit Circumpolar Conference on the Arctic Climate Impact Assessment," ⟨http://inuitcircumpolar.com/index.php?ID=267&Lang=En⟩.

40. The International Court of Justice (ICJ) was created in 1945 under the Charter of the United Nations. See ⟨http://www.icj-cij.org/icjwww/generalinformation/ibbook/Bbookframepage.htm⟩.

41. The Court of Justice of the European Communities, the legal institution of the European Union, whose charge is to enforce "community law . . . separate from, yet superior to national law," was initially created under the Treaties of Paris and Rome in 1952. See ⟨http://europa.en.int/institutions/court/index_en.htm⟩. The European Court of Human Rights (ECHR), the judicial arm of the Council of Europe, started out as the Convention for the Protection of Human Rights and Fundamental Freedoms (1950), and became consolidated as a single, full-time court on 1 November 1998. The International Criminal Court (ICC) was established on 17 July 1998 when 120 states adopted the Statute of Rome. The statute provides for its entry into force sixty days after sixty states have ratified it, which happened on 11 April 2002. Accordingly, the ICC went into effect on 1 July 2002.

42. ⟨http://www.inuitcircumpolar.com/index.php?ID=316&Lang=En⟩.

43. Ibid., 2–3.

44. ⟨http://www.msnbc.com/id/16920923⟩.

45. See, for instance, ⟨http://www.cbc.cn/north.story/2007/04/27/north-award.html⟩.

46. ⟨http://www.earthjustice.org/news/press/007/inter-american-commission-on-human-rights-Hearing-on-global-warming.html⟩.

American Studies in an Age of Extinction

ROBERT S. LEVINE

With the help of Edgar Allan Poe and Nathaniel Hawthorne, this essay asks how we might think about the critical work of American studies in an age of extinction. Concerns that life on the planet may be coming to an end are pervasive, and arguably they define our present moment. Anxieties about nuclear annihilation were everywhere in the 1950s and 1960s, and those anxieties remain with us today. But at the turn into the twenty-first century there are added fears about global warming, apocalyptic terrorist plots, mutating killer viruses, and sundry other dark scenarios (such as computers one day turning against their creators, genetic engineering leading to unforeseen disasters, and so on). There are also heightened concerns in Protestant evangelical culture about the imminence of the end. Hal Lindsey's *The Late, Great Planet Earth* (1970), the best-selling book of the 1970s, discerned in the unfolding events of the Middle East and elsewhere signs of the approach of the Antichrist, and such fears (or, actually, desires to be present during the Last Days) now inform the phenomenally popular series of Left Behind books and movies.[1] But it is human-induced climate change that has generated the greatest concerns about the possibility that the planet will soon be unable to support life. The World Conservation Union's 2007 report lists 16,306 species on the verge of extinction, up from the 16,118 species listed in its 2006 report. Several months after the release of that report, the United Nations' Intergovernmental Panel on Climate Change warned that carbon emissions growth must end by the year 2015 in order to avoid "widespread extinction of species, a slowing of the global currents, decreased food production, loss of 30 percent of global wetlands, flooding for millions of people and higher deaths from heat waves." The UN report, which imagines only sporadic efforts to control emissions, implies that such devastation may be a best-case scenario. Indeed, in March 2008, in the journal *Geophysical Research Letters*, scientists from the United States, Canada, Germany, and several other countries warned that without a relatively quick reduction of carbon output to near zero, the world will soon be without water.[2] And that, truly, would be the end.

Visions of the end have had a long tradition in American culture and in important respects have informed American studies scholarship. In *Redeemer Nation* (1968), a classic work in the field, Ernest Tuveson discusses two distinct modes of end-of-the-world thinking in the United States: millennialist and millenarian. The dominant mode is millennialist, or postmillennialist, a belief that history, and specifically the U.S. nation, is working steadily to produce the triumph of Christian principles, culminating in a thousand-year reign of Christ with his saints. Such a reign would, in effect, lead to the end of the world as we know it by bringing forth heaven on earth, from sea to shining sea. Whereas the postmillennialist regards the United States as the "redeemer nation," the millenarian, or premillennialist, has virtually no use for the nation and rejects the progressive historical vision of a steady march to a thousand-year reign. For the millenarian, the end will come through apocalyptic destruction orchestrated by Christ (figured as a Jehovah avenger), who would subsequently take the saints to a better world elsewhere.[3]

The millenarian generally thinks outside of time and nation; the millennialist is firmly located within time and nation. At the risk of some critical reductionism, we could say that American studies scholarship as traditionally practiced is postmillennialist. Whether we're talking about the field-defining scholarship of Leo Marx or the revisionary scholarship of Paul Lauter, American studies has generally been concerned with examining the nation over time, with the redemptive aspiration of helping to bring about the "millennial" triumph of such valued principles as democratic equality and justice for all within the United States. But for a competing, more recent school of American studies scholarship, represented, for example, by the "New Americanists" in Donald E. Pease and Robyn Wiegman's *The Futures of American Studies* (2002), there is much skepticism about the value of the nation-state as a critical frame and a rejection of traditional chronological or progressive notions of history. Practicing what I would term a critical millenarianism, these revisionary critics seek to liberate the field from the constraints of time and nation through temporal displacements and reorientations that, as Pease and Wiegman put it, "construct multiple pasts and imagine disparate futures out of . . . nonsynchronous historical materials."[4] An important influence on the new critical millenarianism is Walter Benjamin, whose "Theses on the Philosophy of History" (1940) envisioned the emergence of a liberatory "Messianic time," not as the culmination of an orderly progressive movement but rather as a revolutionary irruption, a "Judgment Day," that would reconfigure conceptions of time and space through a "cessation of happening."[5] Pease and Wiegman echo such messianism when they write of the "utopian possibilities" inhering in "alternative futures," proclaiming that future-oriented projects forged in temporal realignments "would release the field's most creative aspects." What they and the contributors to their volume fail to confront is the possibility that one of those futures might be extinction.

This essay addresses the critical challenge of contemplating the "cessation of happening." But rather than imagining the post–Judgment Day or postrevolutionary introduction of what Benjamin calls "a new calendar,"[6] I consider the end of calendars — the end of humankind — by focusing on the mid-nineteenth century, when end-of-the-world thinking permeated U.S. popular culture, including works by Poe and Hawthorne. As Pease and Wiegman might have predicted, these writers in fact did experience a release of creative energy when contemplating the future, however dire their visions of that future might have been. In this respect, their contemplations have renewed relevance for assessing the place of critical thought, and specifically the work of American studies, in our own age of extinction. Before turning to Poe, Hawthorne, and their contemporaries, however, a few additional remarks on end-of-the-world thinking in our own time are in order.

To some extent, such thinking has become a form of entertainment that avoids questions of critical consciousness. Recent movies such as *Judgment Day* (1999), *I Am Legend* (2007), and *WALL-E* (2008) make apocalypse into a divertingly fun hundred minutes or so. Entertainment is also crucial to Alan Weisman's international best seller, *The World without Us* (2007), which announces at the outset that "human extinction is a fait accompli," and then takes the reader on a jaunty science-based tour of a world without humans. As Weisman makes clear, the immediate consequence of man's disappearance is that nature will make a comeback: "On the day after humans disappear, nature takes over and immediately begins cleaning house — or houses, that is. Cleans them right off the face of the Earth. They all go." Because Weisman is interested in tracing the impact that nature would have on human products over time (and vice versa), he avoids the question of what sort of critical or artistic work one might do at a moment in history when we are contemplating the end (beyond writing or reading a best seller on the subject). He does implicitly suggest through the global reach of his study that we might rethink the primacy of the nation, given that human planetary damage crosses national boundaries. In this respect, he makes an argument relevant to American studies scholarship about the importance of transnational thinking at a time of environmental crisis, but that is about as far as he goes in addressing questions of critical consciousness. The millenarianism that informs his study is intended to instruct and entertain, which is perhaps why his book has found such a wide readership and inspired a number of popular film "documentaries" on the same subject. It is worth mentioning, however, that as part of his tour of the post-human world he points out that, contrary to popular belief, paper can do just as well as plastic in surviving the ravages of time. As one of his experts reports, "That's why we have 3,000-year-old papyrus scrolls from Egypt. We pull perfectly readable newspapers out of landfills from the 1930s. They'll be down there for 10,000 years."[7] Here Weisman at least offers the consolation to scholars in an age of extinction that whatever sort of critical work we manage to get into print will perhaps survive for millennia, even if there are no readers.

A considerably more thoughtful meditation on human extinction can be found in Jack Miles's "Global Requiem: The Apocalyptic Moment in Religion," an essay published in 2001, a time when, as Miles reports, "the rate of extinction [of species] is estimated at one every five minutes." Miles makes the logical leap from species extinction to human extinction, stating that "time after time extinction has followed on the loss of habitat when the species at risk was not able to adapt." The extinctions that take place approximately every five minutes wreak havoc on the human habitat, which leads Miles to accuse humankind of "species suicide." One of the main purposes of his essay is to prompt people to take action to save their world and themselves. But his darker suggestion is that inertia and human stupidity will ultimately reign, and that it is not too soon to begin contemplating the end. In his own contemplations, Miles insists on the importance of asking "what the consequences for religion and for the arts, especially literature, will be if and when we conclude that the effort to produce a sustainable society has definitely failed?" He suggests that a new religion and a new art could arise out of the consciousness of the end, but he's not sure what that new religion and art would look like and whether a revitalized religion and art would lead to any significant rethinking of the nation. Because the diminishment of resources may only exacerbate international conflict, thereby refueling nationalism, he concludes that the "prospects for a religion [or art, or critical consciousness] that would subordinate national interests to species survival cannot be called good."[8] In this formulation, American studies in an age of extinction may persist as American studies as we know it.

Then again, it may not; for it is one of the ironies of Miles's rather gloomy essay that Miles himself as a millenarian evinces a surprising optimism about the possibilities for enlarging rather than closing down how we might think about doing critical work. Published in a volume addressing the place of religion in U.S. cultural studies, Miles's essay ultimately turns against the fatalism that typically attends the contemplation of the end of humankind, suggesting how such contemplation can inspire and reinvigorate critical thinking. Despite the essay's publication in a volume focused on U.S. cultural studies, Miles also departs from both traditional and revisionary forms of American studies scholarship, which tend to engage national ideologies from a variety of perspectives. In his view, the most important end-of-the-world thinking will adopt new forms and perspectives existing apart from the nation and other forms of local attachment. But Miles leaves his reader on a precipice, for he is ultimately unable to imagine the shape that those new forms and perspectives would take, and exactly how they would break from such familiar categories as the nation. We are left with questions about religion, art, and nation in an age of extinction, which would seem to be his large point. The final days are when we begin to ask the questions that matter.

In order to address some of the end-of-the-world questions about art, religion, and nation that Miles raises (and, I am suggesting, are implicitly raised on a daily basis by the increasing sense that we may well be approaching the end), I want now to loop back to the American 1830s and 1840s, when a surprisingly large number of people believed that they were approaching the end. The historian Whitney R. Cross notes that "well over fifty thousand people in the United States became convinced that time would run out in 1844, while a million or more of their fellows were skeptically expectant."[9] To be more exact, thousands of people thought that human history would come to an end on 21 March 1843, then 21 March 1844, and finally 22 October 1844. Their spiritual leader was William Miller (1782–1849), a farmer from Low Hampton, New York, who claimed that Scripture presented irrefutable evidence that Christ planned to return to the world in order to destroy it. In his numerous sermons delivered to upwards of a half million people during the 1830s and early 1840s, Miller spoke of a final holocaust, a purging conflagration, which would rid the world of humans and all other forms of life. After the apocalypse, he said, the righteous would be resurrected into a new world, Christ's Kingdom, which may or may not have a material presence (Miller was never clear about that).[10] Many of those known as Millerites sold their property and gave up their jobs, waiting for the final day. When they awoke on 23 October 1844 to discover that the world remained intact, they were understandably confused. Some joined the Shakers; others worked to form the Seventh-Day Adventists; and others simply struggled along in the still temporal world, confused and disillusioned.

Miller was a product of what historians have dubbed the Second Great Awakening, the upsurge of evangelical fervor in the United States in the opening decades of the nineteenth century. The majority of the evangelicals and their followers shared a postmillennial optimism, seeing in the Book of Daniel, St. John's Book of Revelation, and other prophetic texts in the Old and New Testament unambiguous evidence that Christ would return to the world for a glorious spiritual reign with his saints. That reign, they believed, would be ushered in by the converts, who would help to bring about a thousand years of social and religious perfection, whereupon Christ would descend in all of his glory, wipe out the sinners, end the world as we know it, and reunite with his saints. U.S. postmillennialists thus had a progressive vision of history in which the saints recurrently defeated the forces of evil, bringing about an ever-greater spiritual perfection in the nation and throughout the world. This postmillennial vision may appear to be postnational as well, but in early national and antebellum U.S. culture, nationalism and millennialism often went hand in hand. Jan Stieverman observes that "the convergence of (post-)millennialism and nationalism . . . [was] one of the major organizing principles of an emerging collective identity in nineteenth-century America." By the 1840s the postmillennial religious vision of the Second Great Awakening had been thoroughly absorbed into nationalist ideologies, to the extent that the continental expansionism of Manifest Destiny itself was infused with beliefs that the United States was the New Israel ushering in the millennium.[11]

But not all U.S. millennialists of the pre–Civil War period were nationalistic postmillennialists. Miller was among a sizable group of millennially inclined Americans who rejected notions of temporal progress and spiritual redemption through human effort and also silently rejected U.S. nationalism. These premillennialists or millenarians were antiprogressives, convinced that humans could accomplish nothing meaningful in the world other than turning to God. For these premillennialists, there was no hope for social perfection; instead, they had a vision of human frailty and evil. Thus, instead of believing in the possibility of a thousand-year reign of the saints ushering in Christ, they saw a vengeful Christ simply descending one day to obliterate the world, eventually resurrecting those he chose to save in some sort of heavenly place. Miller and his tens of thousands of followers in the northeast region and elsewhere were convinced that that day was just about at hand.[12]

Miller elaborated his end-times views in his lectures, which he collected as a volume, *Evidence from Scripture and History of the Second Coming of Christ, about the Year 1843*, published in Troy, New York, in 1838, and republished in Boston in 1842. As a premillennialist, Miller focuses on Judgment Day. For Miller, death and destruction (the Last Days) are all that humankind has to look forward to: "I say I can find nothing in the word of God to warrant me to believe that we ought to look for or expect a happier period than we now enjoy, until he who has promised to come, shall come the second time without sin until salvation, and cleanse us, the world, and make all things new." As is clear from this passage, Miller's prognostications are based on his reading of the Bible ("the word of God"), especially the prophecies of Isaiah, Daniel, and John, which he regards as crucial evidence of the imminence of what he terms "the judgment of the great day." That Judgment, or "day of vengeance," will bring utter devastation, sparing only "the wise," which is to say the regenerate saints. Miller remains unclear about the location of the post-Judgment world, positing that the reign of the saints "will be on earth" or "in the air." What he is clear about is the timing, which he understands in terms of simple schemas of chronology. In one of many numerico-typological readings that he develops from his close attention to Scripture, Miller proclaims that biblical "days" have to be read metaphorically as "years," and he adduces as a starting point for his countdown a passage in Daniel 8 on the 2,300 days before God offers humans sanctuary. He asks the key question — "When did the 2300 years begin?" — and provides this answer: "Let us begin in where the angel told us, from the going forth of the decree to build the walls of Jerusalem in troublous times, 457 years before Christ; take 457 from 2300, and it will leave A.D. 1843." As even Miller himself seems to acknowledge, all of this may be a stretch, but as he points out to his readers, the truth (or lack of truth) of his vision will become evident in short order: "If I have erred in my exposition of the prophecies, the time being so near at hand will expose my folly."[13]

In the manner of some end-of-the-world millennialists, Miller works with clear chronologies that move in linear fashion from type to antitype, from specific prophecies to the day of fulfillment, which is imagined as bringing an end to time as we know it. But because there would appear to be no jags or ruptures in his vision, he differs somewhat from those premillennialists who emphasize the irruption of apocalypse. He is more typically premillennialist in presenting his prophecies as lacking in nationalist exceptionalism and devoid of any sort of progressive schema. Thus, such key events as the American Revolution and the War of 1812 have no place in his chronological schema. Again and again in his lectures, he appeals to the wise, saintly, and potentially regenerate among "ye inhabitants of the earth." Miller's nonnational or postnational vision becomes clear in the closing page of his volume, when he asks rhetorically: "Will God punish nations, and not individuals? That cannot be, for nations are composed of individuals, and God is just, for he hath appointed a day in which he will judge the world in righteousness."[14]

As a critical millenarian, then, Miller offers a postnational vision, encompassing a spiritual history of humankind that is metaphorical, text-based, and disconnected from U.S. nationalism. But because he can never release his hold on the Bible as the key to making sense of the universe, Miller can never look beyond "extinction" to new ways of thinking about time and space, or, to put this somewhat differently, he can never use his awareness of extinction to challenge his consciousness. But what happens to such an awareness when untethered from the Bible? How can such a consciousness affect our critical thinking about time, space, and nation? Poe's and Hawthorne's Miller-inspired sketches open up possibilities by addressing some of the same questions about the prospects of a new critical millenarianism that Jack Miles addresses in his essay of 2001.

Approximately one year after the appearance of Miller's widely publicized lectures, Poe published a Millerite-inspired end-of-the-world tale, "The Conversation of Eiros and Charmion," in the December 1839 issue of *Burton's Gentleman's Magazine*. He republished the tale in his 1840 *Tales of the Grotesque and Arabesque* and (with the revised title of "The Destruction of the World") his 1845 *Tales*. Like Miller, he imagines the destruction of the world as an apocalyptic event that has little to do with nation. Though Poe follows Miller and other premillennialists in imagining some sort of life beyond the end of calendar time, indeed beyond the end of the world, he departs from Miller in disconnecting the final cataclysm from scriptural prophecy. The emphasis of the story is ultimately on the question of how we might think about human history and culture, and the planet itself, when confronting the imminence of extinction, or a Judgment Day, without the affirmations offered by biblical hermeneutics. Arguably, Poe finds something of even greater value in his end-of-the-world imaginings than a Millerite spiritual cleansing: a reconception of time and space, somewhat on the order of a Benjaminian revolutionism, that has the liberating potential of producing new knowledge from previously unimagined vantage points.[15]

The tale is framed as a conversation between two angelic spirits, Eiros and Charmion (the names of Cleopatra's servants in Shakespeare's *Antony and Cleopatra* and Dryden's *All For Love*), who now exist in "Aidenn," a place that critics have traditionally identified as a type of "heaven" but which the spirit Eiros identifies more complexly as "the speculative Future merged in the august and certain Present."[16] Right from the start, there is a collapse of present and future, with a Benjaminian sense that the collapse has reoriented the present as "the 'time of the now,'"[17] as opposed to a time linked to particular histories, national or otherwise, dependent on narrativized chronologies. There is also a sense, drawn from Miller and other pre- and postmillennialists, that the end of the world as described by Eiros and Charmion has brought about what Miller terms a "reign . . . in the immortal state,"[18] though clearly a reign without Christ.

Charmion initiates the conversation between the two immortals by referring to humankind's "last hour," asserting that it would be best to "converse of familiar things, in the old familiar language of the world which has so fearfully perished" (359). Of course, the narratological truth of the matter is that if the spirits really spoke in a new, unfamiliar language, Poe's readers would be unable to understand the conversation, which is clearly being staged for eavesdroppers. Once Charmion initiates the conversation, Eiros basically takes over, with the final two-thirds of the sketch consisting of Eiros's monologue on how the world has come to an end. Because it is the specter of world's end that inspires new thinking, it would be useful to jump to the end of the tale itself, which, like "The Fall of the House of Usher" (also first published in *Burton's* in 1839), merges the end of the world described in the fiction with the end of the fiction itself.[19] In an ending that also bears some resemblance to the apocalyptic ending of *The Narrative of Arthur Gordon Pym* (1838), Eiros tells Charmion what he or she already knows:

For a moment there was a wild lurid light alone, visiting and penetrating all things. Then — let us bow down, Charmion, before the excessive majesty of the great God! — then, there came a shouting and pervading sound, as if from the mouth itself of HIM; while the whole incumbent mass of ether in which we existed, burst at once into a species of intense flames, for whose surpassing brilliancy and all-fervid heat even the angels in the high Heaven of pure knowledge have no name. Thus ended all. (363)

An apocalypse brought about by flames beyond description eerily anticipates our own concerns about nuclear annihilation, even as Poe draws on the rhetoric of Miller and other millennialists (including the colonial postmillennialist Jonathan Edwards), who typically warn of a retributive Jehovah subjecting sinners to the flames of hell. Crucial to the modernistic feel of "The Conversation of Eiros and Charmion," however, is that the Jehovah figure — "HIM" — remains vague, and the cessation of happening is not simply about retribution. It is about postapocalyptic knowledge, a "pure knowledge" that, because of the unprecedented occasion of the end, has no name. But, as in other fiction by Poe, it is the very fact that all has "ended" that allows for the possibility of meaning. Poe writes in his aesthetic manifesto "The Philosophy of Composition" (1846): "It is only with the *dénouement* constantly in view that we can give a plot its indispensable air of consequence."[20] Given that the denouement here is extinction (the story suggests that there are no humans remaining on Earth, and no Earth that remains), Poe has the opportunity to use his spirits to address the matter of how the knowledge of impending human extinction changes everything (just before the end).

As we learn from Eiros, that which eventually brings about the end is a comet. In a critique of mere Earth-bound thinking, Eiros scoffs at those scriptural prognosticators whose end-of-the-world messages are guided by "fear-enkindled . . . biblical prophecies" (361), remarking that their various predictions are ultimately limited, "having reference to the orb of the earth alone" (359). Whether or not they are swayed by such prophecies, the masses fail to consider Earth in relation to the larger solar system, and thus for a long while remain in denial about the distinct possibility, recognized by just "two or three astronomers of secondary note" (360), that the world would soon be no more. Even those whom Eiros terms the "learned" speak of only "probable alterations in climate" (361), although as people consider the new evidence of climate change, they become increasingly convinced that the changes would be catastrophic. As Eiros recalls, climate change soon becomes the main focus of human concerns: "It could not be denied that our atmosphere was radically affected; the conformation of this atmosphere and the possible modifications to which it might be subjected, were now the topics of discussion" (362). Scientists begin to worry that a steady loss of nitrogen in the climate could lead to an oxygen-based "combustion irresistible, all-devouring, omni-prevalent, immediate" (363). And yet before too long it becomes clear that such combustion wouldn't even matter, for the speeding comet, all realize, is on a direct path to Earth.[21]

The knowledge of imminent extinction is ultimately what inspires urgent new efforts to know. As Eiros reports to Charmion (but more insistently to the reader who would not know all of this), the knowledge of a new telos — the imminent end of everything — brings about a complete revolution in conventional thought, something like a messianic moment but without a messiah and without any sort of use-value beyond the attainment of "perfected knowledge" (362). Eiros remarks on the comet itself: "We could no longer apply to the strange orb any *accustomed* thoughts. Its *historical* attributes had disappeared" (362; emphasis in the original). With the recognition of the imminent end of history comes a reorientation of time and space, a revolutionary reconceptualization that resembles Benjamin's imaginings of the heightened immediacy of the present "shot through with chips of Messianic time."[22] What Eiros says about the comet appears to be true about all phenomena under inquiry in the final days: sedimented thought falls by the wayside as "*Truth* arose in the purity of her strength" (361). Such is Poe's artful indirection that the nature of that "*Truth*," as in Miles's essay, remains vague, though it is that very vagueness which underscores the urgency of pursuing some sort of "perfected knowledge" outside of the conventionally historical or national. In the midst of what Eiros describes as the "frenzy of mankind" (363), people across the planet "felt an unusual elasticity of frame and vivacity of mind" (363). Like Miller, Poe's angelic spirits are unconcerned about nations, just as the comet itself takes no account of nations. Instead, the comet becomes "the consummation of Fate" (363). That consummation is precisely what is described at the tale's end, where there is a blending of Fate and God for that brief knowledge-infused duration between the moment the danger has been identified and annihilation.

The large thrust of Poe's story, then, with its materialist account of the discovery of a new comet, is that there are good reasons to regard any age as a possible age of extinction, and that the contemplation of the end is incumbent upon all serious thinkers. The end-of-the-world "Conversation" is not a tragic story. In the tale, Poe insists that critical thought in an age of extinction, rather than closing down avenues of investigation, inevitably opens them up, rejuvenating a tired and sleepy age that has for too long functioned with "the old familiar language of the world." Eiros's initial remark on how the two angels exist in "the speculative Future merged in the august and certain Present" thus speaks both to the fictional fate of the angelic characters and to the reconceived temporal consciousness that Poe seeks to evoke in his Miller-inspired tale: a present infused with meaning because of the abrupt recognition of a future without a future. Such a perspective, however vaguely or suggestively, liberates the present from the constraints of time, from the additive or progressive. Still, the tale enacts a certain nostalgia for "the old familiar language of the world," for without that language Poe would be unable to evoke the world to come. And without readers in the old familiar world, his vision would be lacking in any sense of urgency.

In 1843, a year after the Boston publication of Miller's *Evidence from Scripture and History*, Hawthorne published two Millerite-inspired sketches that place an even greater emphasis on the tension between the familiar and the millenarian.[23] These sketches emerged from Hawthorne's own short-lived commitment to millennial reform, as exemplified by his seven-month stay in 1841 at the socialist reform community Brook Farm, in West Roxbury, Massachusetts (which he would later take as the subject of *The Blithedale Romance* [1852]). Hawthorne is generally regarded as a social conservative, but during the 1830s and 1840s he was a Jacksonian democrat who was opposed to aristocratic privilege, and for a while he was genuinely inspired by the reformers in the Boston-Concord circle who were convinced that they could help to create a better United States and world. Although Hawthorne was initially enthusiastic about Brook Farm's prospects, by late 1841 he had come to believe that the reformers themselves needed reforming. From this perspective, the premillennialist vision of the Millerites, with its images of destruction *preceding* actual human reform, spoke to his disillusionment with the postmillennial notion that humans could bring about their own redemption. And yet, for much of his career, he retained his interest in what could be termed millennial reform, attacking aristocratic privilege in many of his fictional works and on several occasions voicing his objections to slavery, going so far as to sign a Free Soil petition in 1852. In his 1843 "The Hall of Fantasy," Hawthorne put his competing visions of reform into conflict.

In the sketch, the narrator provides the reader with a guided tour of the reformers scattered throughout the Hall of Fantasy, a sort of "public Exchange" with a white marble floor, pillars, and an impressive dome.[24] The reformers are presented as "dreamers" touched by a "contagious" form of "madness" (738), but also as serious people who have genuine (and admirable) desires for social change. Thus, the narrator states that even a "conservative," perhaps not unlike the sketch's author, "could hardly have helped throbbing in sympathy with the spirit that pervaded these innumerable theorists" (741). After describing various reformers who believe they can "cast off the whole tissue of ancient custom, like a tattered garment" (740), the narrator leads the reader to the unlikely figure of "Father Miller himself," described as "an elderly man of plain, honest, trustworthy aspect," who with "the sincerest faith in his own doctrine ... announced that the destruction of the world was close at hand" (741–42). The narrator subsequently underscores the stark differences between the postmillennialist and the premillennialist: "They [the secular-postmillennial social reformers] look for the earthly perfection of mankind, and are forming schemes, which imply that the immortal spirit will be connected with a physical nature, for innumerable ages of futurity. On the other hand, here comes good Father Miller, and, with one puff of his relentless theory, scatters all their dreams like so many withered leaves upon the blast" (742). The question posed by the sketch's grouping of optimistic worldly reformers with the premillennialist Miller himself is in some respects the same question posed by our own historical moment: What should people do if the end of the world is "close at hand"? How might they think, act, teach, or write?

Hawthorne brings these large questions to a focus when he grants Miller his donné and imagines the coming of the end. Like Miller and Poe, he envisions the world going up in flames. The force of the sketch thus lies in the conjectural imagining of apocalypse. But Hawthorne offers no postapocalyptic commentary from angels, no insight or spiritual "solution" to what the narrator terms the "riddle" (742) of life. Instead, he simply worries over the challenge of gaining larger meaning from cataclysmic destruction. As the narrator confesses to the reader, should the world be "burnt to-morrow morning, I am at a loss to know what purpose will have been accomplished, or how the universe will be wiser or better for our existence and destruction" (742). Poe aggressively challenges the reader to rise to the occasion of imagining new ways of thinking; Hawthorne remains "at a loss" and allows for a retreat into a nostalgic recovery of the conventional. At the sketch's end, he depicts parents who are desirous that "their new-born infant should not be defrauded of his life-time" by "the consummation, prophesied by Father Miller" (743). Domestic ideals thus prevail over end-of-the-world imaginings. Still, in an intriguing moment, Hawthorne implicitly addresses the fate of writing in an age of extinction, presenting us with a "youthful poet" who, in response to Miller's prophecies, glumly "murmured, because there would be no posterity to recognize the inspiration of his song" (743). The suggestion is that if one is writing for posterity in an age of extinction, some adjustments may be in order (though Hawthorne never even hints at what those adjustments might entail).

Hawthorne directly addresses connections between writing and posterity in a subsequent Miller-inspired sketch, "The New Adam and Eve," also published in 1843. If in "The Hall of Fantasy" Hawthorne momentarily entertains Miller's end-of-the-world prophesy, only to take refuge in conventional notions of domesticity, here he bases an entire story around Miller's prognostications. Right from the start, the narrator of "The New Adam and Eve" asks the reader to imagine that Miller is correct: "Let us conceive good Father Miller's interpretation of the prophecies to have proved true. The Day of Doom has burst upon the globe, and swept away the whole race of men. From cities and fields, sea-shore and mid-land mountain region, vast continents, and even the remotest islands of the ocean — each living thing is gone" (746).

Taking the end of the world as the tale's pretext and point of departure, Hawthorne anticipates Alan Weisman's *The World without Us* by focusing on the marks that humans have left on the world. The narrator surveys the initially humanless scene: "No breath of a created being disturbs this earthly atmosphere. But the abodes of man, and all that he has accomplished, the foot-prints of his wanderings, and the results of his toil, the visible symbols of his intellectual cultivation and moral progress — in short, everything physical that can give evidence of his present position — shall remain untouched by the hand of destiny" (746). In *The World without Us*, Weisman guides his reader through that post-human world as he imagines it with the help of his wide scientific reading. Hawthorne, on the other hand, offers his readers a "half-sportive and half-thoughtful" (746) tour of the postextinction world with the help of the mysterious advent of a new Adam and Eve, who view what remains of that previous human world through their innocent and constantly bewildered eyes. There is a Thoreauvian thrust to Hawthorne's sketch, as he depicts his new Adam and Eve baffled by Parisian fashion, prisons, courts, banks, jewelers' shops, alcoholic beverages, and the detritus of nineteenth-century life — in short, what the new Adam terms "heaps of rubbish of one kind or another" (758). As a Jacksonian democrat, Hawthorne is especially intent on using the innocence of his new Adam and Eve to highlight, from the point of view of their incomprehension, the evidence of class inequities, which they see just about everywhere they look. Because they lack the verbal gifts and historical consciousness that would enable them to articulate the meaning of what they see, the narrator has to do that work for them in rhetorical fashion: "When will they comprehend the great and miserable fact, — the evidences of which appeal to their senses everywhere, — that one portion of earth's lost inhabitants was rolling in luxury, while the multitude was toiling for scanty food?" (759).

It is important to note that the narrator's critique of class inequities focuses on the "earth" and not the nation. And yet Hawthorne's readers would have recognized, through the description of Adam and Eve's wanderings, that the story is examining humans' "foot-prints" in Boston and nearby areas. The very localness of the sketch becomes especially clear when the new Adam and Eve journey "into the suburbs of the city" and "stand on a grassy brow of a hill, at the foot of a granite obelisk." When the new Adam regards the obelisk as "a visible prayer" (759), the narrator cannot resist identifying it as the monument "on far-famed Bunker Hill" (759–60). Here is a point in the sketch when the national could be recuperated through the invocation of American Revolutionary ideals. Instead, Hawthorne uses the occasion to meditate on war apart from nationalist ideologies, anticipating (and perhaps influencing) Melville's equally satirical account of the Bunker Hill Monument in the preface to his antinationalist American Revolutionary novel *Israel Potter* (1855). Using the prospect of the end of the world to demythify a battle that had come to be celebrated as a founding moment of the new nation, the narrator remarks (in the same year that the monument was completed and dedicated): "Could they guess that the green sward on which they stand so peacefully, was once strewn with human corpses and purple with their blood, it would equally amaze them, that one generation of men should perpetuate such carnage, and that a subsequent generation should triumphantly commemorate it" (760).[25] The fact of the extinction of all humans prior to the new Adam and Eve thus allows the narrator to think about war apart from the ideological imperatives of particular national histories. War becomes simply war, with no clear beginning, middle, or end, and no clear sense of purpose. After all, a key consequence of human extinction is that historical narrative, too, becomes extinct, a relic of the past. In "The Hall of Fantasy," the murmuring poet imagines a time when his poems can no longer be fathomed because there is no longer a posterity; thus, he chooses simply to follow his inspiration. To some extent the narrator of "The New Adam and Eve" takes a similar path by adopting a historical perspective unconstrained by ideological expectations. Nevertheless, like the poet, he is concerned about posterity. His critical millenarianism does not quite achieve the boldness of Poe's.

Consistent with Hawthorne's interest in posterity, near the end of the sketch he describes the new Adam and Eve's journey to "the rich library of Harvard University" (760), the penultimate stopping point of these indefatigable wanderers. There they are confronted by innumerable mysterious objects lined up on shelves, books from the past that have come to have no meaning. Written at a moment when thousands of Americans are considering the possibilities of extinction, the sketch itself, we might say, reflects on its own eventual lack of meaning. And more: given that Harvard Library has volumes from the past and present, the sketch raises questions about the historical traditions of literature, the monumentalization of certain types of literature, and the creation of the institution of the library. As the perplexed Adam puzzles over the "mystic characters" and "unintelligible thought" contained in the volumes, the scene is fraught with tension. He feels the pull of the characters, and such is the force of the pull that the narrator steps forth to express his desire that Adam abandon his efforts and return to the natural world: "Oh Adam, it is too soon, too soon by at least five thousand years, to put on spectacles, and busy yourself in the alcoves of a library!" (760). Within the fictional frame of the sketch, Eve does the work for the narrator, coaxing Adam outside. By resisting the temptations of "the mysterious perils of the library" (761), Adam and Eve keep alive the possibility that the new human race will one day produce works of art with "a melody never yet heard on earth" (762).

The new Adam and Eve make one final stop before they sleep, journeying to Cambridge's Mount Auburn cemetery, where they find a "Child, in whitest marble" (762). As in "The Hall of Fantasy," Hawthorne concludes his postapocalyptic tale with an evocation of family. But this is perhaps the eeriest evocation of family in nineteenth-century literature, as the marble child is of course a monument to a dead child. Thus, when Adam says to Eve, "Let us sleep, as this lovely little figure is sleeping" (763), we are left with a final image of the new Adam and Eve joining the figure of a dead child in an image presaging their inevitable end. In this respect, Hawthorne's sketch suggests somewhat sentimentally that even if his is not an age of extinction, death (extinction) will always remain the final stop in every individual's worldly journey.

Much more than Poe, then, Hawthorne in contemplating extinction is drawn to the local and familiar—the Bunker Hill Monument, the Harvard library, Mount Auburn Cemetery, and tropes of the family central to nineteenth-century domestic ideology. But despite their differences, both writers use their contemplations of the end to challenge progressive notions of history and to dissent from the nationalist exceptionalism that Miller had little use for as well. Even with all of its attendant horrors, catastrophe has the potential to be liberating, particularly in the way that it reframes the present. Pease and Wiegman remark in their introduction to *The Futures of American Studies* that the temporal realignments and reimaginings that they are calling for must beware "the self-satisfactions of presentism" (ironically, the very charge that critics regularly level against the so-called New Americanists).[26] But what Poe, Hawthorne, and other end-of-the-world writers show is that contemplation of the end works to heighten attention to the present, in ways that can free critical thought from the conventional and historical. In this sense we move from mere presentism to a more spiritual, even messianic notion of what Poe terms "the august and certain Present" as reconfigured by the "speculative Future" of no future at all. Thinking about temporality in this way pushes us in Emersonian directions to regard the work that we do as part of a new beginning, even if it is the beginning of the end.

I CONCLUDE this reflection on American studies in an age of extinction with a Poe- and Hawthorne-inflected consideration of recent efforts to understand a catastrophe in our own time, Hurricane Katrina and its aftermath. In a complex analysis, Wai Chee Dimock proposes that the most effective frame for talking about Katrina is the planetary, particularly the dynamics of climate change that have little respect for borders, boundaries, and conceptions of national sovereignty. Taking account of the ongoing work of MIT's Department of Earth, Atmospheric, and Planetary Sciences, she calls for "the study of the planet as an integral unit," and imagines a reconceived American studies that would move beyond the artificial boundaries of national histories to develop "as a body of knowledge aggregated on a different scale, with connecting threads running through other dimensions of the planet." In a formulation that seems greatly indebted to the rhetoric of extinction, and in the tradition of Poe's vision of catastrophe in "The Conversation of Eiros and Charmion," she elaborates on her notion of the planetary: "The 'planetary' emerges here as the bearer of a scale indifferent to human institutions and indifferent to the human species itself." Dimock's insistence on such indifference seems intended to underscore that humans may not be around all that much longer. The question that one might raise about her analysis is whether it has truly transcended the local. After all, from the galactic vantage point of Eiros, Dimock's planetary frame could be regarded as small and artificial, as "local" in its own way as the nation. In Dimock's defense, changing conceptions of the local may be just what we need to develop new approaches to time and space in American studies, and her work can be usefully read in relation to recent hemispheric approaches that consider Katrina in the context of the Gulf of Mexico and longer histories of transamerican catastrophes.[27]

This is not to say that the national, and even the town, city, or neighborhood, are not also useful locales for the consideration of catastrophe. As both Poe and (especially) Hawthorne suggest, the "familiar" will continue to exert its pull. While Dimock has enlarged our vision by offering a planetary frame for Katrina, Spike Lee's HBO documentary *When the Levees Broke: A Requiem in Four Acts* (2006), a bracing work in American studies, forces us to look as closely as possible, often from street and house level, at the day-by-day unfolding of the catastrophe in relation to what could be termed nation-time. For Lee, the sufferings in New Orleans had much to do with the failure of local and national government, such as the long history of neglecting the levees and ignoring the urban poor. In a companion text, *Teaching the Levees: A Curriculum for Democratic Dialogue and Civic Engagement*, published by The Rockefeller Foundation in 2007, the editors' "Hurricane Katrina Timelines" deploy old-fashioned chronological timelines as powerful explanatory frameworks. Whereas Dimock links Katrina to climate change, with the possibilities of even greater catastrophes to come, Lee and his collaborators underscore that by the time Katrina hit New Orleans, it had become a category 1 or 2 hurricane, and that the disaster would have occurred even if carbon emissions had been curbed years ago, extinction was less of a prospect, and category-5 storms were still a rarity. His four-hour film moves back and forth between New Orleans's present and past, for the most part ignoring larger planetary and hemispheric contexts, in order to show that national policies based on racial and class hierarchies were ultimately to blame for the suffering that he so powerfully records.

The local, national, hemispheric, and global-planetary have all come into play in the very best work on Katrina, which has helped to reinvigorate the field of American studies by pushing critics to think anew about geographical and temporal frames, perhaps in preparation for what we all suspect will be the greater catastrophes to come. Had he been around in 2005, William

Miller may have proclaimed that the flooding in New Orleans was foretold in the Revelation of St. John, which prophesies that among the apocalyptic events preceding Christ's Second Coming will be a "second vial . . . poured out 'upon the sea'" (Rev. 16.3). Even if one does not share such a text-based millennial notion of apocalypse, it is difficult at the current moment not to contemplate catastrophic possibilities of the end. In an age of extinction, practitioners of American studies may well find themselves adopting a Benjaminian phenomenology of "a present which is not a transition, but in which time stands still and has come to a stop,"[28] a perspective that is not so very different from the "elasticity of frame and vivacity of mind" that Poe's Eiros describes taking hold just before the destruction of the planet. But as Hawthorne suggests in both "The Hall of Fantasy" and "The New Adam and Eve," it is not so easy, or even wise, to toss aside the familiar; and Poe, too, gestures to the familiar in order to push his readers toward something new. What I am suggesting in this essay, through my deployment of Poe and Hawthorne in particular, is the potential for productive exchanges between the millennialist, nation-based traditions of American studies and the even longer tradition of a postnationalist (critical) millenarianism. Such a dialectical approach, difficult as it might be to chart out with any sort of methodological precision, may offer the best possible hope for helping us to see where the meanings are before we are no more.

NOTES

1. See Melani McAlister, "Rethinking the 'Clash of Civilizations': American Evangelicals, the Bush Administration, and the Winding Road to the Iraq War," in *Race, Nation, and Empire in American History*, ed. James. T. Campbell, Matthew Pratt Guterl, and Robert G. Lee (Chapel Hill: University of North Carolina Press, 2007), 352–74.

2. Doug Struck, "Emissions Growth Must End in 7 Years, U.N. Warns: Report Lays out Stark Choices to Avoid the Death of Species," *Washington Post*, 18 November 2007, A10; Juliet Eilperin, "Carbon Output Must Near Zero to Avert Danger, New Studies Say," *Washington Post*, 10 March 2008, A1. See also Eilperin, "188 More Species Listed as Near Extinction," *Washington Post*, 13 September 2007, A10; and David A. Fahrenthold, "Climate Change Brings Risk of More Extinctions," *Washington Post*, 17 September 2007, A7.

3. See Ernest Lee Tuveson, *Redeemer Nation: The Idea of America's Millennial Role* (Chicago: University of Chicago Press, 1968), esp. 1–34. For a consideration of millennialism in the comparative context of the Americas, see Thomas O. Beebee, *Millennial Literatures of the Americas, 1492–2002* (New York: Oxford University Press, 2009).

4. Donald E. Pease and Robyn Wiegman, "Futures," in *The Futures of American Studies*, ed. Pease and Wiegman (Durham: Duke University Press, 2002), 22. I should note that

distinctions between critical millennialists and critical millenarians in American studies are not always so clear. Paul Lauter, whose *Canons and Contexts* (New York: Oxford University Press, 1991), is a classic of the millennialist strain in American studies scholarship, has an essay in *The Futures of American Studies*, a volume which concludes on a classically millennial note with its hope for the achievement of "radical democracy" (38) in our own time.

5. Walter Benjamin, "Theses on the Philosophy of History," in *Illuminations*, ed. Hannah Arendt (New York: Schocken Books, 1969), 263, 254, 263; Pease and Wiegman, "Futures," 3, 38. Benjamin's "Theses" was completed in 1940 and first published in 1950.

6. Benjamin, "Theses on the Philosophy of History," 261.

7. Alan Weisman, *The World without Us* (New York: St. Martin's Press, 2007), 4, 15, 119. Weisman's best-selling book has been translated into more than thirty languages and the film rights have been sold. Already, though, two Weisman-inspired films have appeared: "Life without People," which was the History Channel's most widely viewed program of January 2008, and "Aftermath: Population Zero," aired on the National Geographic channel in March 2008.

8. Jack Miles, "Global Requiem: The Apocalyptic Moment in Religion," in *Religion and Cultural Studies*, ed. Susan L. Mizruchi (Princeton: Princeton University Press, 2001), 194, 196, 208.

9. Whitney R. Cross, *The Burned-Over District: The Social and Intellectual History of Enthusiastic Religion in Western New York, 1800–1850* (1950; New York: Harper Torchbooks, 1965), 287. For additional background, see David L. Rowe, *Thunder and Trumpets: Millerites and Dissenting Religion in Upstate New York, 1800–1850* (Chico, Calif.: Scholars Press, 1985). On the European tradition of premillennialism, dating back to the medieval period, see Norman Cohn, *The Pursuit of the Millennium: Revolutionary Millenarians and Mystical Anarchists of the Middle Ages* (1957; rev. ed., New York: Oxford University Press, 1970).

10. See Gary Scharnhorst, "Images of the Millerites in American Literature," *American Quarterly* 32 (1980): 19–36. Scharnhorst reports that there were more than 100 Millerite tent-meetings in the early 1840s with a cumulative attendance of around 500,000 worshipers and the curious (21).

11. Jan Stieverman, "The Discursive Construction of American Identity in Millennialist Tracts during the War of 1812," in *Millennial Thought in America: Historical and Intellectual Contexts, 1630–1860*, ed. Bernd Engler, Joerg O. Fichte, and Oliver Scheiding (Trier: Wissenschaftlicher Verlag, 2002), 283, 297. Seminal studies of American millennialism and nationalism include Tuveson, *Redeemer Nation*; and James West Davidson, *The Logic of Millennial Thought: Eighteenth-Century New England* (New Haven: Yale University Press, 1977). Also useful is Steven Mintz, *Moralists and Modernizers: America's Pre–Civil War Reformers* (Baltimore: Johns Hopkins University Press), 16–49.

12. There was also transatlantic interest in Miller. On Millerites in Great Britain, see Penelope J. Corfield, *Time and the Shape of History* (New Haven: Yale University Press, 2007), 113–21.

13. William Miller, *Evidence from Scripture and History of the Second Coming of Christ, about the Year 1843: Exhibited in a Course of Lectures* (Troy, N.Y.: Elias Gates, 1838), 22, iii,

iii, 166, 16, 51, vii. The slightly revised and expanded edition was published in Boston in 1842 by Joshua V. Himes.

14. Ibid., iii, 267, 278.

15. Scharnhorst, "Images of the Millerites," 21–22, argues for the direct influence of Miller on the tale. See also Douglass Robinson, "Poe's Mini-Apocalypse: 'The Conversation of Eiros and Charmion,'" *Studies in Short Fiction* 19 (1982): 329–37.

16. Poe, "The Conversation of Eiros and Charmion," in Edgar Allan Poe, *Poetry and Tales*, ed. Patrick F. Quinn (New York: Library of America, 1984), 359. Page references to this tale are provided parenthetically in the main body of the text.

17. Benjamin, "Theses on the Philosophy of History," 263.

18. Miller, *Evidence from Scripture and History*, 166.

19. See Paul John Eakin, "Poe's Sense of an Ending," *American Literature* 45 (1973): 1–22. For an influential analysis of connections between fictional narrative endings and conceptions of the Last Judgment, see Frank Kermode, *The Sense of an Ending: Studies in the Theory of Fiction, with a New Epilogue* (1967; New York: Oxford University Press, 2000), 3–31.

20. Poe, "The Philosophy of Composition," in Edgar Allan Poe, *Essays and Reviews*, ed. G. R. Thompson (New York: Library of America, 1984), 13. There is also a materialist, physical-science dimension to Poe's sense of an ending, which comes across most clearly in his 1848 prose poem *Eureka*, where he talks about the Godhead as being the force within the matter of the universe that is forever imploding and thus moving toward "*Inevitable Annihilation*" (*Poetry and Tales*, 1261).

21. According to Martin Rees, the statistics suggest that we face our own possibilities of a runaway comet or asteroid. The last major hit was sixty-five million years ago, probably resulting in the extinction of the dinosaurs. Because, as Rees writes, a "ten-kilometre asteroid, harbinger of worldwide catastrophe and major extinctions, is expected to hit Earth once every fifty to one-hundred-million years," we could say that in some ways we are fifteen millions years overdue. See *Our Final Hour: A Scientist's Warning: How Terror, Errors, and Environmental Disaster Threaten Humankind's Future in this Century — On Earth and Beyond* (New York: Basic Books, 2003), 90–91.

22. Benjamin, "Theses on the Philosophy of History," 263.

23. In addition to the two Hawthorne sketches I discuss, see also "The Christmas Banquet" (1844), which has an allusion to Miller, and "Earth's Holocaust" (1844), which focuses on book burning. In a recent essay, James Hewitson argues that Hawthorne makes use of Miller to attack reformism ("'To Despair at the Tedious Delay of the Final Configuration': Hawthorne's Use of the Figure of Father Miller," *ESQ: A Journal of the American Renaissance* 53 [2007]: 89–111), presenting Hawthorne as considerably more skeptical about reform than he actually was. Hewitson ignores Scharnhorst's much more nuanced analysis of Hawthorne's and other American writers' responses to Miller (see "Images of the Millerites"). For discussions of the influence of millennial thought on Hawthorne's writings of the 1840s, see also Jonathan A. Cook, "New Heavens, Poor Old Earth: Satirical Apocalypse in Hawthorne's *Mosses from an Old Manse*," *ESQ* 39 (1993): 208–51; and Beebee, *Millennial Literatures of the Americas*, 110–15. On Hawthorne as a conflicted reformer during the 1840s and 1850s, see Robert S. Levine, *Dislocating Race and Nation:*

Episodes in Nineteenth-Century American Literary Nationalism (Chapel Hill: University of North Carolina Press, 2008), chap. 3.

24. Hawthorne, "The Hall of Fantasy," in Nathaniel Hawthorne, *Tales and Sketches*, ed. Roy Harvey Pearce (New York: Library of America, 1982), 734. Page references to Hawthorne's writings are to this edition and are cited parenthetically in the main body of the text.

25. The Bunker Hill Monument was dedicated on 17 June 1843, right around the time that Hawthorne published "The New Adam and Eve."

26. Pease and Wiegman, "Futures," 37. For a representative attack on Pease and the so-called New Americanists as presentist in their politics, see G. R. Thompson and Eric Carl Link, *Neutral Ground: New Traditionalism and the American Romance Controversy* (Baton Rouge: Louisiana State University Press, 1999).

27. Wai Chee Dimock, "Afterword: The Hurricane and the Nation," *ESQ: A Journal of the American Renaissance* 50 (2004): 224, 227, 226. See also Anna Brickhouse, "'L'Ouragan de Flammes' ('The Hurricane of Flames'): New Orleans and Transamerican Catastrophe, 1866/2005," *American Quarterly* 59 (2007): 1097–1127; and Kirsten Gruesz, "The Gulf of Mexico System and the 'Latinness' of New Orleans," *American Literary History* 18 (2006): 468–97.

28. Benjamin, "Theses on the Philosophy of History," 262.

CONTRIBUTORS

SRINIVAS ARAVAMUDAN is professor of English and the Program in Literature and Dean of Humanities in the Trinity College of Arts and Sciences at
Duke University. He specializes in eighteenth-century British and French literature and in postcolonial literature and theory. He is the author of essays in
Diacritics, ELH, *Social Text, Novel, Eighteenth-Century Studies, Anthropological Forum, South Atlantic Quarterly*, and other venues. His *Tropicopolitans:
Colonialism and Agency, 1688–1804* won the outstanding first-book prize
of the Modern Language Association in 2000. He has also edited *Slavery,
Abolition and Emancipation: Writings of the British Romantic Period*, volume
6. His most recent book is *Fiction Guru English: South Asian Religion in a
Cosmopolitan Language*. He is working on two book-length studies, one on
the eighteenth-century French and British oriental tale, and the other on
sovereignty and anachronism. He is also editor of William Earle's antislavery
romance, *Obi; or, The History of Three-Fingered Jack*.

IAN BAUCOM is professor of English at Duke University. He is the author
of *Out of Place: Englishness, Empire and the Locations of Identity* and *Specters of the Atlantic: Finance Capital, Slavery, and the Philosophy of History*
and coeditor of *Shades of Black: Assembling Black Arts in 1980s Britain*. He
has edited special issues of *South Atlantic Quarterly* on Atlantic studies and
romanticism and is currently working on a new book project tentatively entitled *The Disasters of War: On Inimical Life*.

CHRISTOPHER CASTIGLIA is professor of English and senior scholar at the
Center for American Literary Studies at the Pennsylvania State University.
He is the author of *Bound and Determined: Captivity, Culture-Crossing and
White Womanhood from Mary Rowlandson to Patty Hearst* and *Interior States:
Institutional Consciousness and the Inner Life of Democracy in the Antebellum
U.S.*

RUSS CASTRONOVO is Jean Wall Bennett Professor of English and American Studies at the University of Wisconsin at Madison. He is author of three books: *Beautiful Democracy: Aesthetics and Anarchy in a Global Era*; *Necro Citizenship: Death, Eroticism, and the Public Sphere in the Nineteenth-Century United States*; and *Fathering the Nation: American Genealogies of Slavery and Freedom*. He is also coeditor (with Dana Nelson) of *Materializing Democracy: Toward a Revitalized Cultural Politics*.

WAI CHEE DIMOCK is William Lampson Professor of English and American Studies at Yale University. Her recent work includes *Through Other Continents: American Literature across Deep Time* and a collaborative volume, *Shades of the Planet: American Literature as World Literature*. She is now at work on a textbook, *American Literature and the World*.

NAN ENSTAD is professor of history at the University of Wisconsin at Madison. She is author of *Ladies of Labor, Girls of Adventure: Popular Culture and Labor Politics at the Turn of the Twentieth Century* and is writing a book tentatively entitled *The Jim Crow Cigarette: Following Tobacco Road from North Carolina to China and Back*.

SUSAN GILLMAN is professor of literature at the University of California at Santa Cruz, where she is affiliated with the curricular and research group in world literature and cultural studies. Her first book is *Dark Twins: Imposture and Identity in Mark Twain's America*; her second book extends into African American studies, *Blood Talk: American Race Melodrama and the Culture of the Occult*. Her current book in progress reaches into New World–hemispheric studies, *Incomparably Yours: Adaptation, Translation and American Studies*, and is forthcoming with the University of Chicago Press.

RODRIGO LAZO is associate professor of English and associate dean of humanities at the University of California at Irvine. He is author of *Writing to Cuba: Filibustering and Cuban Exiles in the United States* and has published numerous articles on Latino literature and hemispheric American studies.

ROBERT S. LEVINE is professor of English and Distinguished Scholar-Teacher at the University of Maryland. He is the author of *Conspiracy and Romance: Studies in Brockden Brown, Cooper, Hawthorne, and Melville*; *Martin Delany, Frederick Douglass, and the Politics of Representative Identity*; and *Dislocating Race and Nation: Episodes in Nineteenth-Century American Literary Nationalism* and the editor of a number of volumes, including *The*

Norton Anthology of American Literature, 1820–1865 and (with Caroline Levander) *Hemispheric American Studies.*

ANNE MCCLINTOCK is the Simone de Beauvoir Professor of English and Women's and Gender Studies at the University of Wisconsin at Madison. She is the author of *Imperial Leather: Race, Gender and Sexuality in the Colonial Context*; coeditor of *Dangerous Liaisons* with Ella Shohat and Aamir Mufti; and author of the short biographies, *Olive Schreiner* and *Simone de Beauvoir*, and a monograph called *Double Crossings* on madness, sexuality, and colonialism. She has written widely on issues of gender and sexuality, imperialism, race, nationalism, and visual culture. Her work has been translated into French, Spanish, Portuguese, Swedish, Taiwanese, Mandarin, and Japanese. She is working on a new book called *Paranoid Empire: Specters beyond Guantánamo and Abu Ghraib*. McClintock's creative nonfiction book *Skin Hunger: A Chronicle of Sex, Desire and Money* is under contract with Jonathan Cape, and *Global Intimacies: Essays on Sexuality and Power in a Global Era* is under contract with Routledge.

KENNETH W. WARREN is Fairfax M. Cone Distinguished Service Professor and deputy provost for research and minority issues at the University of Chicago. He is author of two books, *Black and White Strangers: Race and American Literary Realism* and *So Black and Blue: Ralph Ellison and the Occasion of Criticism.*

INDEX

Absence: in queer theory, 69–71, 77, 85 (n. 1)

Abu Ghraib, 88–111; conditions at, 106; containment of crisis at, 97–101; deaths at, 106; innocent people at, 88, 105; investigations of, 98; motives for torture at, 105; paranoia at, 105–7; photos of torture at, 9–10, 96–101, 109–11; pornography and, 98–101; state of emergency and, 9–10; women prisoners at, 100, 105–6

Accountability: expansion of concept of, 152

Adam, 174–76

Adaptation: versus translation, 46, 53 (n. 19)

Afghanistan, U.S. invasion and occupation of: and Bagram Air Base, 111; enemy deficit before, 93; justification for, 95; results of, 25

Africa: law of war in, 126, 127–31

African American studies. See Black studies

Afro-British: concept of, 118, 120

Agamben, Giorgio: on state of exception, 125–27, 138–41; and unjust enemy, 125–27, 138–41, 142 (n. 22); and U.S. as rogue state, 24

Agency: of commodities, 60–61; toxicity and, 60–61

Aggression: in archival process, 43–44

Agricola, 111

AIDS, 69–85; in American studies, 70, 80–81; as crisis, 75, 87 (n. 18); end of crisis of, 74, 75; forgetting of, 69–76; and post-traumatic disorder, 76–80, 85 (n. 2); queer theory's neglect of, 69–70; scale of, 11, 70; as trauma, 71–76, 85 (n. 2), 87 (n. 18); treatment for trauma of, 72, 86 (n. 7)

Albright, Madeleine, 26

Ali, Tariq: *The Clash of Fundamentalisms*, 30

Al Jazeera, 94

All For Love (Dryden), 169

Al Qaeda, 95, 102, 106

Alternative archive, 40

Ambivalence: in queer theory, 70–74, 78–80, 83–85

American cultures programs, 2

American Historical Association, 144

American Indian languages, 44

American Revolution, 175

American studies: definition of, 2; fragmentation of, 19; future of, 22–23, 163; genealogy of, 17; history of field, 17–23; as millennialist versus millenarianist, 162–63; names of field, 2, 18; nation as unit of time in, 144–45; objections to, 13–14; professionalization of, 18, 20–21; progressive thought in, 18, 19–20; relationship between National Archives and, 42; relationship between state and, 17–19, 145–46; state of emergency in, 9. *See also* Object of American studies

189

Genetic mutations: toxins and, 62

Geneva Conventions: and U.S. as rogue state, 24; violations at Abu Ghraib, 106; Yoo's memo on, 26

Genocide, 25

Gentili, Alberico, 132, 133; *De Iure Belli*, 130

Geophysical Research Letters (journal), 162

Georgia Institute of Technology, 153

German-language archives, 50

Germ theory, 61, 62

Gibson, William, 89

Giddens, Anthony, 145

Giers, Corporal, 127

Giles, Paul, 20

Gilroy, Paul: *The Black Atlantic*, 116–22

Global issues: changing conceptions of, 178; climate change as, 153–57, 177–78; human extinction and, 178; hurricanes as, 152–53, 177–78; versus local issues, 56, 58, 178; toxicity and, 56, 58

Globalization: as benign, 89; time in, 59–60; toxins in, 55, 57–60

Globalization studies, 21–22

"Global Requiem" (Miles), 164–65, 168, 171

Global warming: in Arctic, 153–57; and Dutch flood protection, 150; and hurricanes, 153. *See also* Climate change

Goebel, Walter: *Beyond the Black Atlantic*, 122

Gómez, Luis G.: *Mis Memorias*, 38–43, 45–47

Gonzalez, Alberto, 95

Gore, Al: *An Inconvenient Truth*, 154, 155; Nobel Peace Prize to, 157

Gould, Phillip, 120

Gourevitch, Philip, 9–10

Governmentality, 25–27, 29

Graner, Charles, 107, 108–9

Great Awakening, Second, 166

Great Britain. *See* Britain

Greenhouse gases: legal action against emitters of, 155; and ocean temperatures, 153. *See also* Climate change

Greenland, 154

Grief, 70, 72–73

Gross, Robert, 21

Grotius, Hugo, 128–33

Gruesz, Kristen Silva, 53 (n. 19)

Guantánamo Bay, 88–111; bodies as property at, 104; innocent people at, 88, 101–2; purpose of, 88, 101–2, 104–5; sovereignty and, 27; territorializing of paranoia in, 92, 101–5; touchless torture at, 102–5; unjust enemy and, 126, 127

Guha, Ranajit, 23

Gulf of Mexico, 152, 156, 178

Gurstein, Rochelle, 98, 99

Gutiérrez, Ramón A., 48, 49

Habeas corpus, 105

Habitat loss, 164

Haiti, 25

Halberstam, Judith, 77–80

"Hall of Fantasy, The" (Hawthorne), 172–74, 175, 176, 179

Halttunen, Karen, 22

Hare, Joseph, 28

Harm: expansion of concept of, 152

Harpe, Micajah, 28

Harpe, Wiley, 28

Harvard Library, 176

Hawthorne, Nathaniel: on apocalypse, 172–77, 179; *The Blithedale Romance*, 172; "The Hall of Fantasy," 172–74, 175, 176, 179; "The New Adam and Eve," 174–76, 179

Head, Richard, 28

Health effects of toxins, 56, 60–62

Hegel, Georg Wilhelm Friedrich, 5, 15 (n. 10)

Hegemony: of archival claim, 47; consent in, 23; decline of U.S., 23–24

Hemispheric approaches, 178

Hersh, Seymour, 95

Hewitson, James, 181 (n. 23)